SPIDER-MAN loves mary jane

my secret life

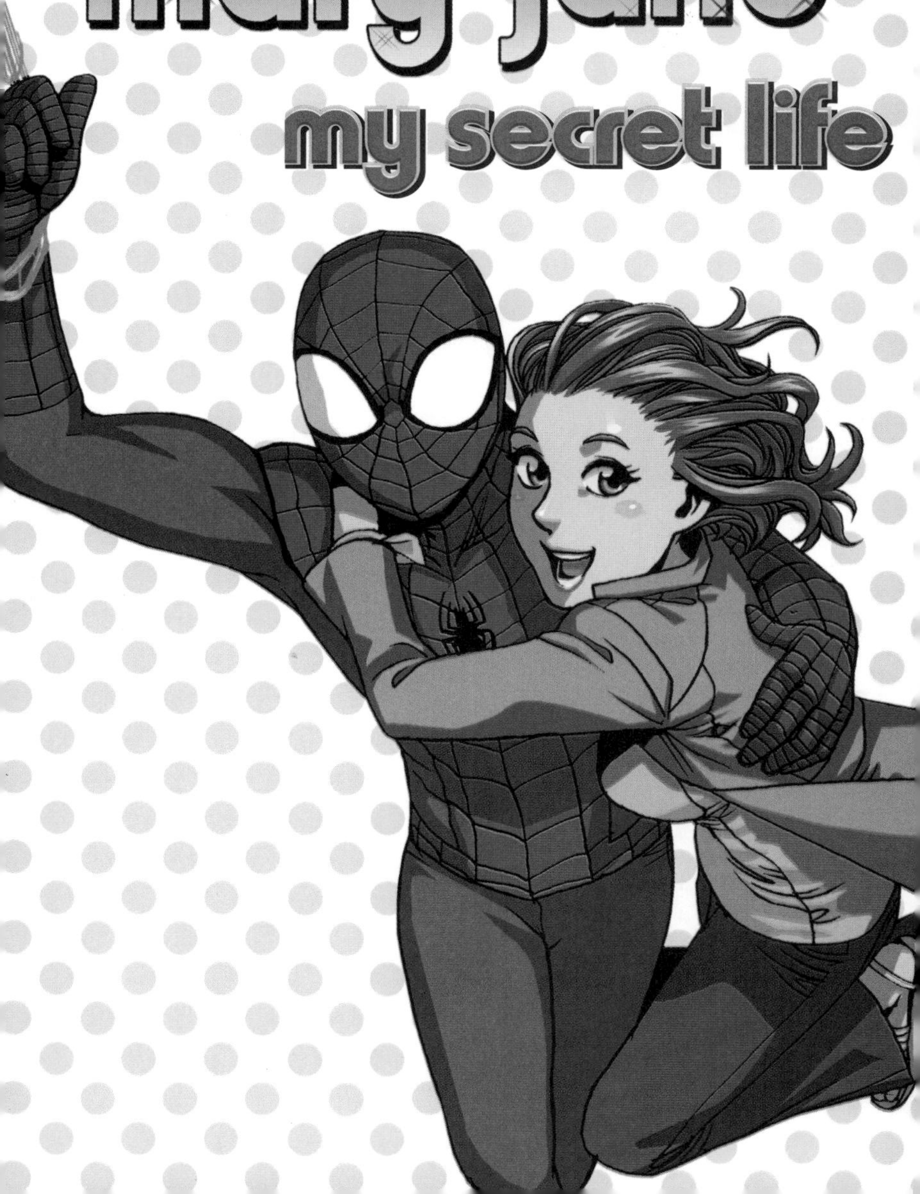

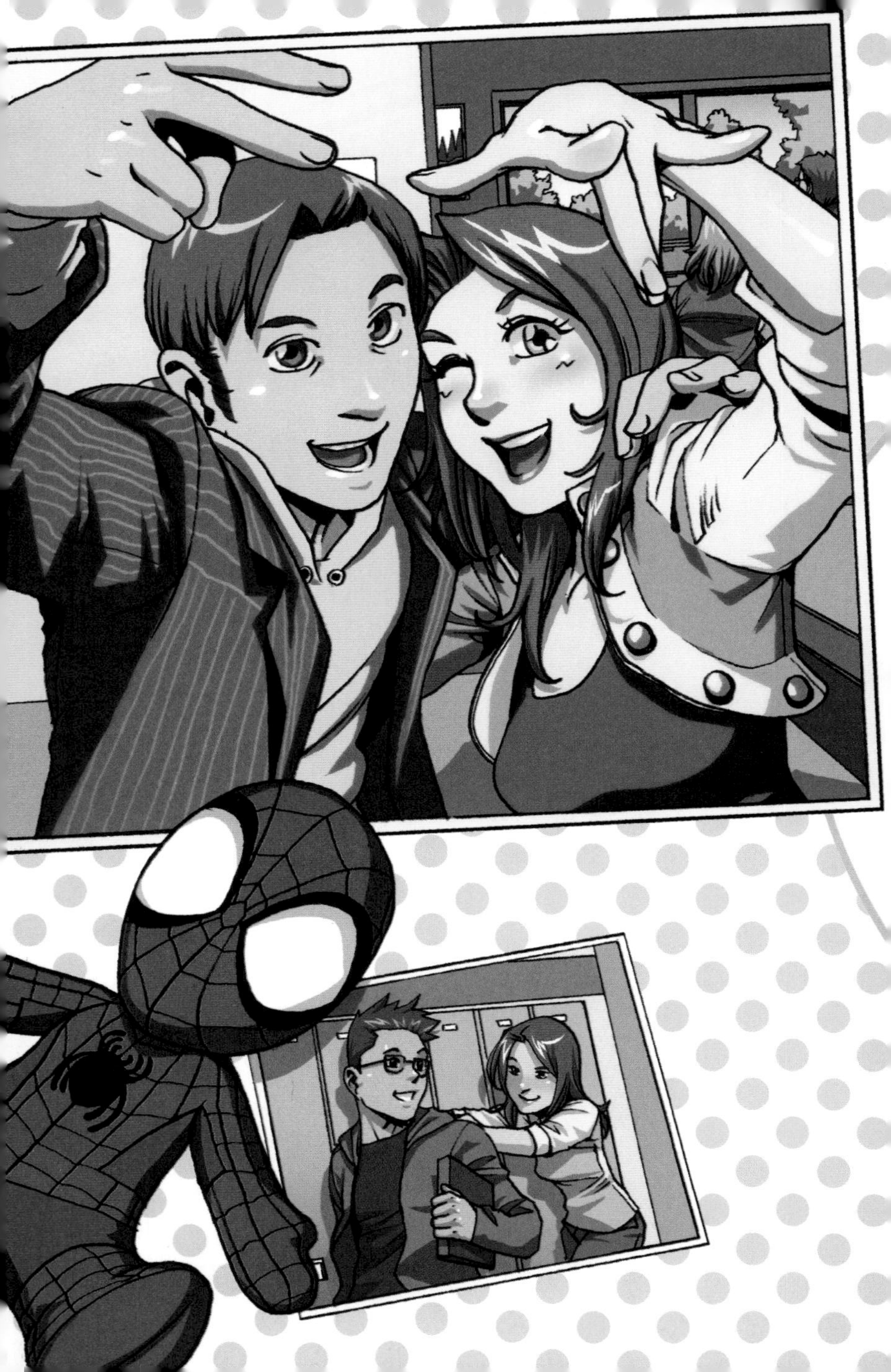

SPIDER-MAN loves mary jane

my secret life

writer
SEAN McKEEVER

art
TAKESHI MIYAZAWA WITH RICK MAYS

colors
CHRISTINA STRAIN

letters
DAVE SHARPE

covers
TAKESHI MIYAZAWA, NORMAN LEE & CHRISTINA STRAIN

assistant editor
NATHAN COSBY

editor
MARK PANICCIA

Special thanks to **MACKENZIE CADENHEAD & DAVID GABRIEL**

collection editor
JENNIFER GRÜNWALD
assistant editors
MICHAEL SHORT & CORY LEVINE
associate editor
MARK D. BEAZLEY
senior editor, special projects

$7.99

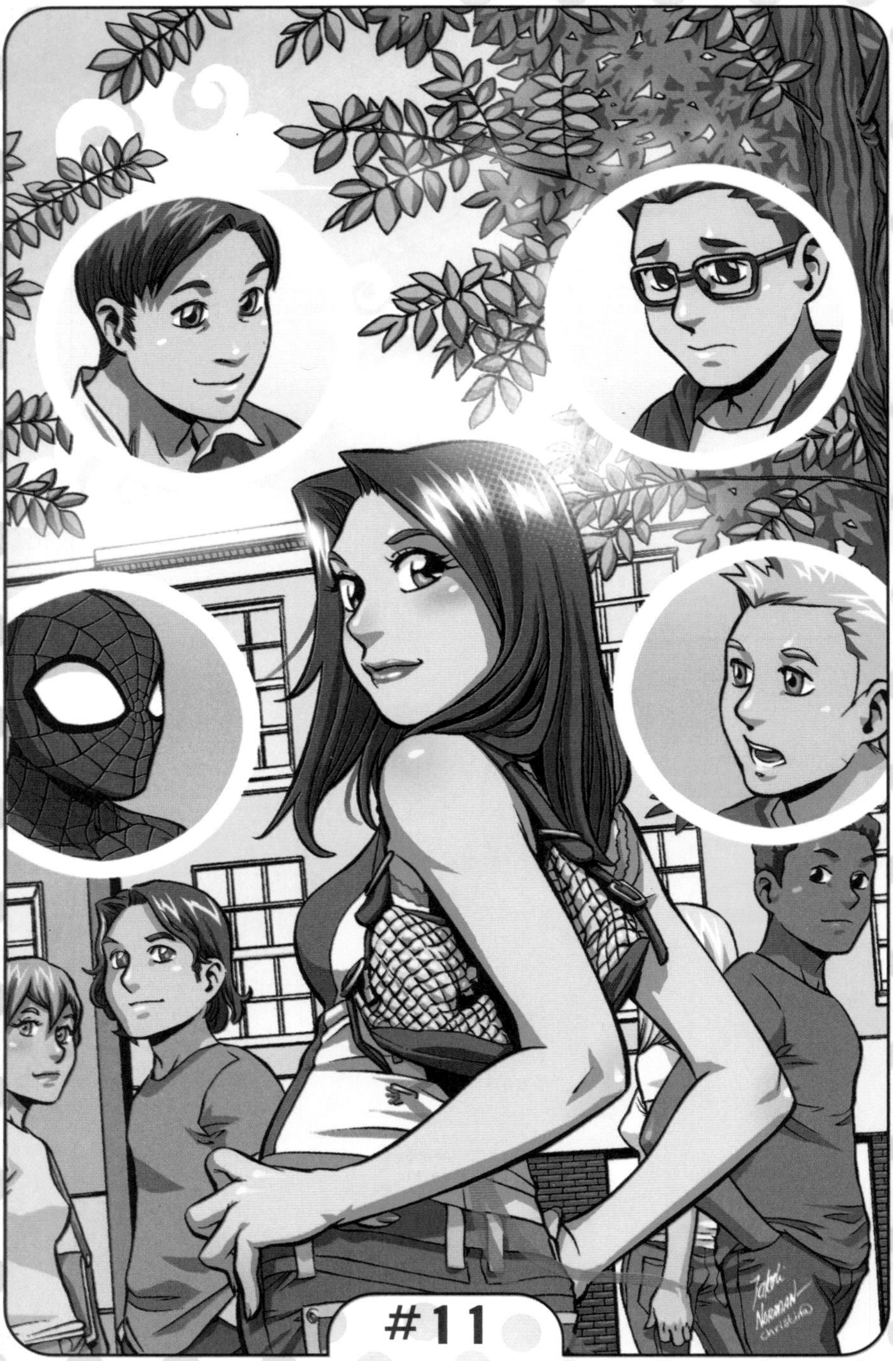
#11

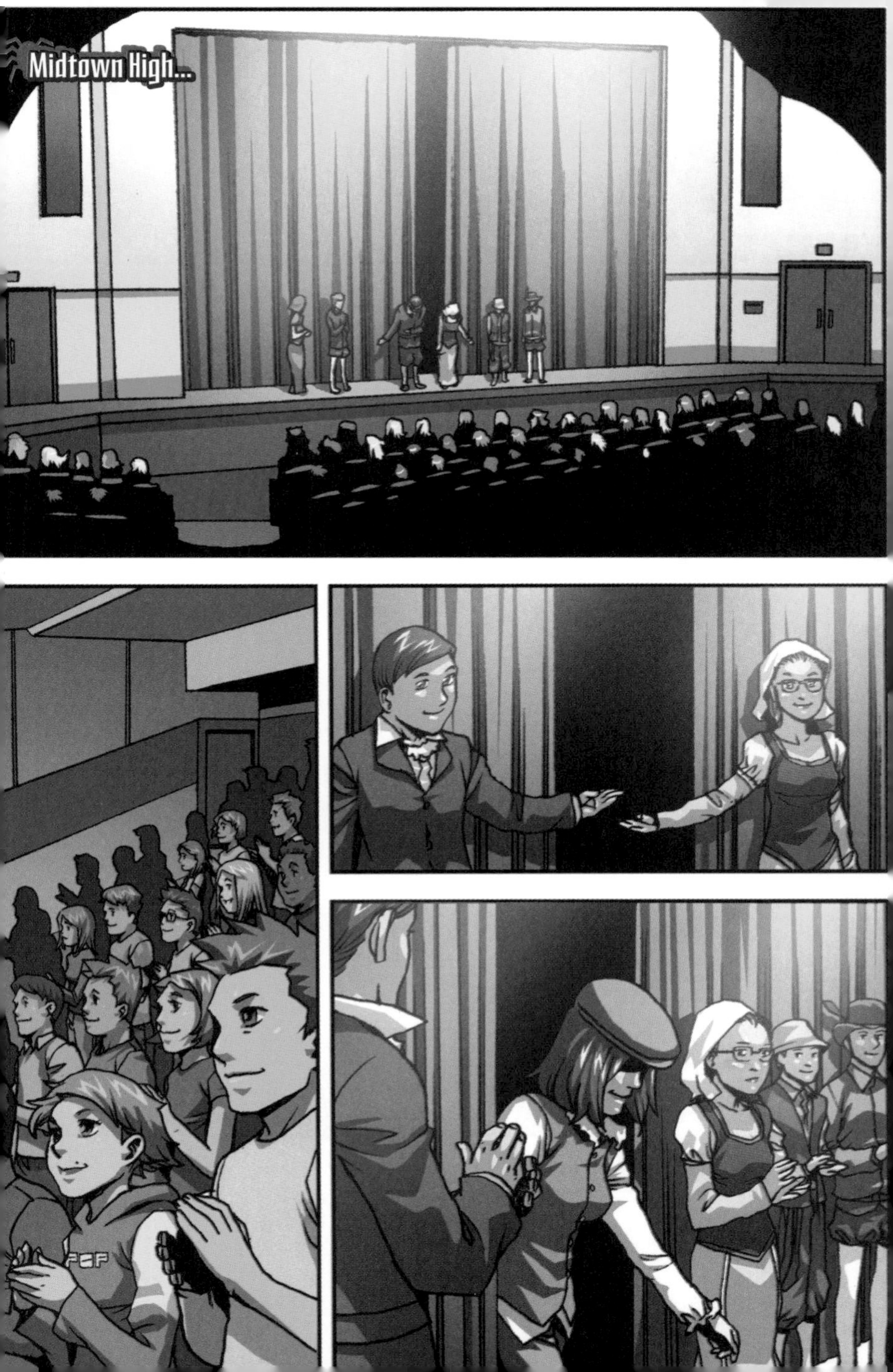
Midtown High...
PCF

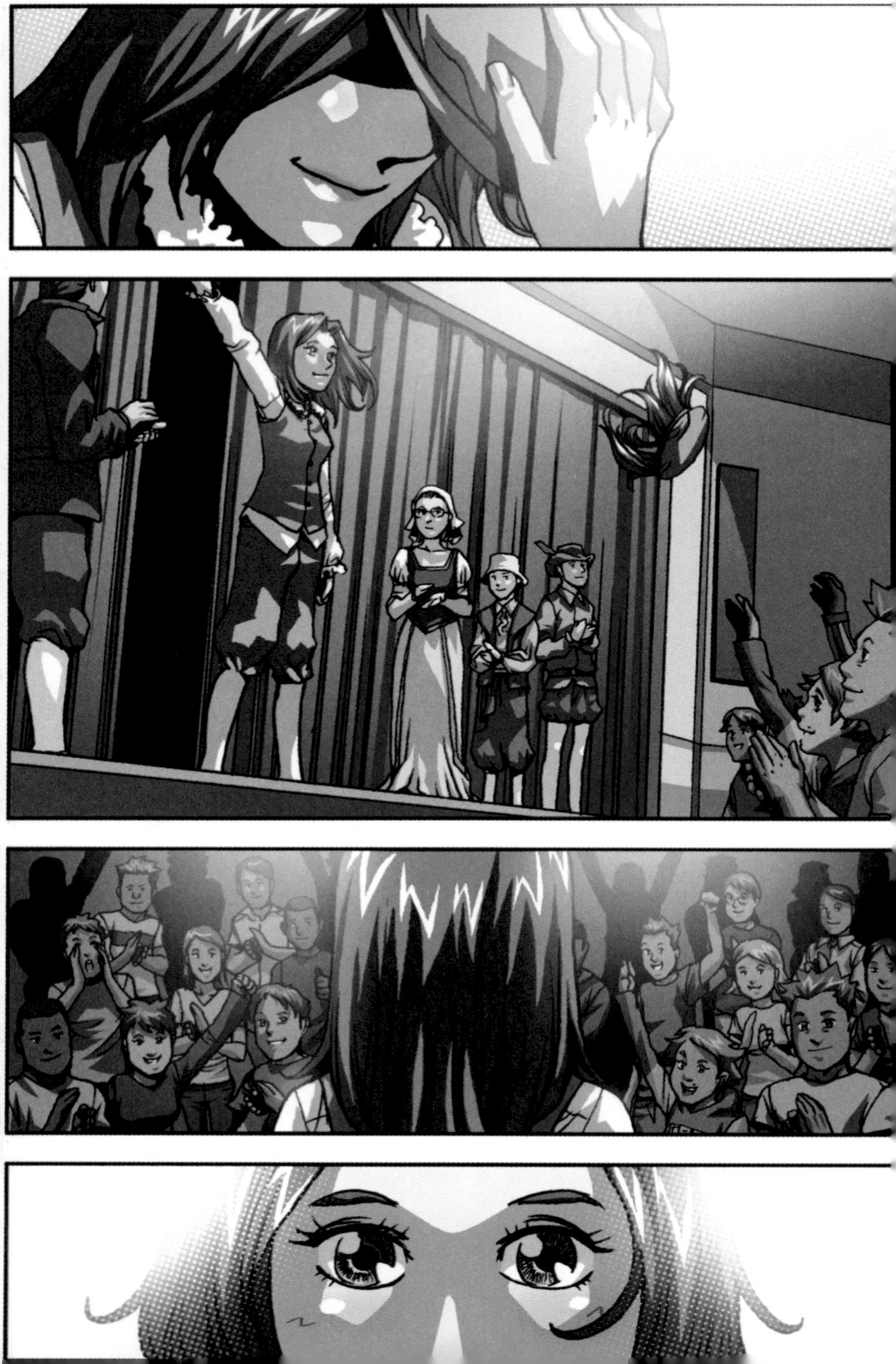

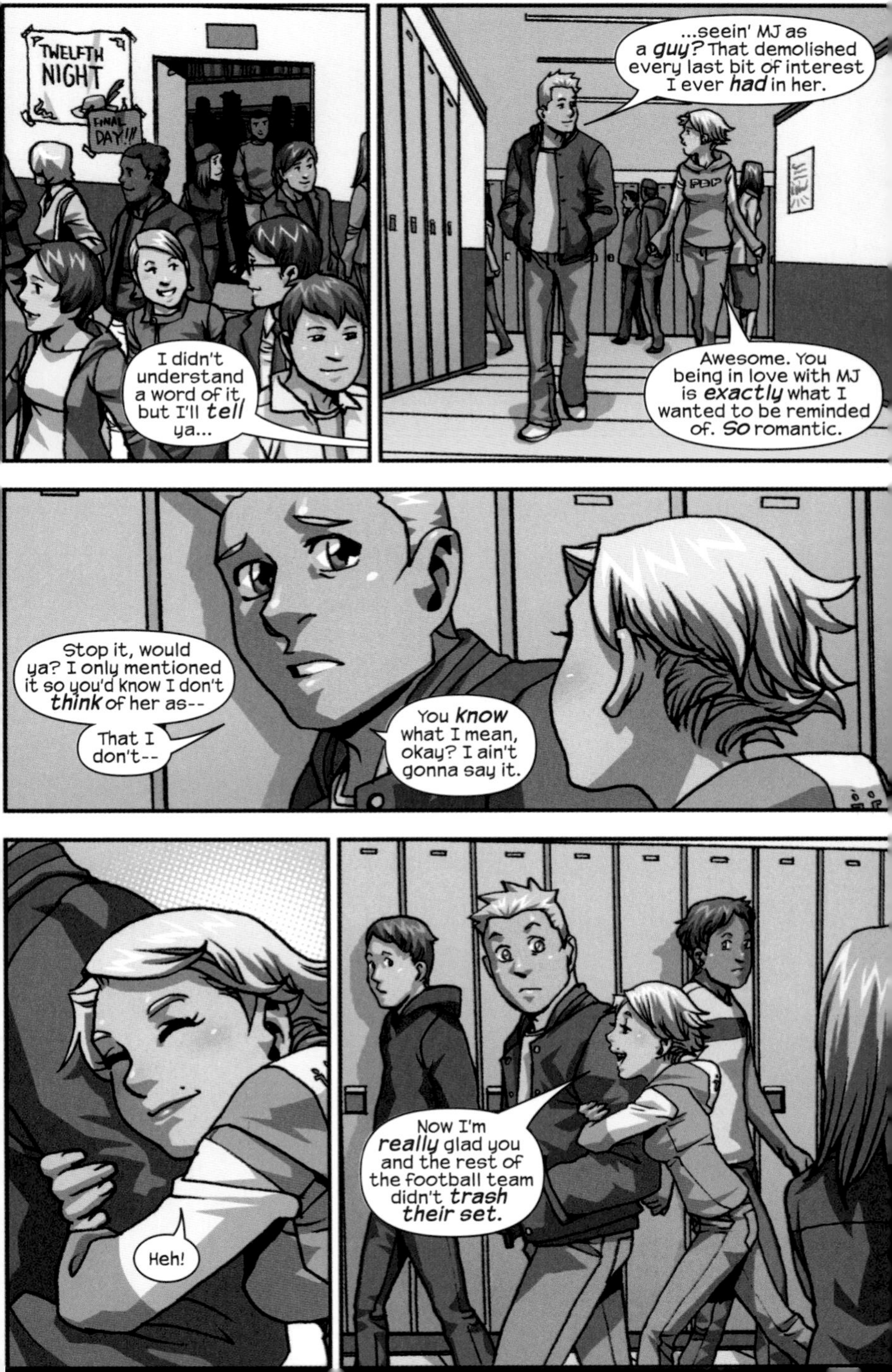
TWELFTH NIGHT
FINAL DAY!!!
I didn't understand a word of it, but I'll *tell* ya...
...seein' MJ as a *guy?* That demolished every last bit of interest I ever *had* in her.
Awesome. You being in love with MJ is *exactly* what I wanted to be reminded of. *SO* romantic.
Stop it, would ya? I only mentioned it so you'd know I don't *think* of her as--
That I don't--
You *know* what I mean, okay? I ain't gonna say it.
Heh!
Now I'm *really* glad you and the rest of the football team didn't *trash their set.*

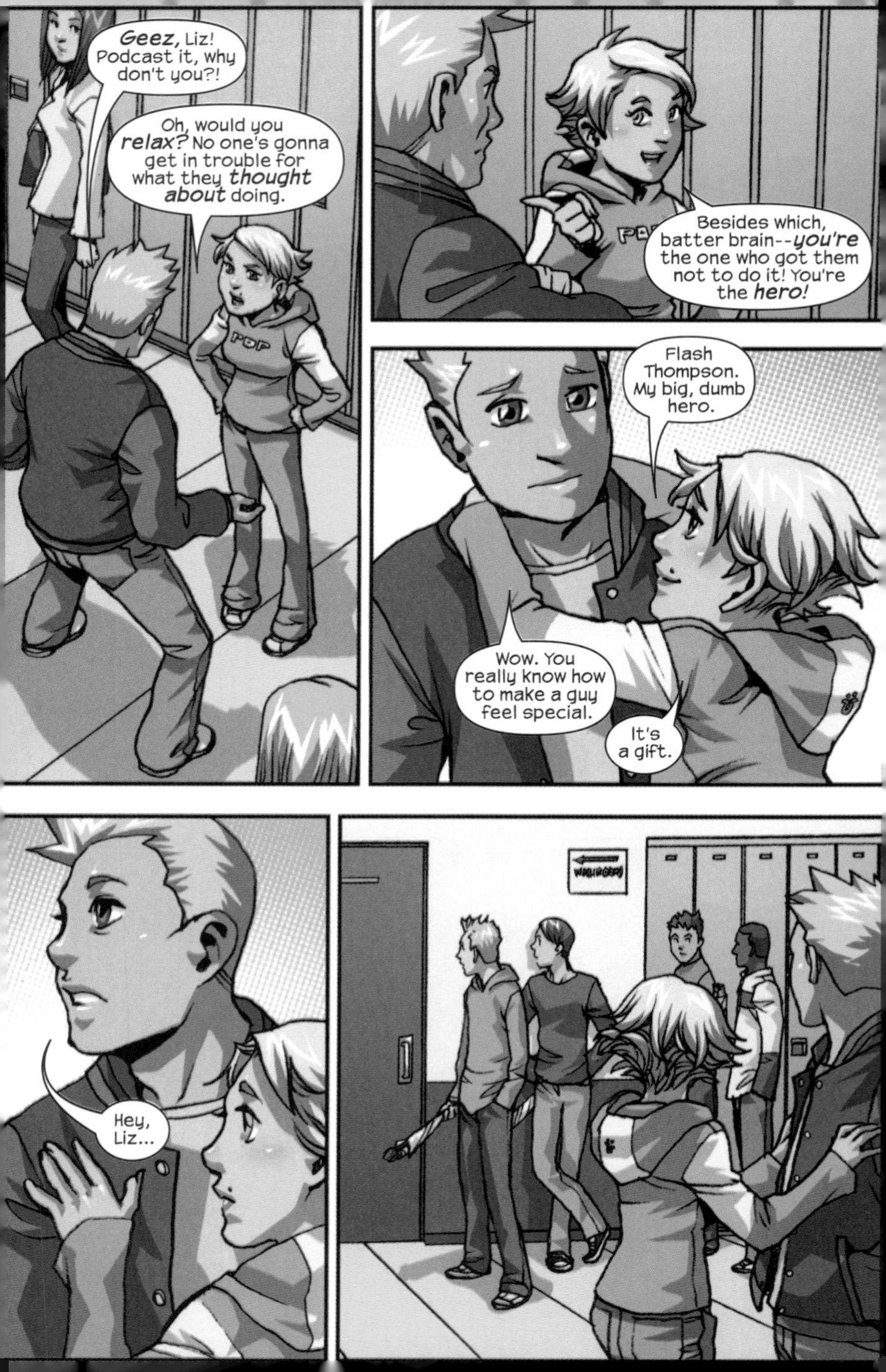
Geez, Liz! Podcast it, why don't you?!
Oh, would you relax? No one's gonna get in trouble for what they thought about doing.
Besides which, batter brain--you're the one who got them not to do it! You're the hero!
Flash Thompson. My big, dumb hero.
Wow. You really know how to make a guy feel special.
It's a gift.
Hey, Liz...

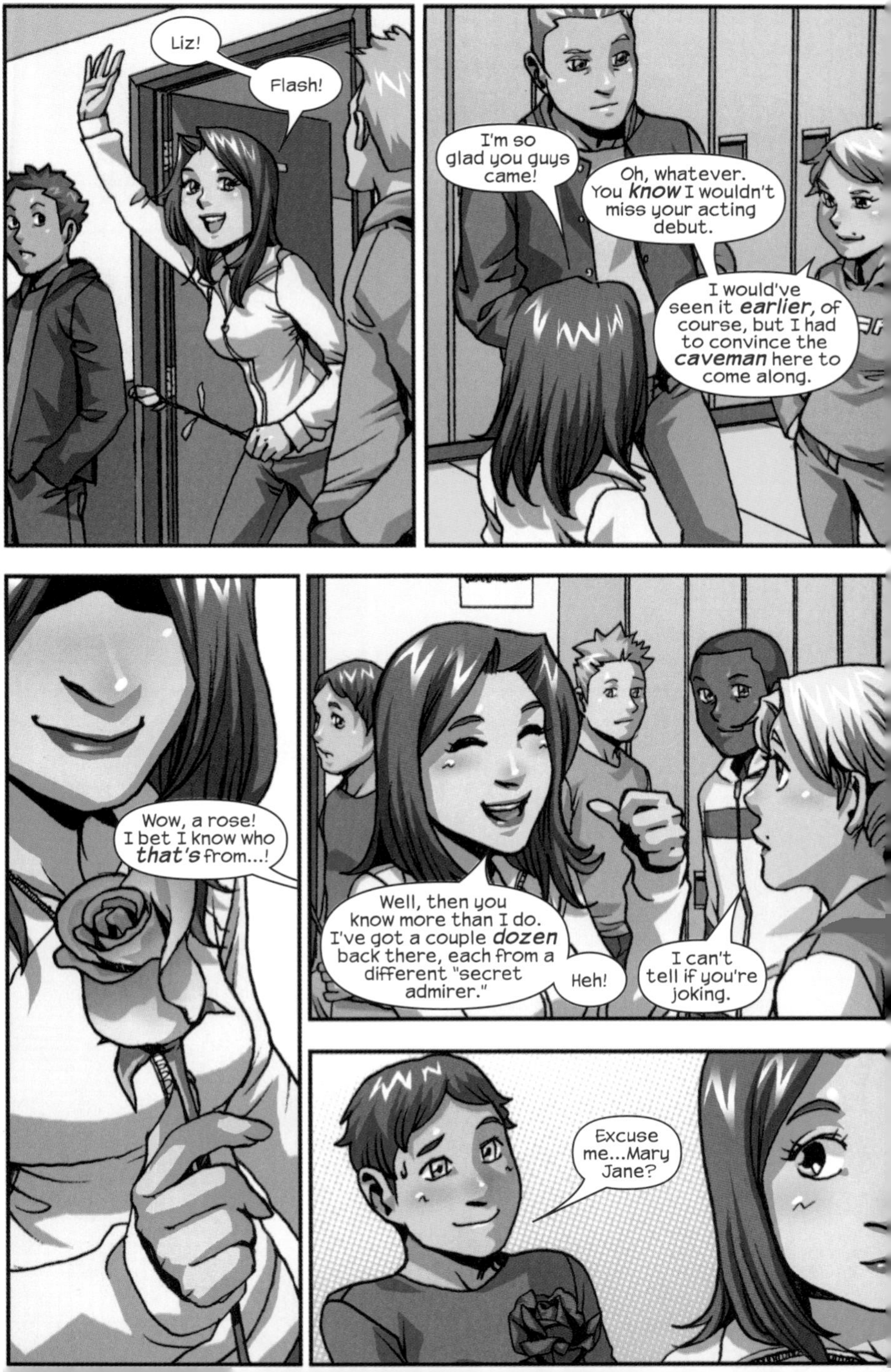
Liz!
Flash!
I'm so glad you guys came!
Oh, whatever. You *know* I wouldn't miss your acting debut.
I would've seen it *earlier,* of course, but I had to convince the *caveman* here to come along.
Wow, a rose! I bet I know who *that's* from...!
Well, then you know more than I do. I've got a couple *dozen* back there, each from a different "secret admirer."
Heh!
I can't tell if you're joking.
Excuse me...Mary Jane?

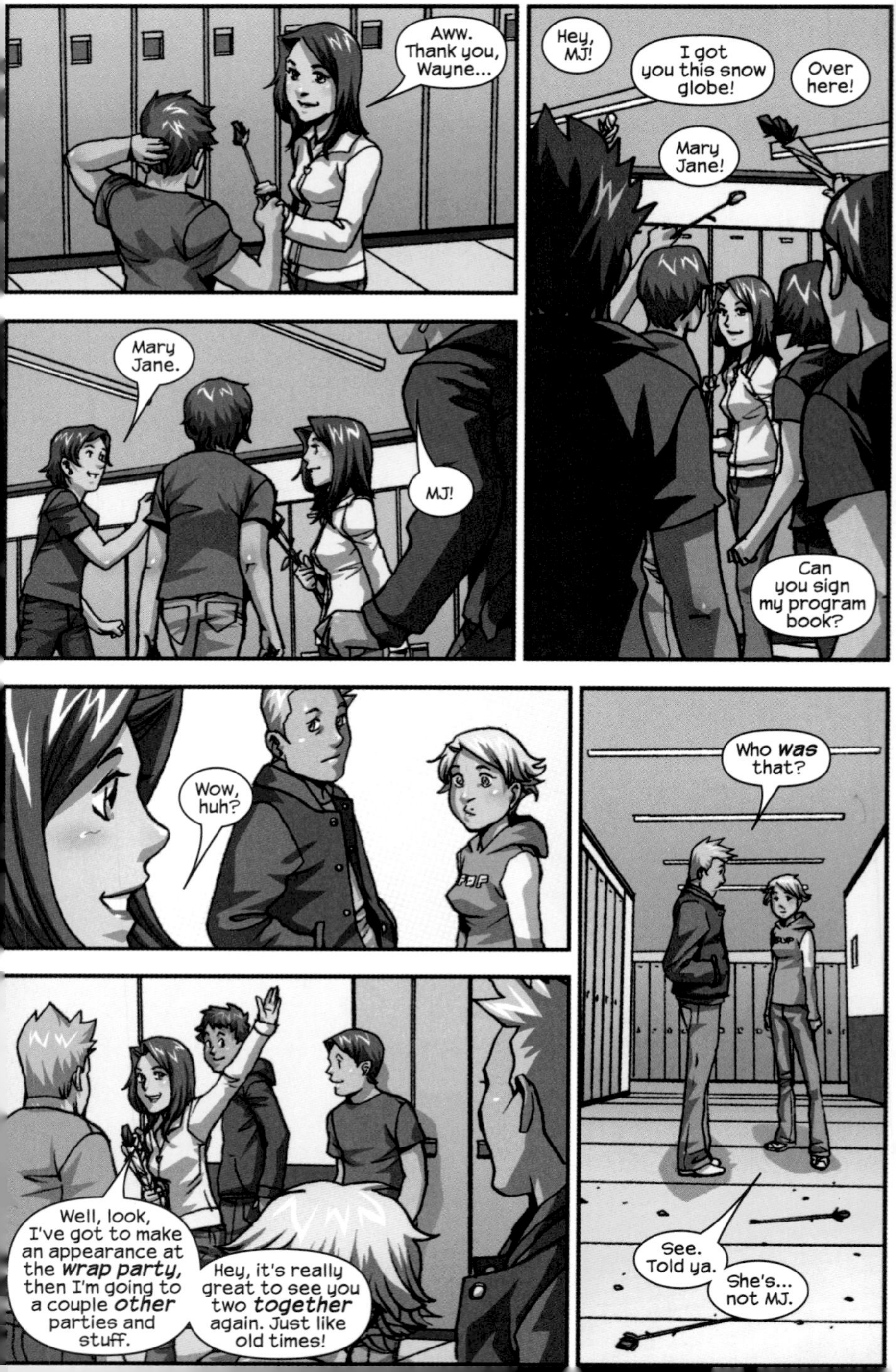
Aww. Thank you, Wayne...
Hey, MJ!
I got you this snow globe!
Over here!
Mary Jane!
Mary Jane.
MJ!
Can you sign my program book?
Wow, huh?
Who *was* that?
Well, look, I've got to make an appearance at the *wrap party,* then I'm going to a couple *other* parties and stuff.
Hey, it's really great to see you two *together* again. Just like old times!
See. Told ya.
She's... not MJ.

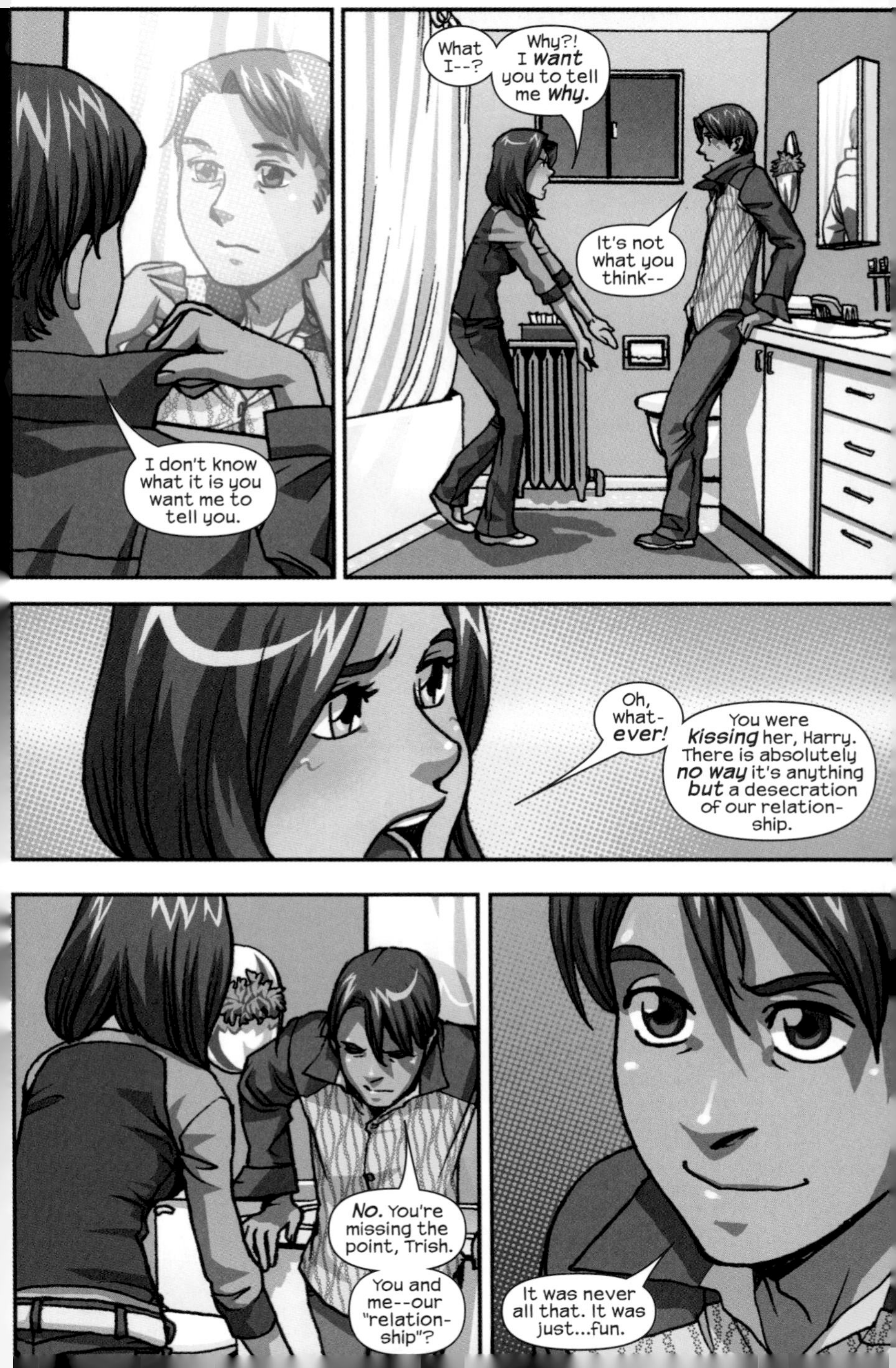
I don't know what it is you want me to tell you.
What I--?
Why?! I *want* you to tell me *why*.
It's not what you think--
Oh, what-*ever!*
You were *kissing* her, Harry. There is absolutely *no way* it's anything *but* a desecration of our relation-ship.
No. You're missing the point, Trish.
You and me--our "relation-ship"?
It was never all that. It was just...fun.

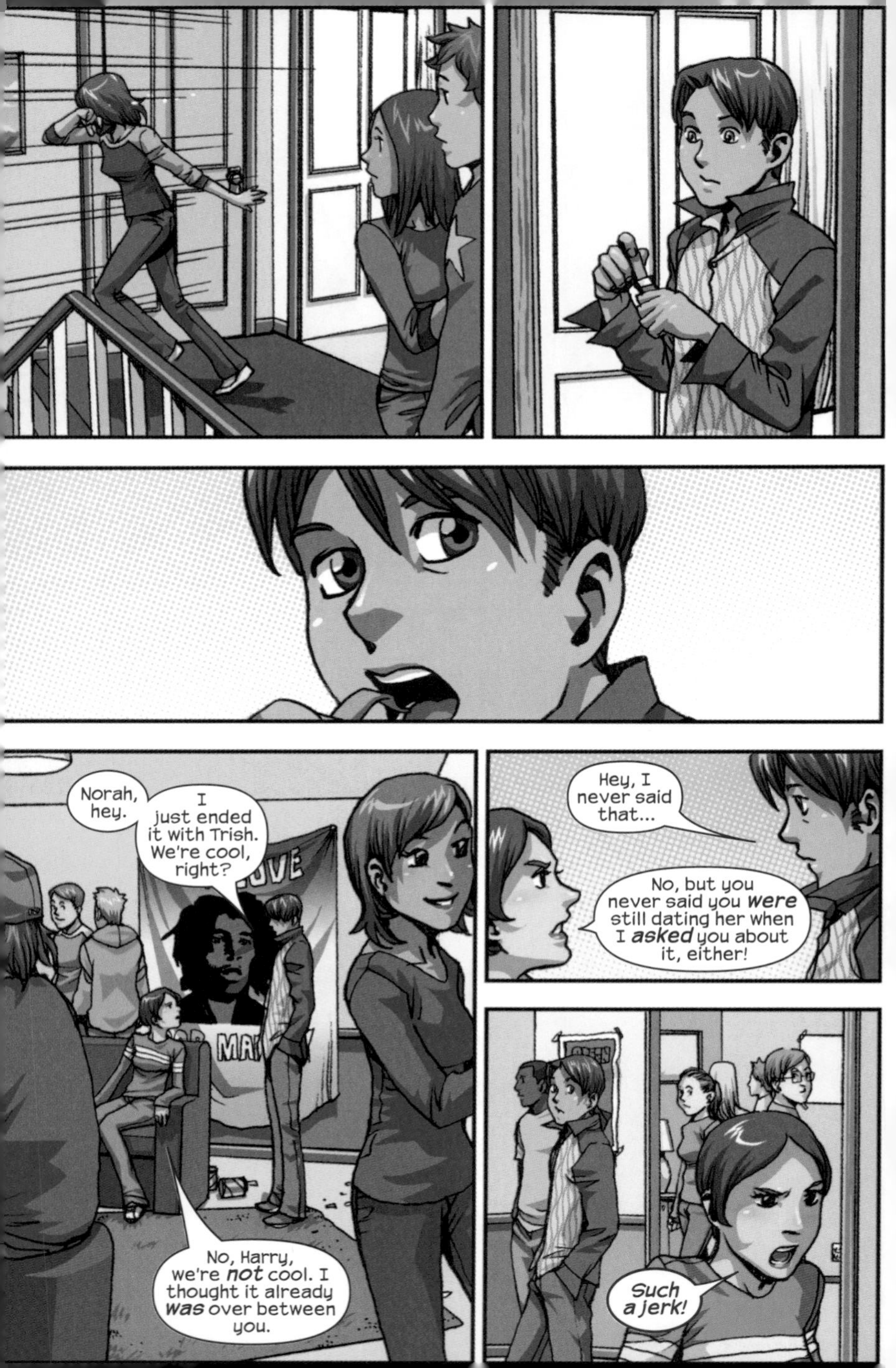
Norah, hey.
I just ended it with Trish. We're cool, right?
No, Harry, we're *not* cool. I thought it already *was* over between you.
Hey, I never said that...
No, but you never said you *were* still dating her when I *asked* you about it, either!
Such a jerk!

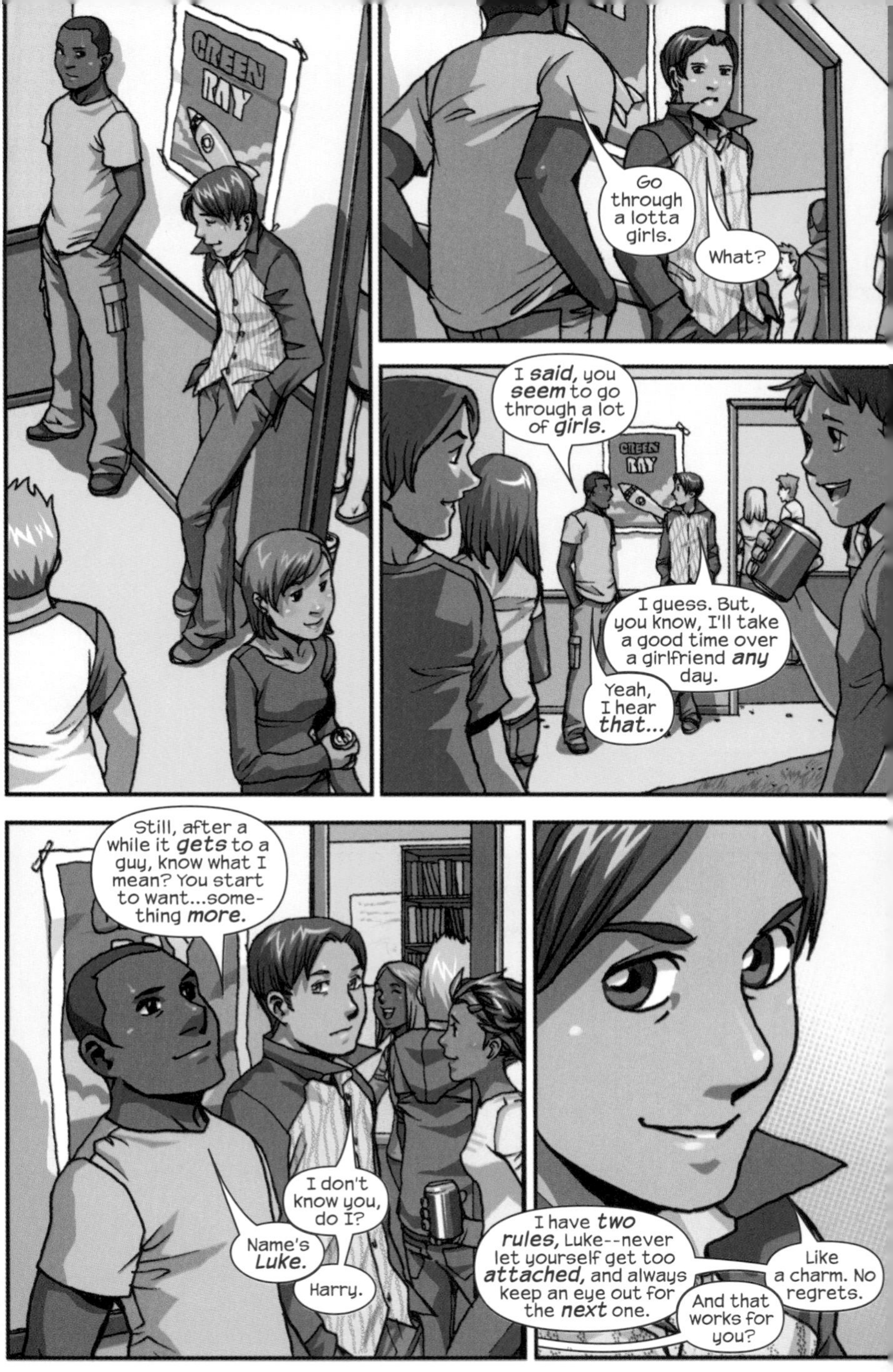
GREEN RAY
Go through a lotta girls.
What?
I said, you seem to go through a lot of girls.
GREEN RAY
I guess. But, you know, I'll take a good time over a girlfriend any day.
Yeah, I hear that...
Still, after a while it gets to a guy, know what I mean? You start to want...some-thing more.
I don't know you, do I?
Name's Luke.
Harry.
I have two rules, Luke--never let yourself get too attached, and always keep an eye out for the next one.
And that works for you?
Like a charm. No regrets.

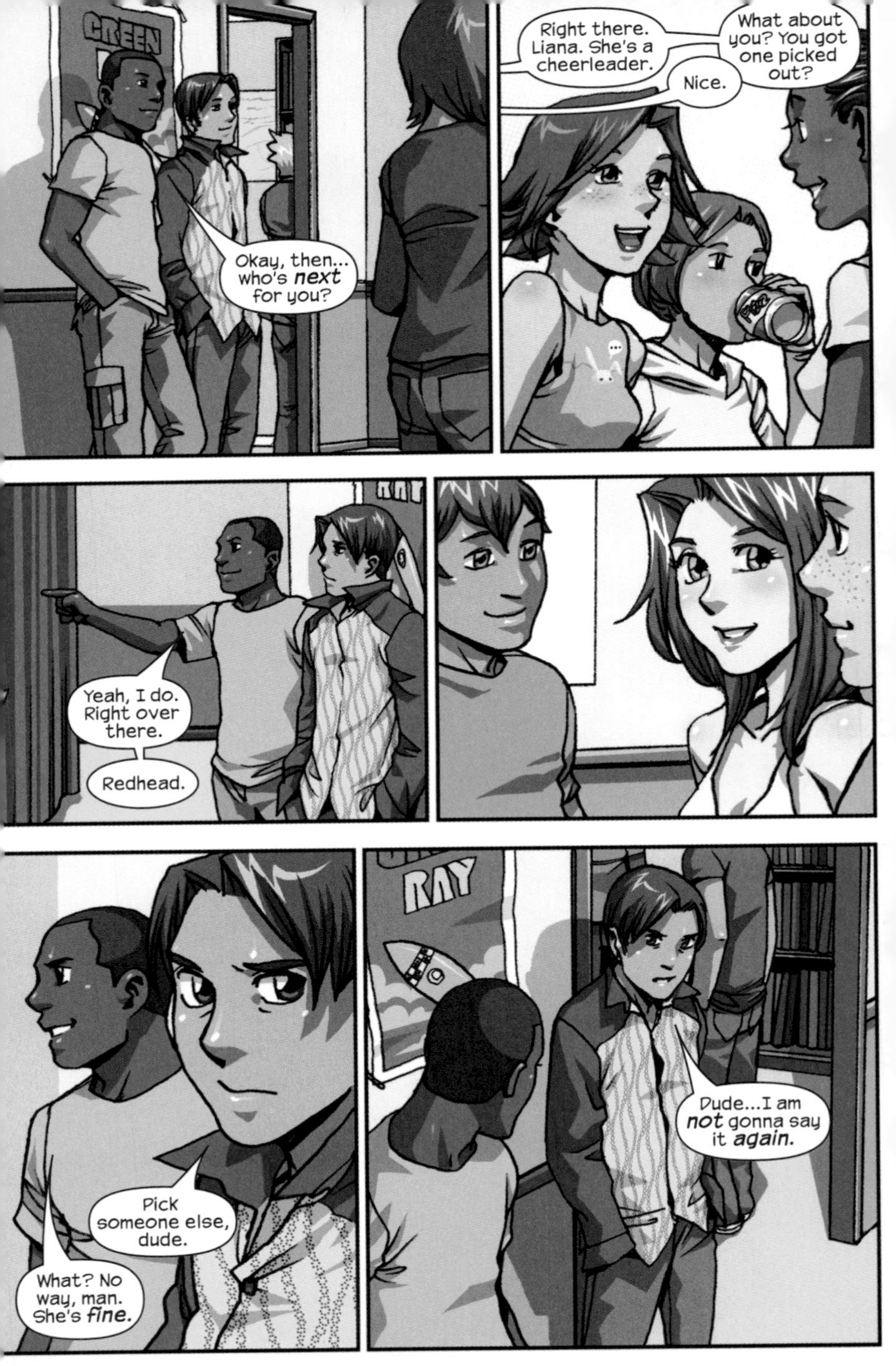
GREEN
Okay, then... who's *next* for you?
Right there. Liana. She's a cheerleader.
Nice.
What about you? You got one picked out?
Yeah, I do. Right over there.
Redhead.
Pick someone else, dude.
What? No way, man. She's *fine.*
RAY
Dude...I am *not* gonna say it *again.*

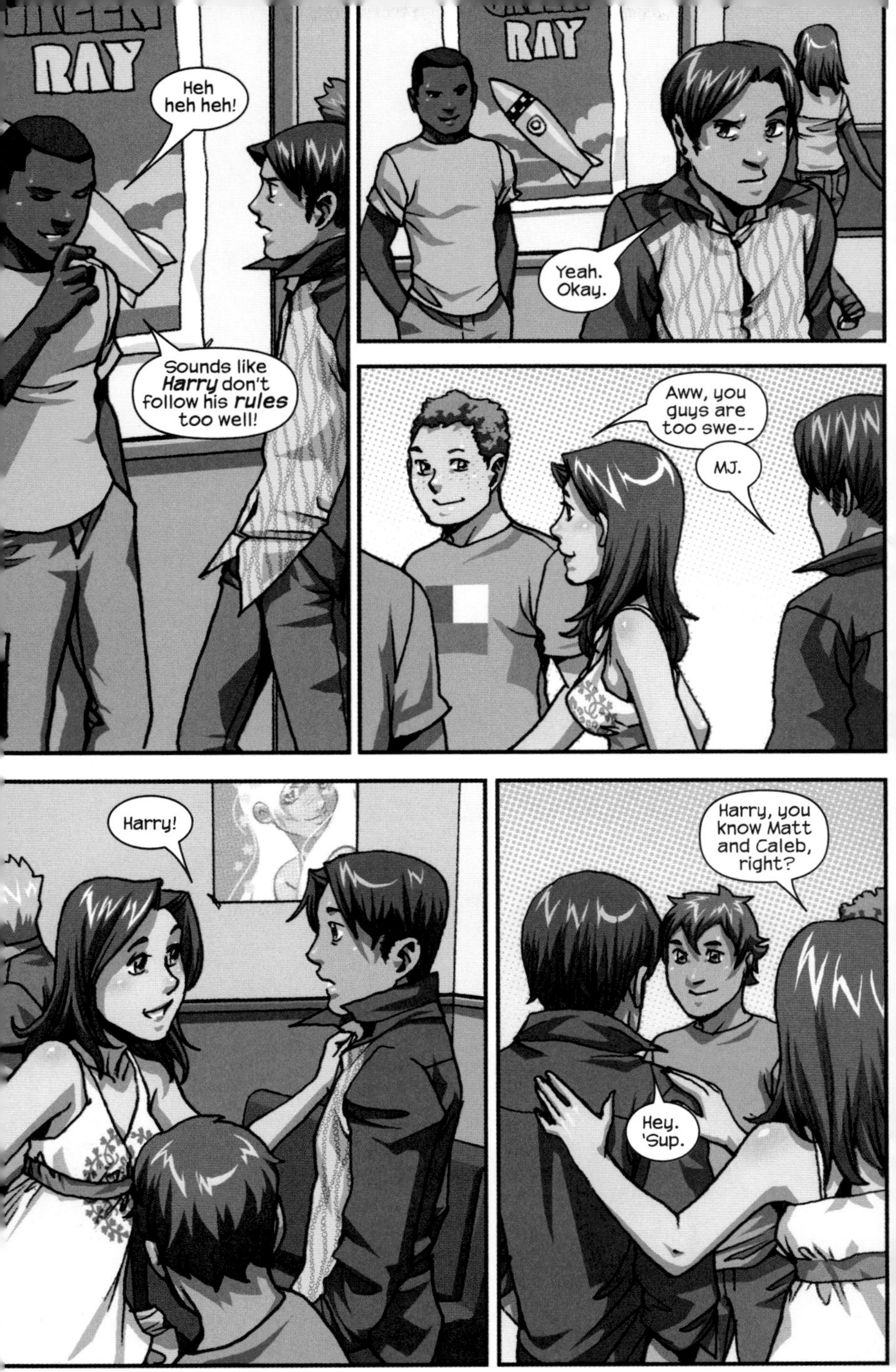
GREEN
RAY
Heh heh heh!
Sounds like Harry don't follow his rules too well!
RAY
Yeah. Okay.
Aww, you guys are too swe--
MJ.
Harry!
Harry, you know Matt and Caleb, right?
Hey. 'Sup.

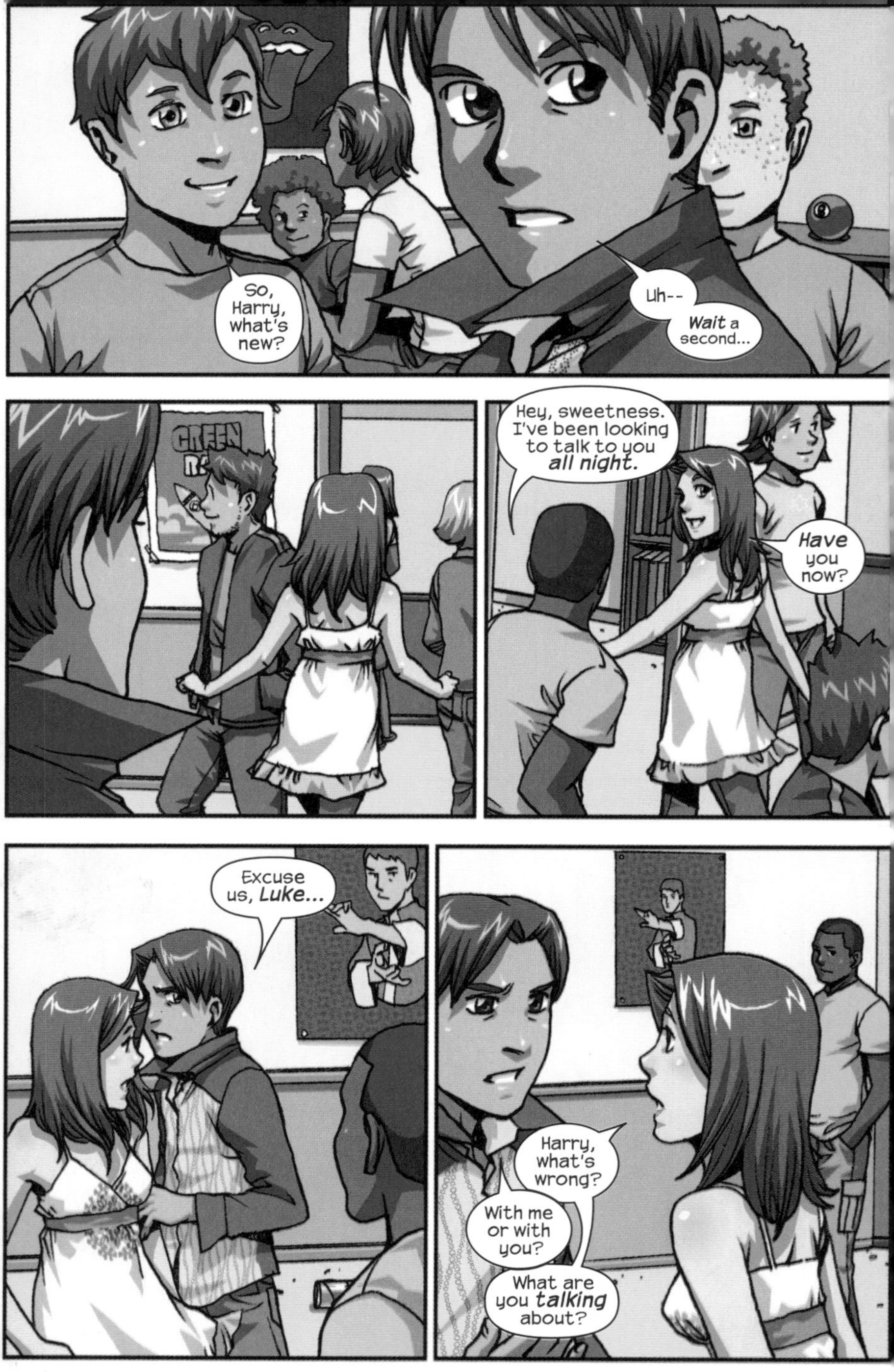
So, Harry, what's new?
Uh--
Wait a second...
Hey, sweetness. I've been looking to talk to you all night.
Have you now?
Excuse us, Luke...
Harry, what's wrong?
With me or with you?
What are you talking about?

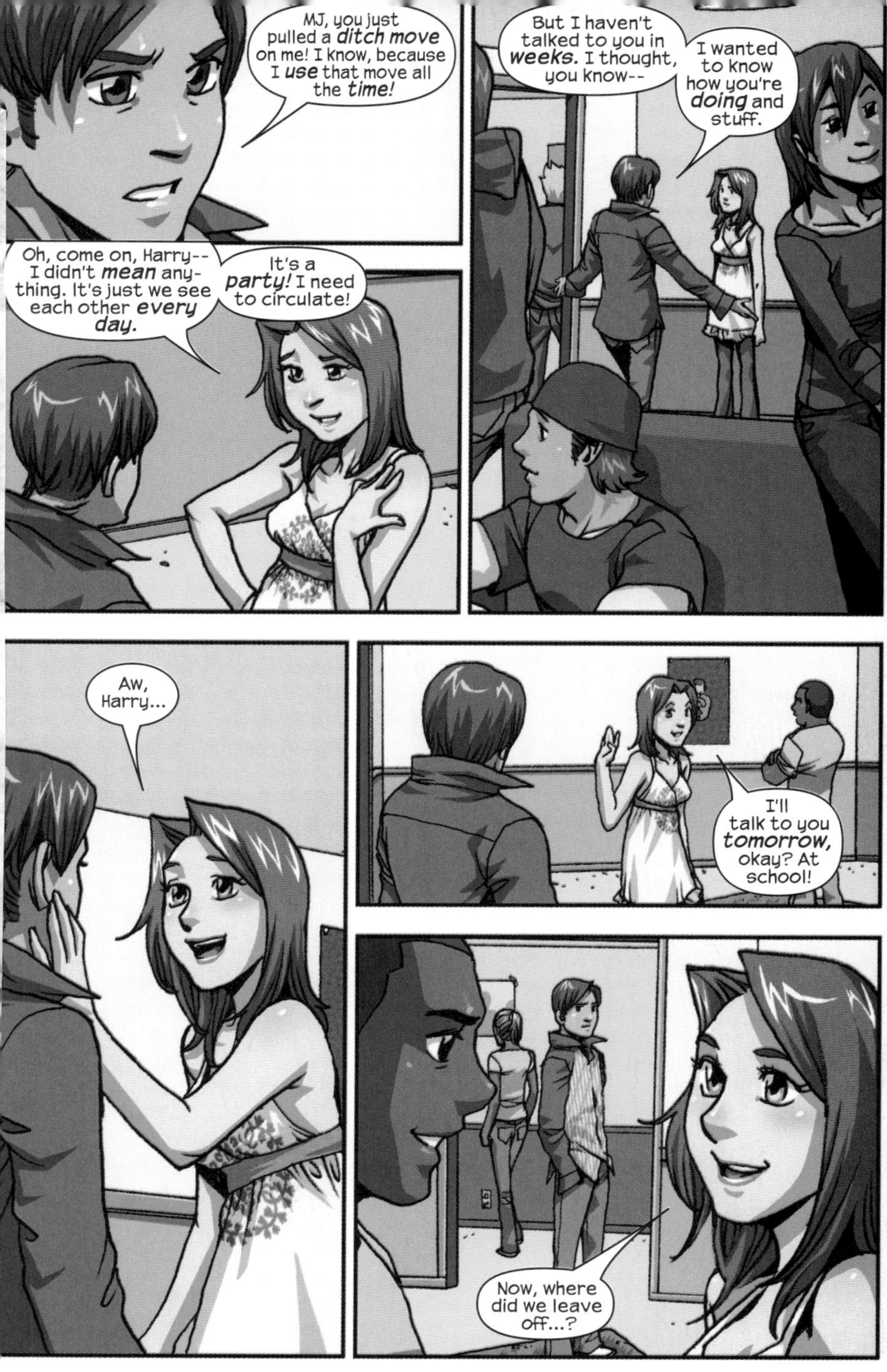
MJ, you just pulled a ditch move on me! I know, because I use that move all the time!
But I haven't talked to you in weeks. I thought, you know--
I wanted to know how you're doing and stuff.
Oh, come on, Harry-- I didn't mean any-thing. It's just we see each other every day.
It's a party! I need to circulate!
Aw, Harry...
I'll talk to you tomorrow, okay? At school!
Now, where did we leave off...?

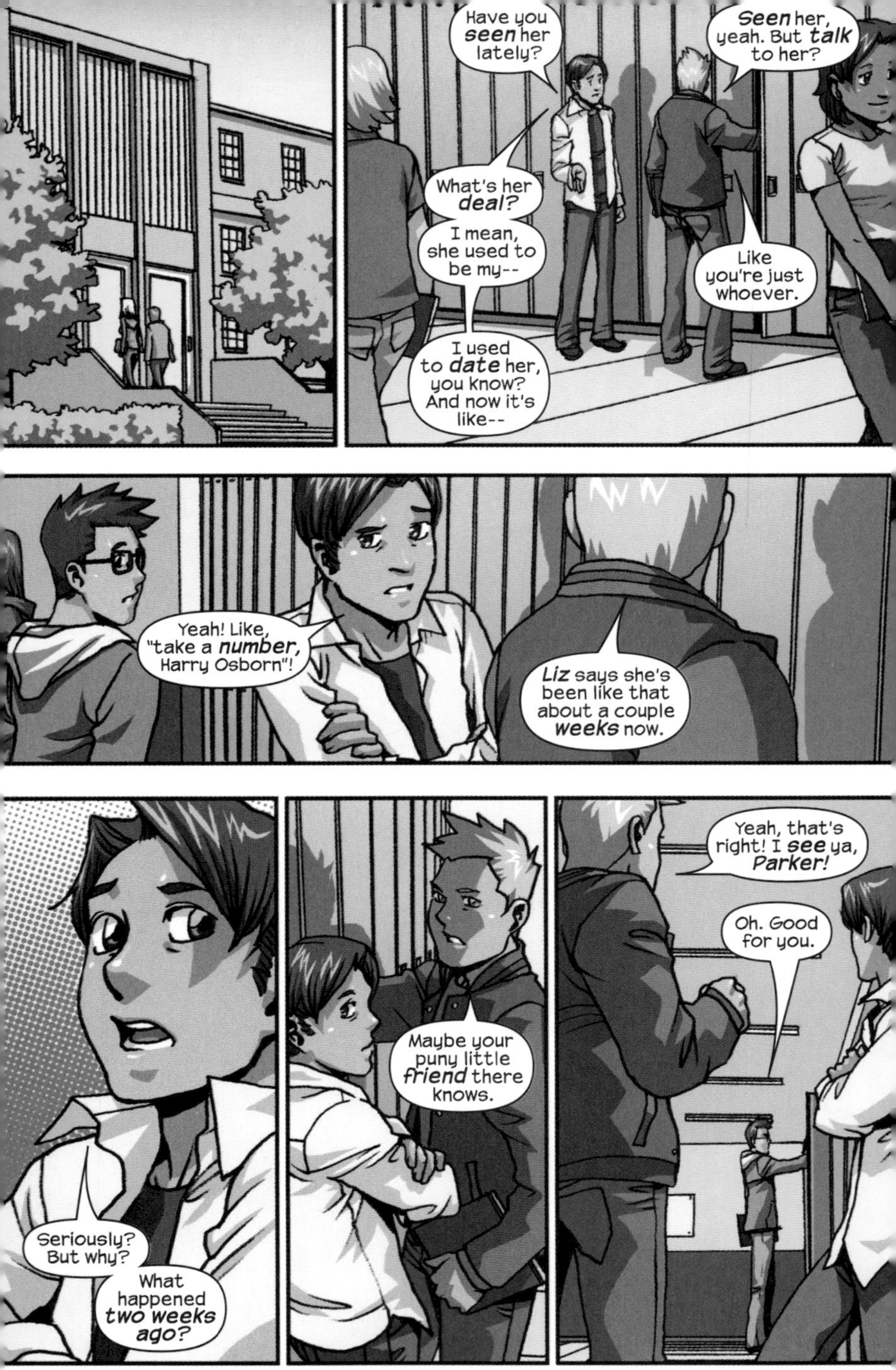
Have you seen her lately?
Seen her, yeah. But talk to her?
What's her deal?
I mean, she used to be my--
Like you're just whoever.
I used to date her, you know? And now it's like--
Yeah! Like, "take a number, Harry Osborn"!
Liz says she's been like that about a couple weeks now.
Seriously? But why?
What happened two weeks ago?
Maybe your puny little friend there knows.
Yeah, that's right! I see ya, Parker!
Oh. Good for you.

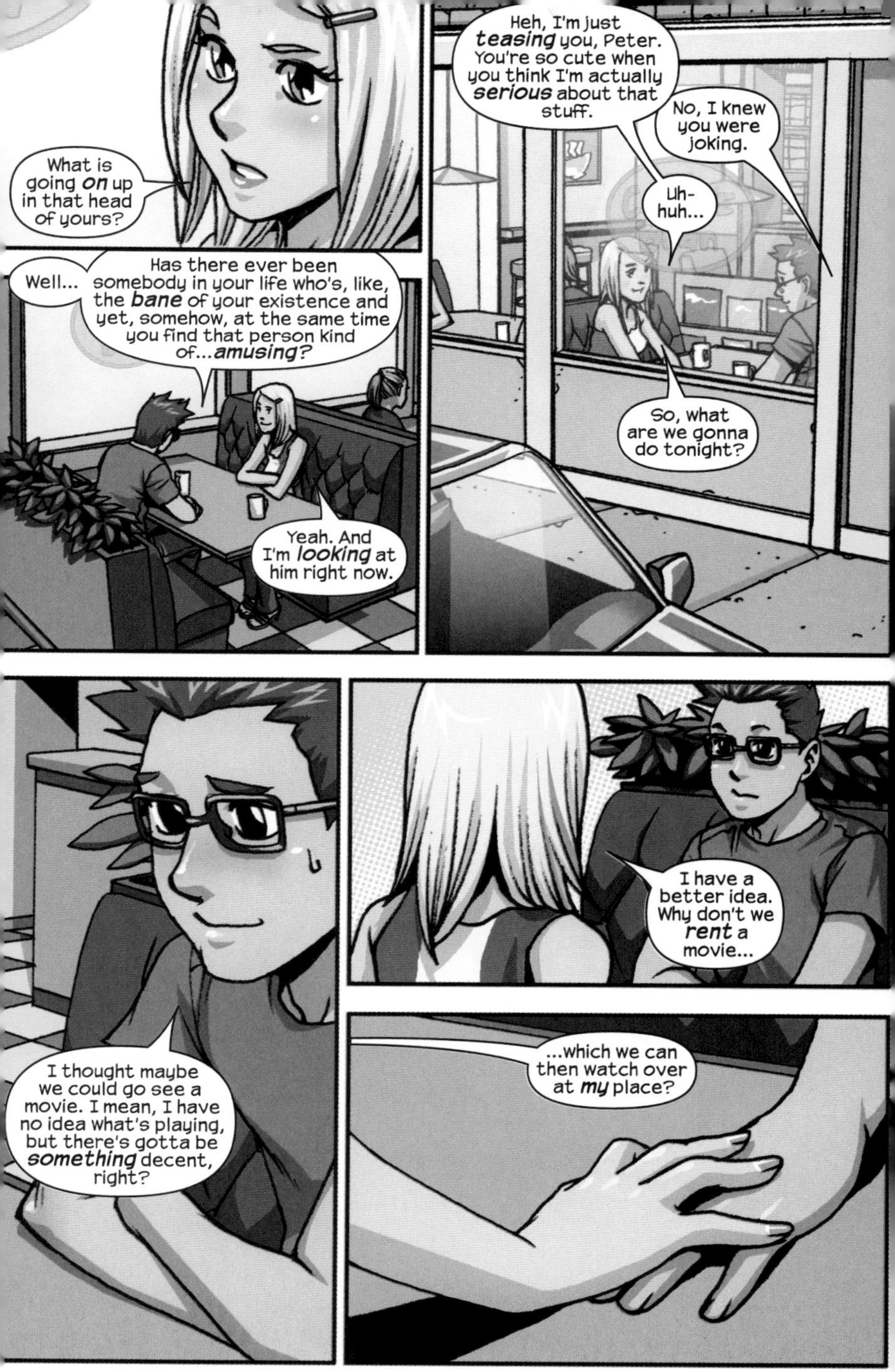
What is going on up in that head of yours?
Heh, I'm just teasing you, Peter. You're so cute when you think I'm actually serious about that stuff.
No, I knew you were joking.
Uh-huh...
Well...
Has there ever been somebody in your life who's, like, the bane of your existence and yet, somehow, at the same time you find that person kind of...amusing?
Yeah. And I'm looking at him right now.
So, what are we gonna do tonight?
I thought maybe we could go see a movie. I mean, I have no idea what's playing, but there's gotta be something decent, right?
I have a better idea. Why don't we rent a movie...
...which we can then watch over at my place?

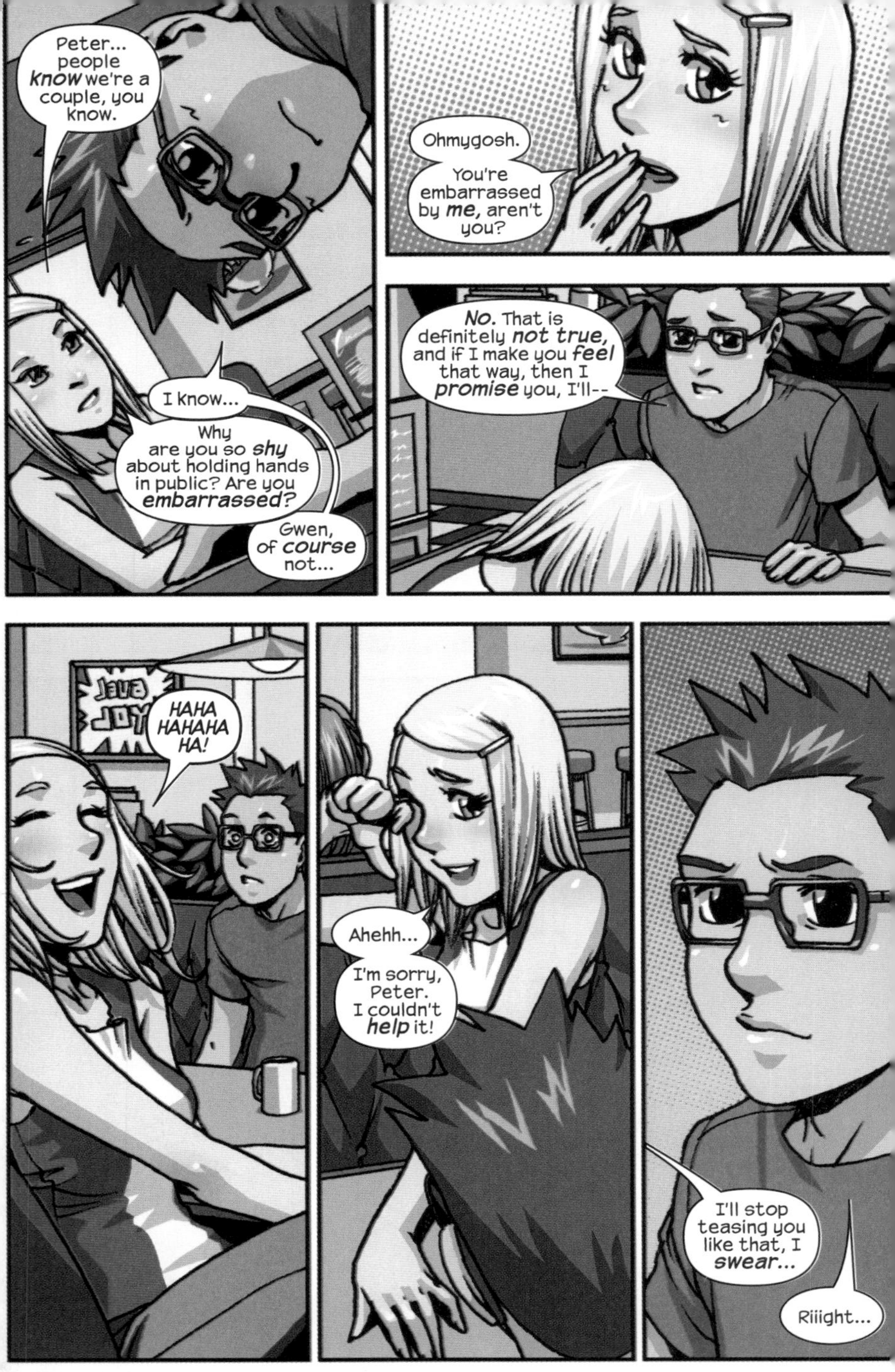
Peter... people KNOW we're a couple, you know.
I know...
Why are you so shy about holding hands in public? Are you embarrassed?
Gwen, of course not...
Ohmygosh.
You're embarrassed by me, aren't you?
No. That is definitely not true, and if I make you feel that way, then I promise you, I'll--
HAHA HAHAHA HA!
Ahehh...
I'm sorry, Peter. I couldn't help it!
I'll stop teasing you like that, I swear...
Riiight...

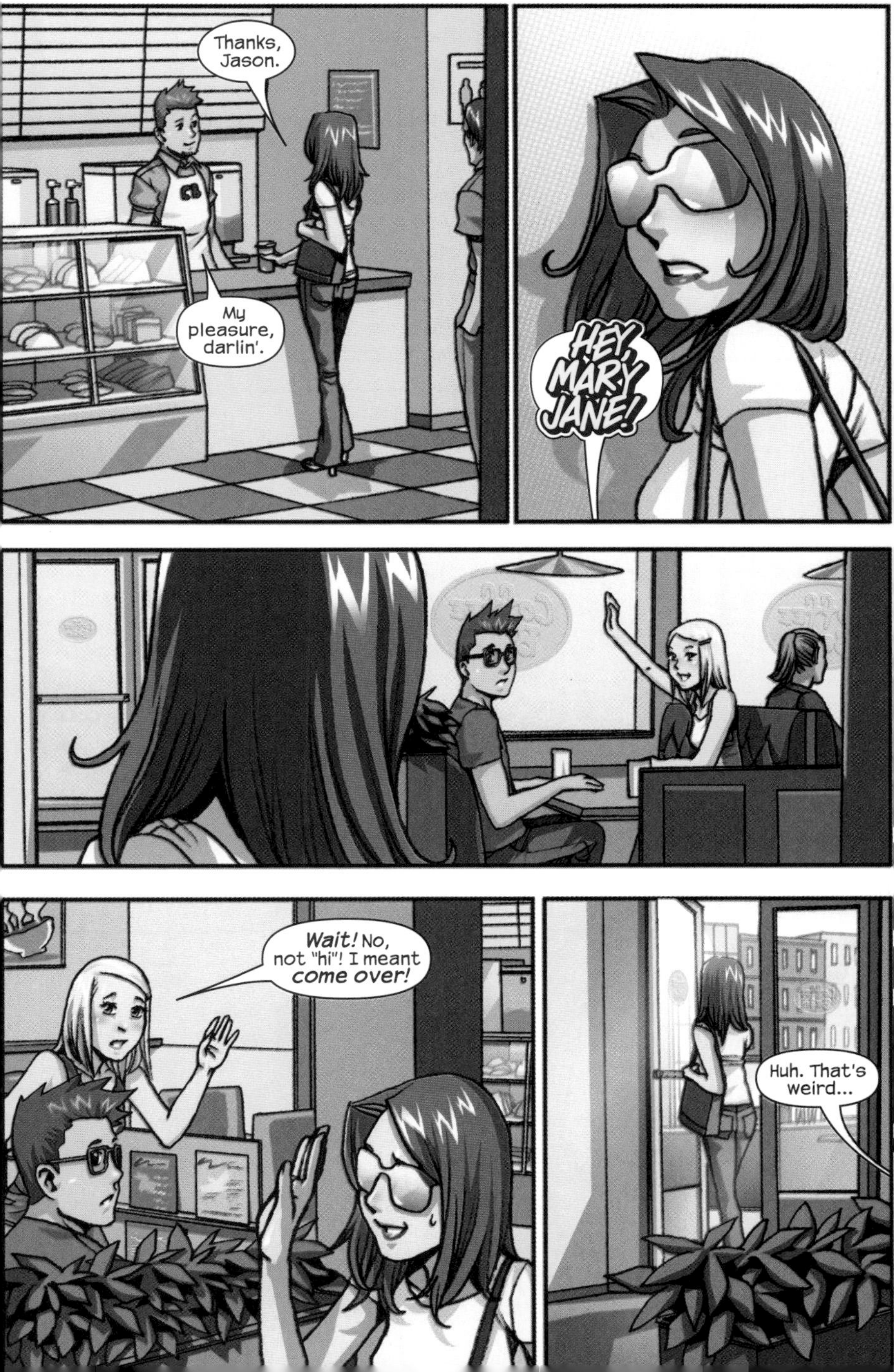
Thanks, Jason.
My pleasure, darlin'.
HEY, MARY JANE!
Wait! No, not "hi"! I meant come over!
Huh. That's weird...

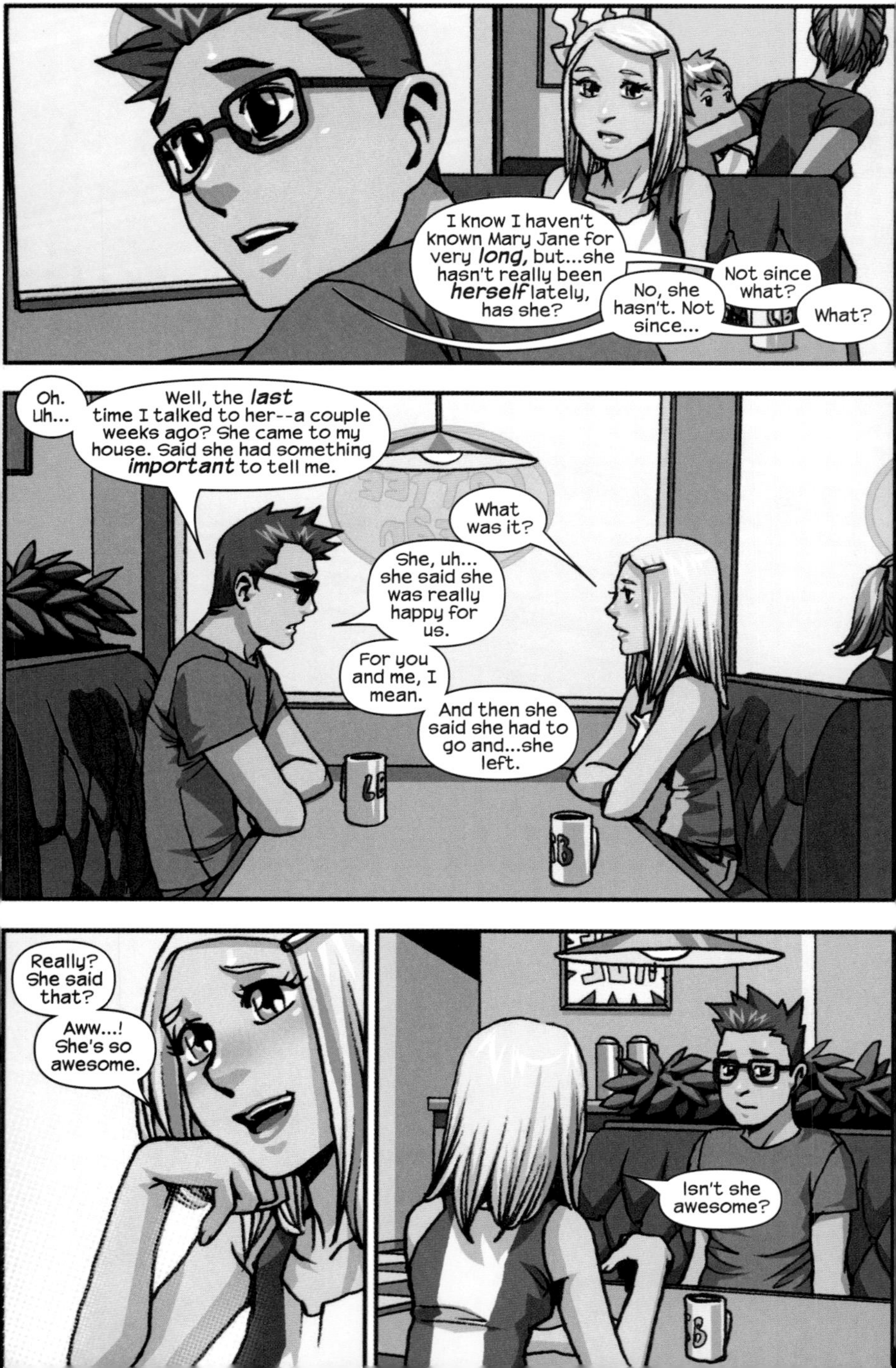
I know I haven't known Mary Jane for very *long,* but...she hasn't really been *herself* lately, has she?
No, she hasn't. Not since...
Not since what?
What?
Oh. Uh...
Well, the *last* time I talked to her--a couple weeks ago? She came to my house. Said she had something *important* to tell me.
What was it?
She, uh... she said she was really happy for us.
For you and me, I mean.
And then she said she had to go and...she left.
Really? She said that?
Aww...! She's so awesome.
Isn't she awesome?

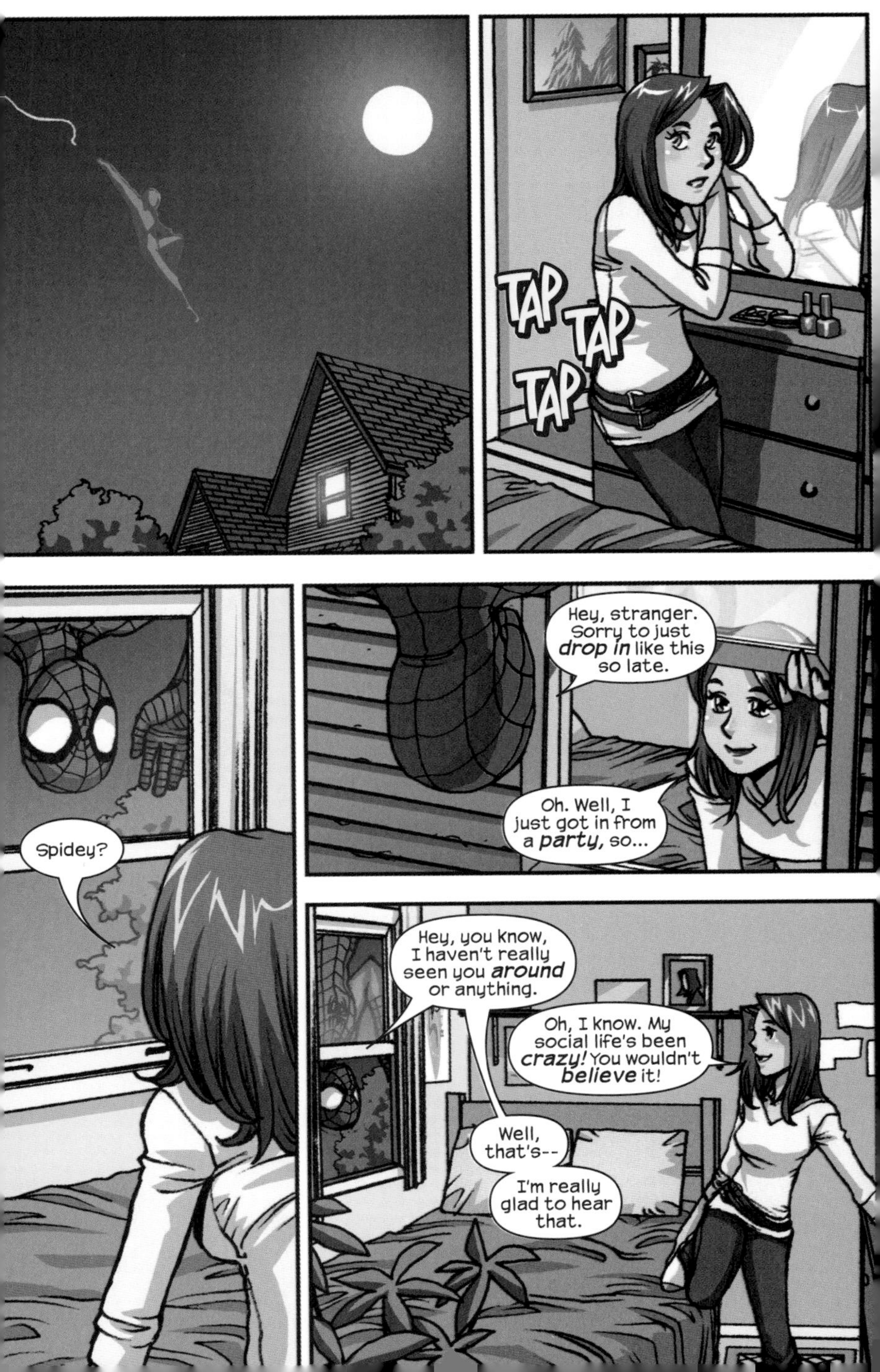
TAP
TAP
TAP
Spidey?
Hey, stranger. Sorry to just drop in like this so late.
Oh. Well, I just got in from a party, so...
Hey, you know, I haven't really seen you around or anything.
Oh, I know. My social life's been crazy! You wouldn't believe it!
Well, that's--
I'm really glad to hear that.

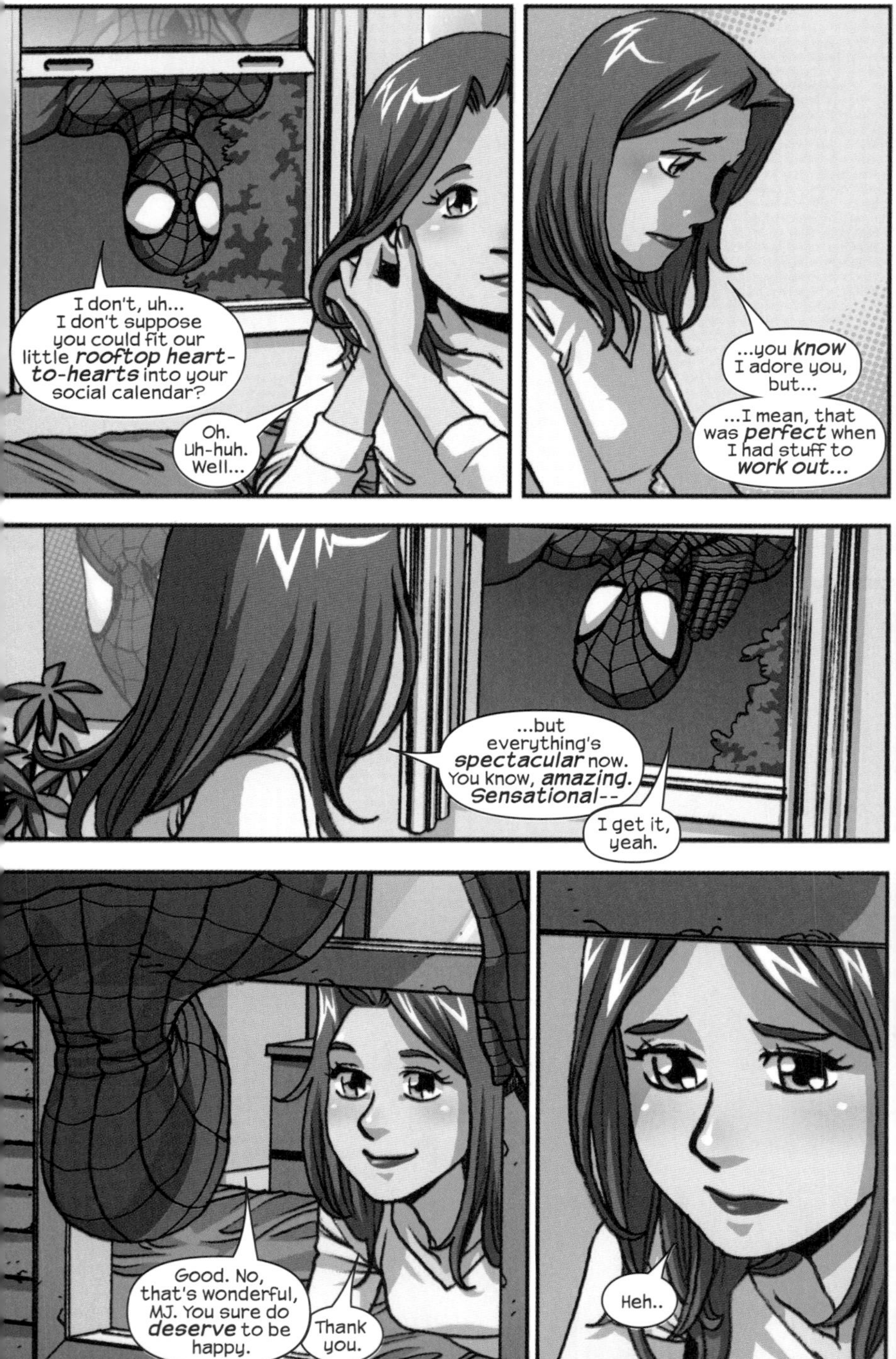
I don't, uh... I don't suppose you could fit our little rooftop heart-to-hearts into your social calendar?
Oh. Uh-huh. Well...
...you know I adore you, but...
...I mean, that was perfect when I had stuff to work out...
...but everything's spectacular now. You know, amazing. Sensational--
I get it, yeah.
Good. No, that's wonderful, MJ. You sure do deserve to be happy.
Thank you.
Heh..

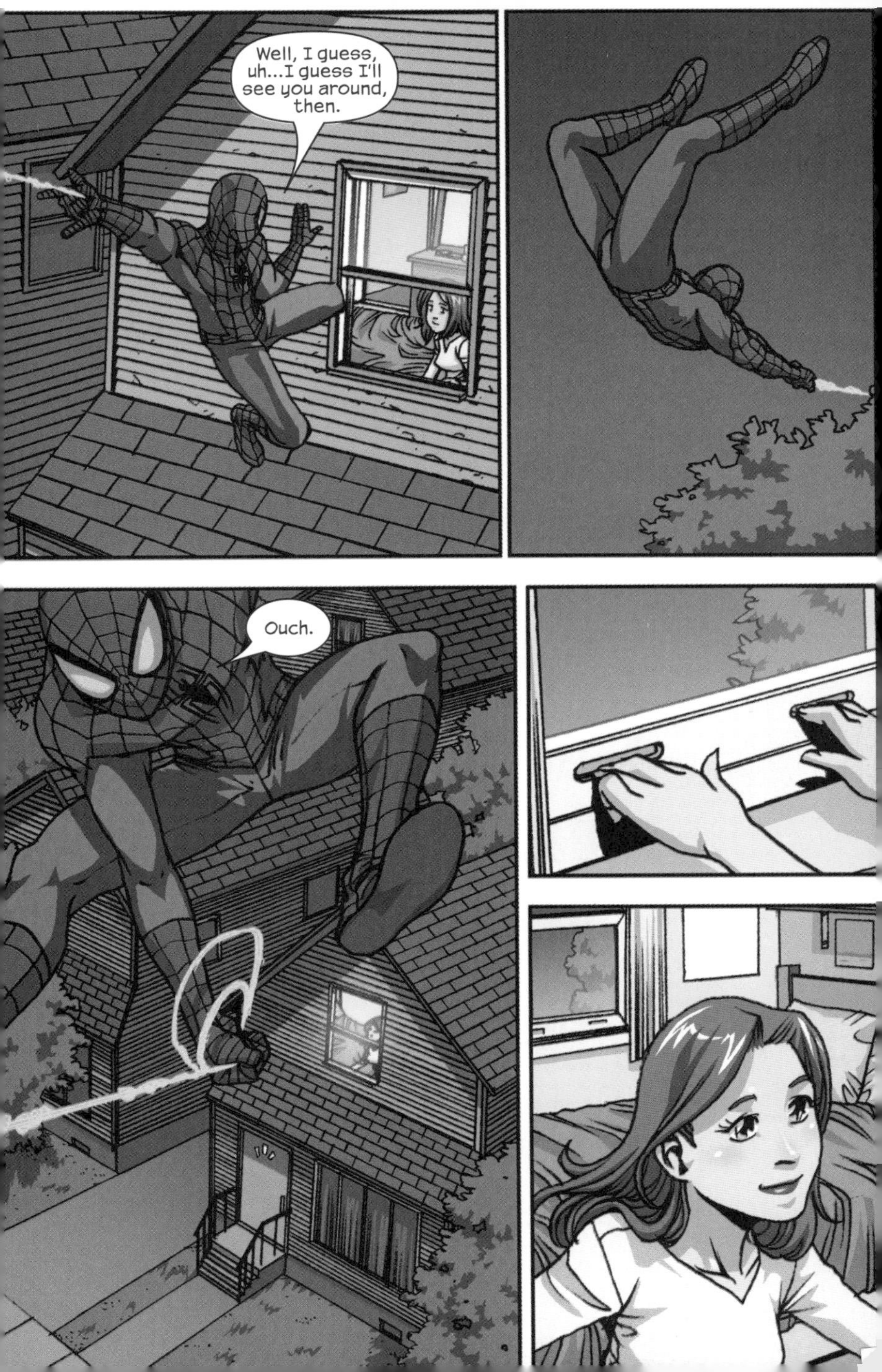
Well, I guess, uh...I guess I'll see you around, then.
Ouch.

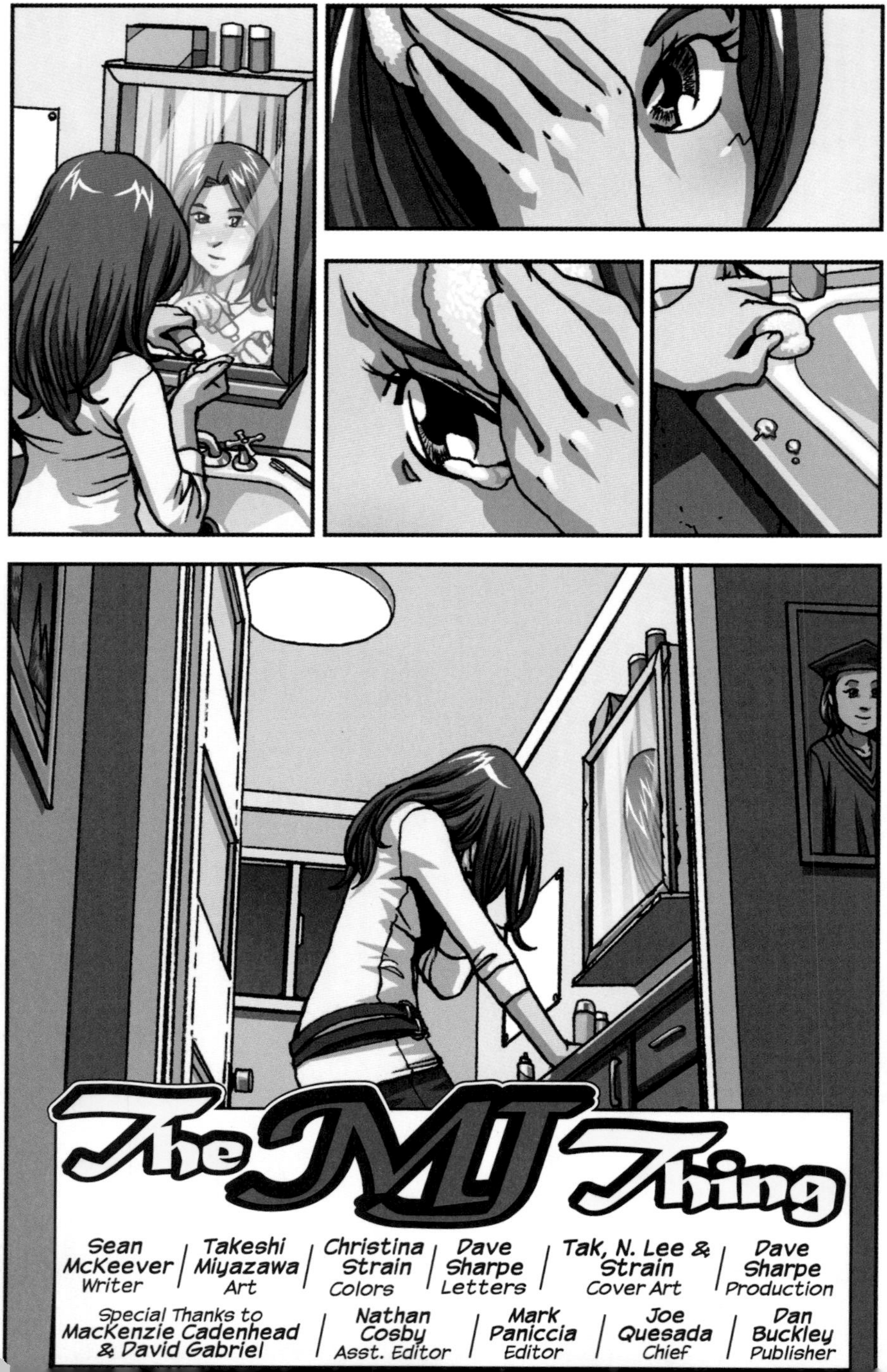
The MJ Thing
Sean McKeever Writer
Takeshi Miyazawa Art
Christina Strain Colors
Dave Sharpe Letters
Tak, N. Lee & Strain Cover Art
Dave Sharpe Production
Special Thanks to MacKenzie Cadenhead & David Gabriel
Nathan Cosby Asst. Editor
Mark Paniccia Editor
Joe Quesada Chief
Dan Buckley Publisher

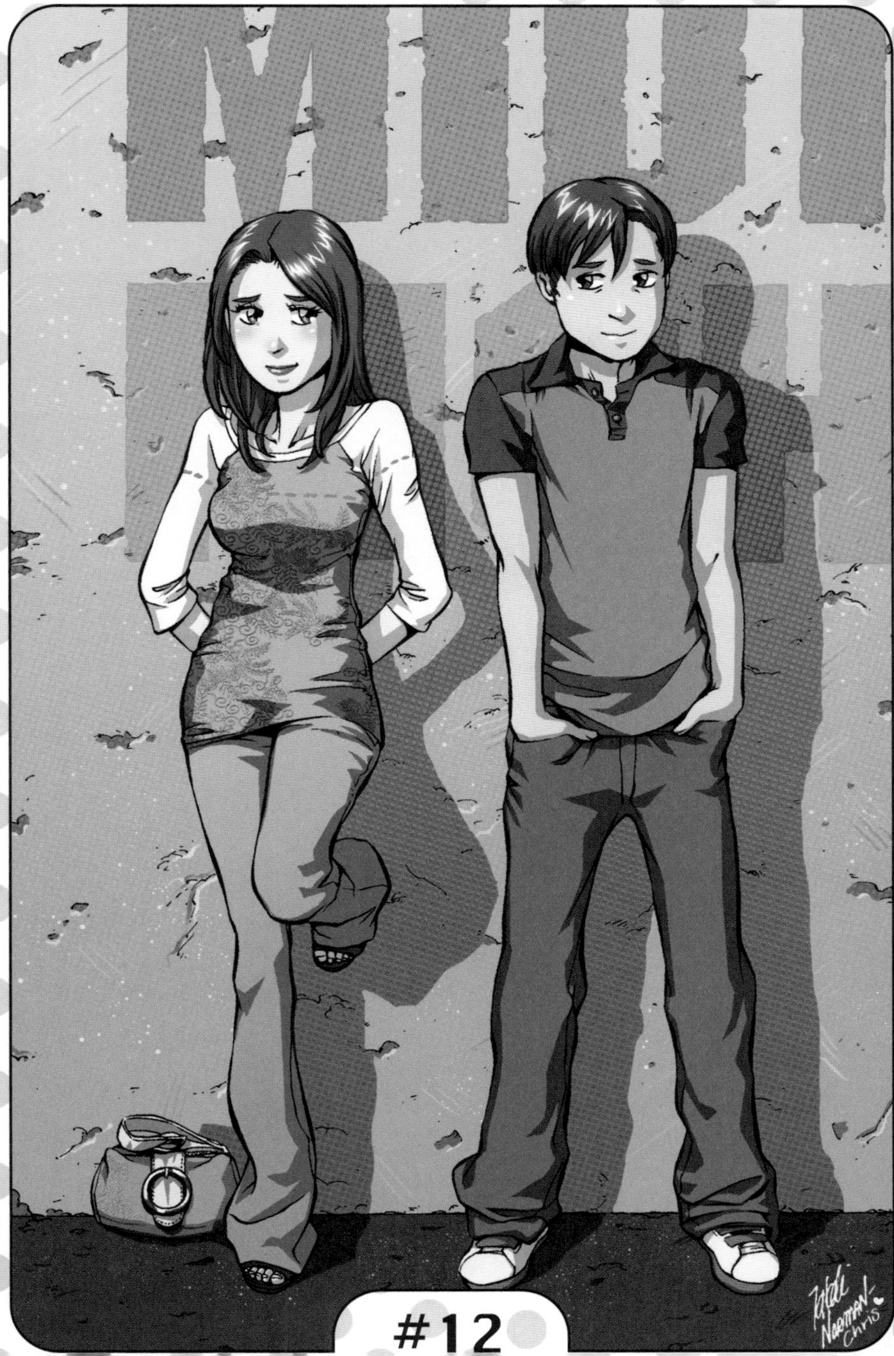
#12

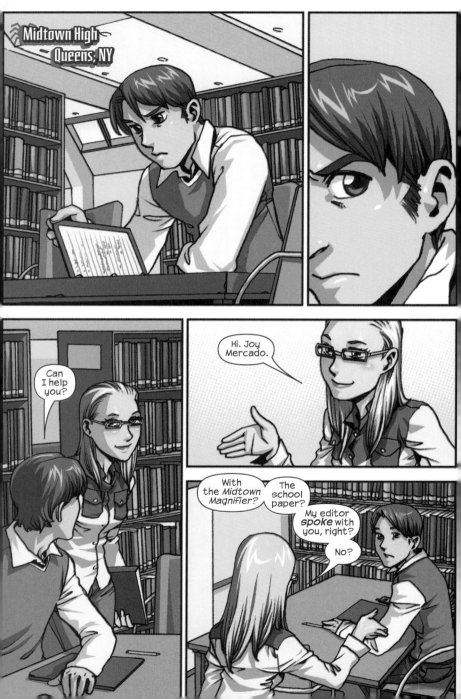

Can I help you?

Hi. Joy Mercado.

With the *Midtown Magnifier*?

The school paper?

My editor *spoke* with you, right?

No?

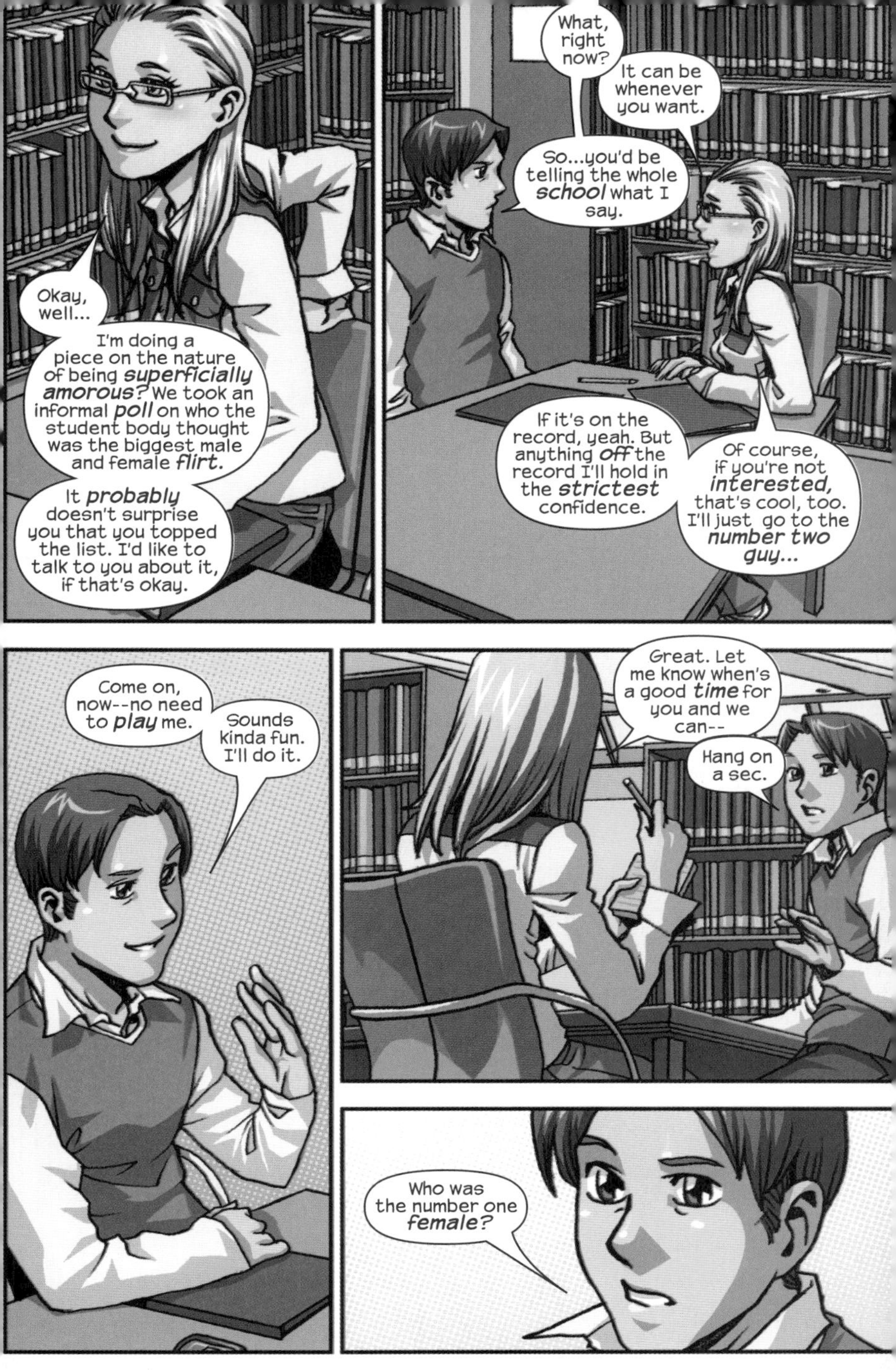
Okay, well...
I'm doing a piece on the nature of being superficially amorous? We took an informal poll on who the student body thought was the biggest male and female flirt.
It probably doesn't surprise you that you topped the list. I'd like to talk to you about it, if that's okay.
What, right now?
It can be whenever you want.
So...you'd be telling the whole school what I say.
If it's on the record, yeah. But anything off the record I'll hold in the strictest confidence.
Of course, if you're not interested, that's cool, too. I'll just go to the number two guy...
Come on, now--no need to play me.
Sounds kinda fun. I'll do it.
Great. Let me know when's a good time for you and we can--
Hang on a sec.
Who was the number one female?

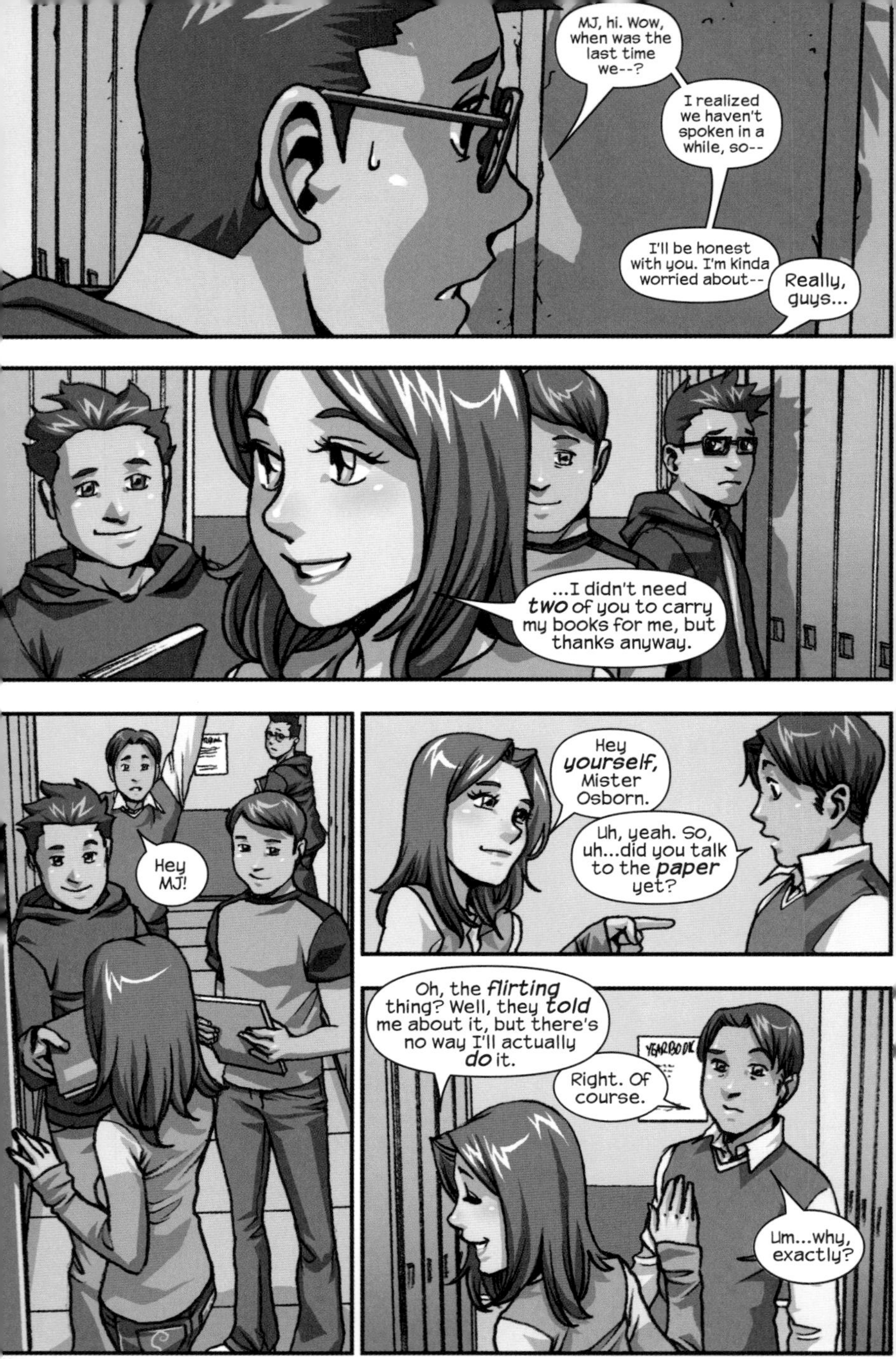
MJ, hi. Wow, when was the last time we--?
I realized we haven't spoken in a while, so--
I'll be honest with you. I'm kinda worried about--
Really, guys...
...I didn't need *two* of you to carry my books for me, but thanks anyway.
Hey MJ!
Hey *yourself,* Mister Osborn.
Uh, yeah. So, uh...did you talk to the *paper* yet?
Oh, the *flirting* thing? Well, they *told* me about it, but there's no way I'll actually *do* it.
Right. Of course.
Um...why, exactly?

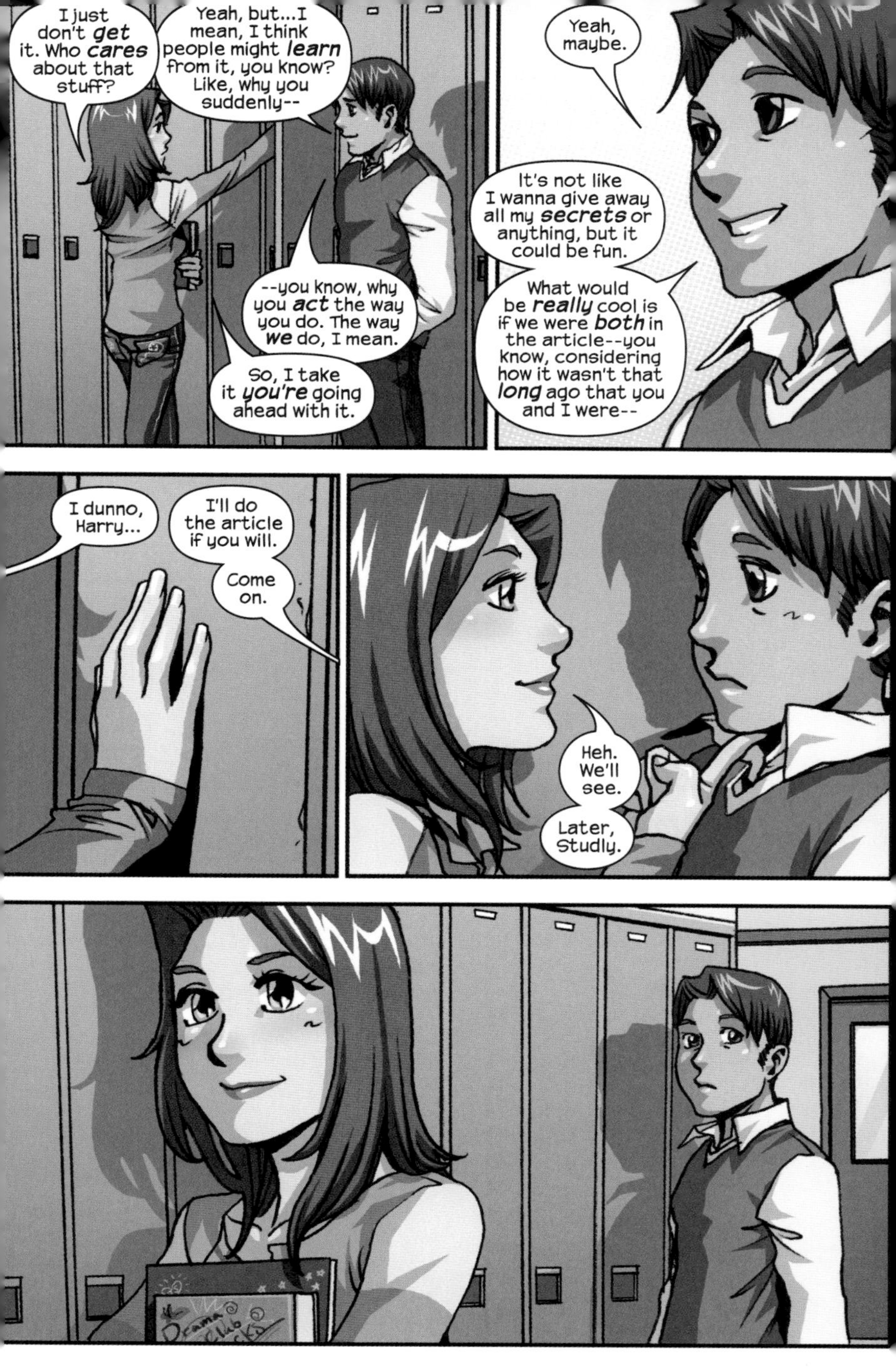
I just don't *get* it. Who *cares* about that stuff?
Yeah, but...I mean, I think people might *learn* from it, you know? Like, why you suddenly--
--you know, why you *act* the way you do. The way *we* do, I mean.
So, I take it *you're* going ahead with it.
Yeah, maybe.
It's not like I wanna give away all my *secrets* or anything, but it could be fun.
What would be *really* cool is if we were *both* in the article--you know, considering how it wasn't that *long* ago that you and I were--
I dunno, Harry...
I'll do the article if you will.
Come on.
Heh. We'll see.
Later, Studly.

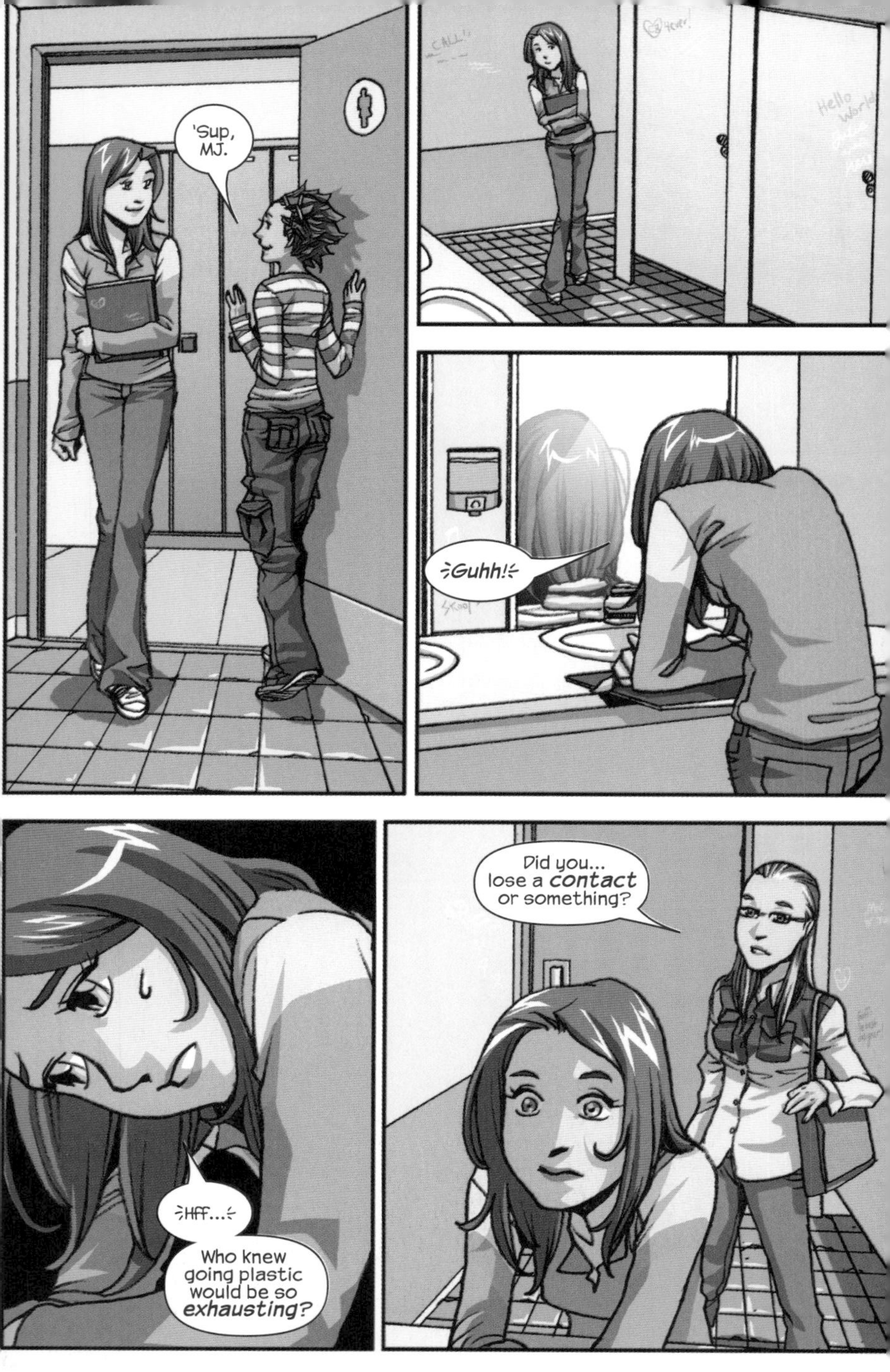
'Sup, MJ.
Guhh!
Hff...
Who knew going plastic would be so *exhausting*?
Did you... lose a *contact* or something?

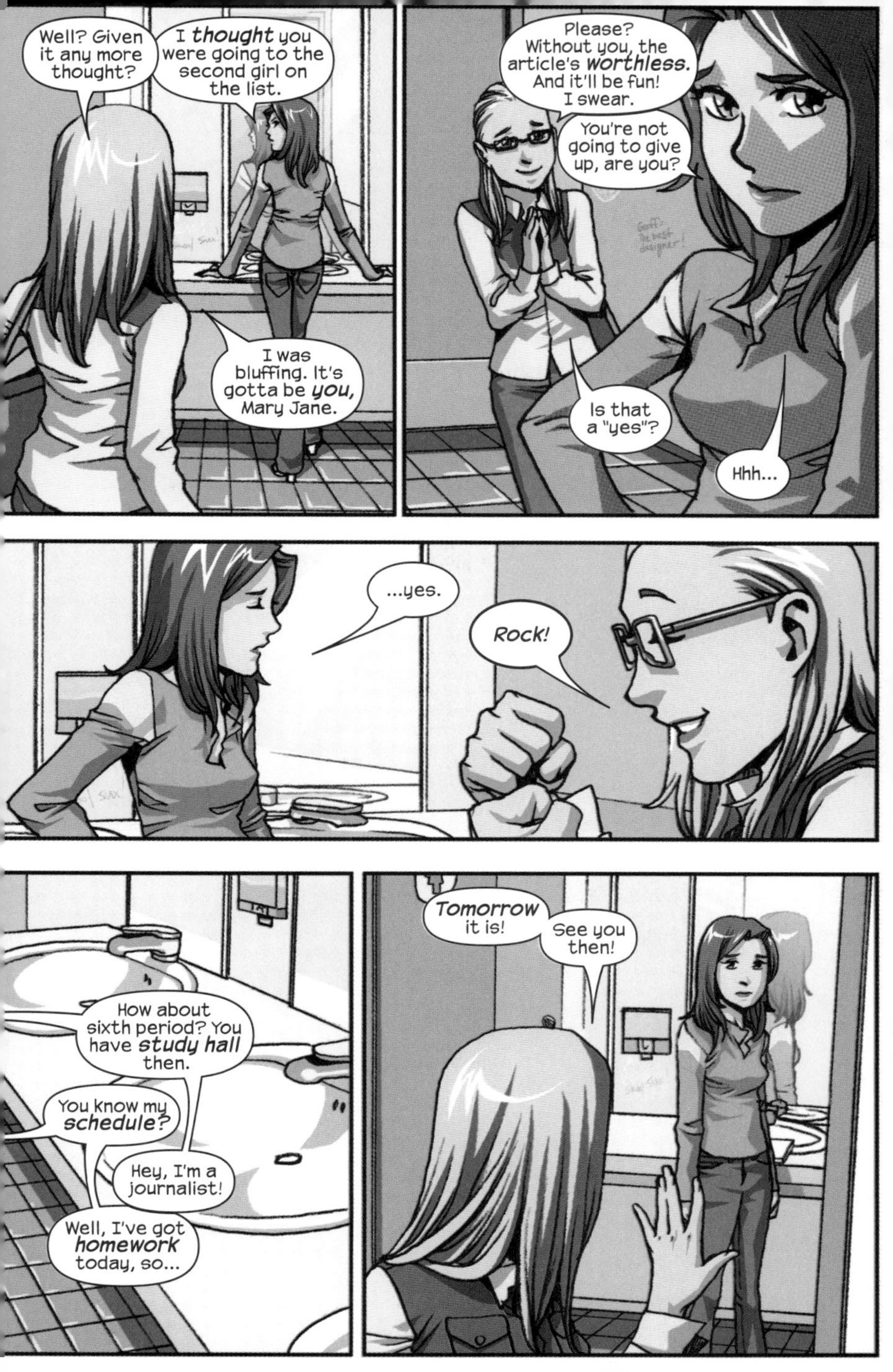
Well? Given it any more thought?
I *thought* you were going to the second girl on the list.
I was bluffing. It's gotta be *you,* Mary Jane.
Please? Without you, the article's *worthless.* And it'll be fun! I swear.
You're not going to give up, are you?
Is that a "yes"?
Hhh...
...yes.
Rock!
How about sixth period? You have *study hall* then.
You know my *schedule?*
Hey, I'm a journalist!
Well, I've got *homework* today, so...
Tomorrow it is!
See you then!

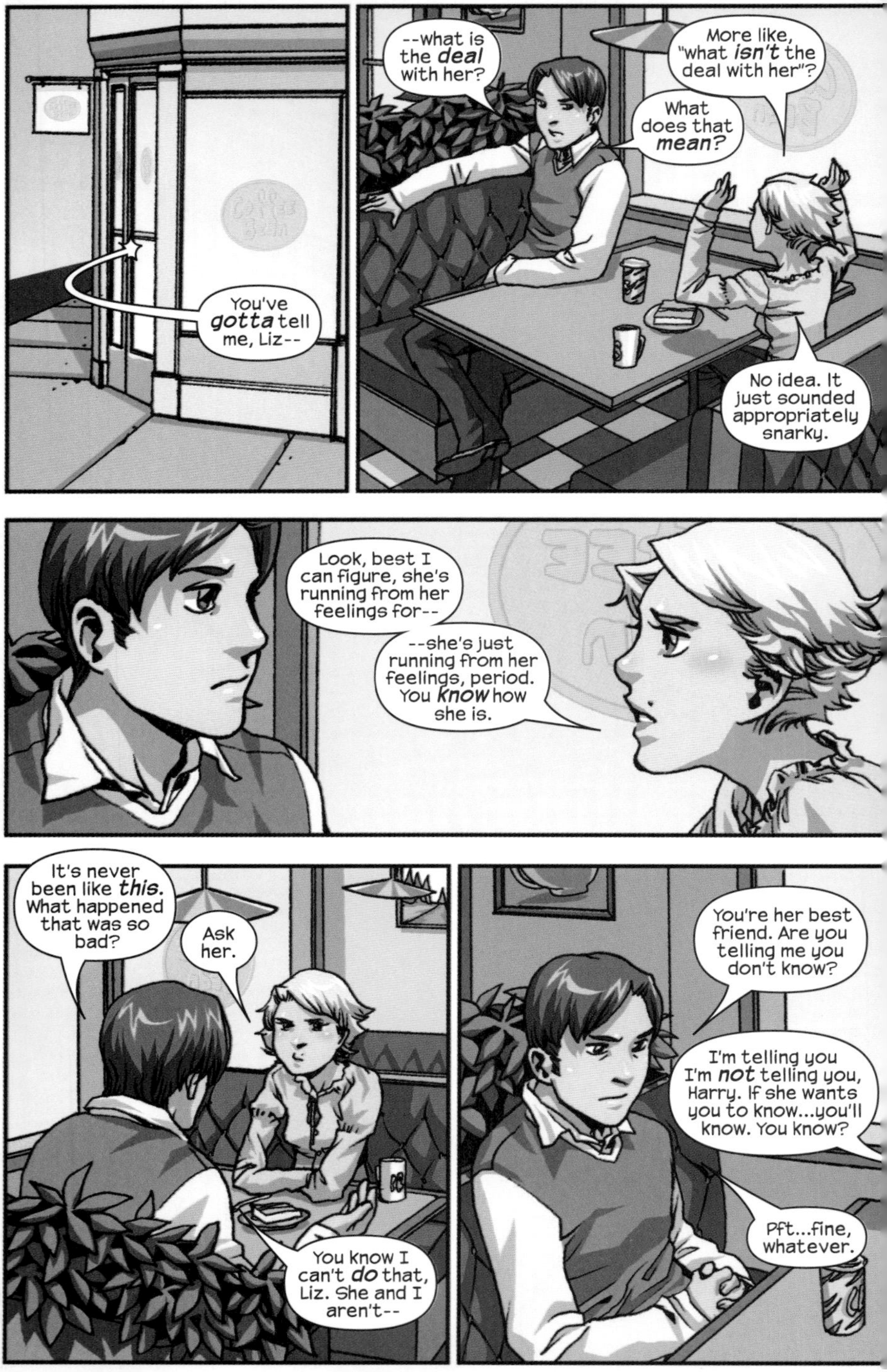
You've *gotta* tell me, Liz--
--what is the *deal* with her?
More like, "what *isn't* the deal with her"?
What does that *mean*?
No idea. It just sounded appropriately snarky.
Look, best I can figure, she's running from her feelings for--
--she's just running from her feelings, period. You *know* how she is.
It's never been like *this*. What happened that was so bad?
Ask her.
You know I can't *do* that, Liz. She and I aren't--
You're her best friend. Are you telling me you don't know?
I'm telling you I'm *not* telling you, Harry. If she wants you to know...you'll know. You know?
Pft...fine, whatever.

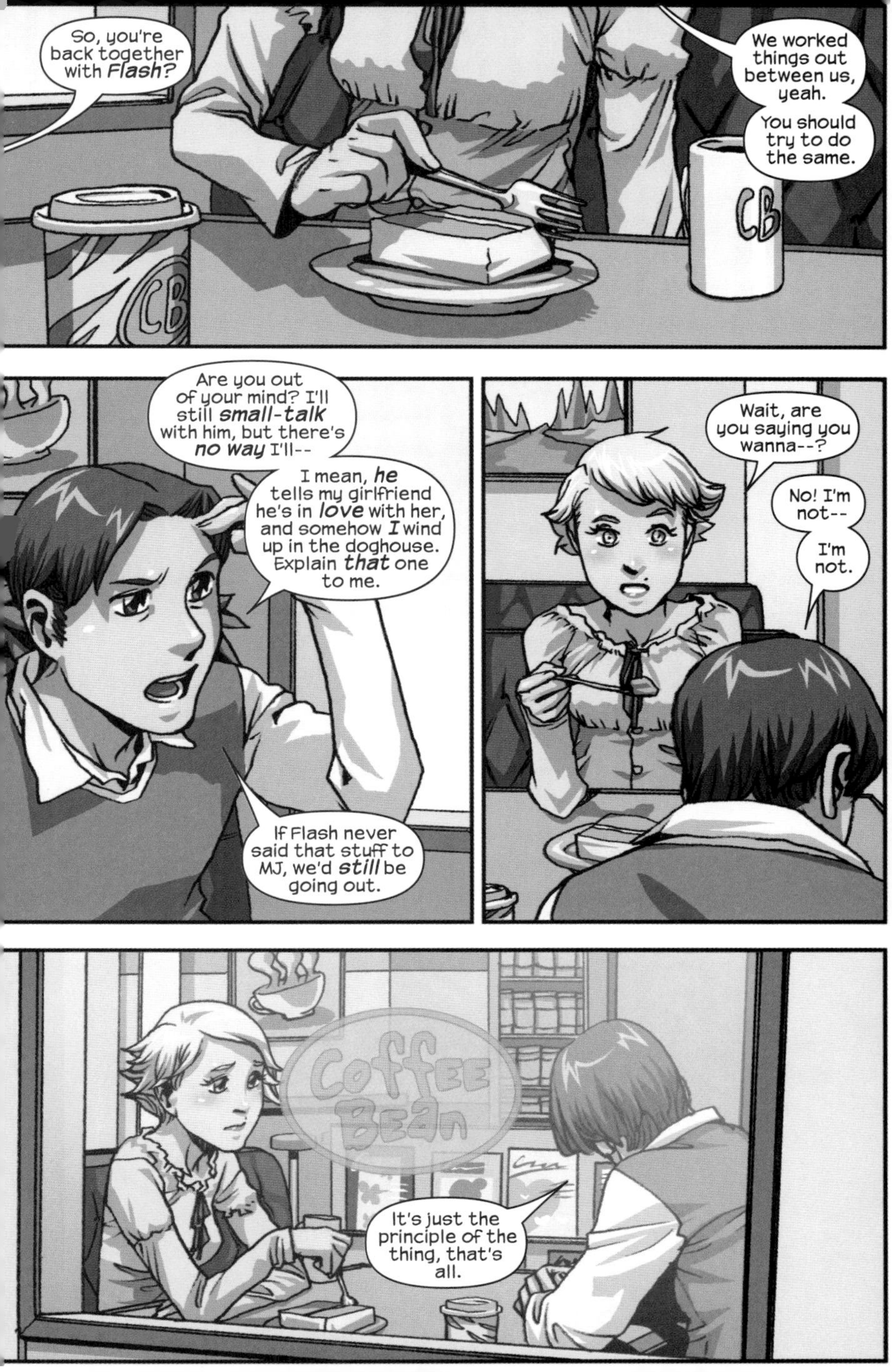
So, you're back together with *Flash?*
We worked things out between us, yeah.
You should try to do the same.
CB
CB
Are you out of your mind? I'll still ***small-talk*** with him, but there's ***no way*** I'll--
I mean, ***he*** tells my girlfriend he's in ***love*** with her, and somehow ***I*** wind up in the doghouse. Explain ***that*** one to me.
If Flash never said that stuff to MJ, we'd ***still*** be going out.
Wait, are you saying you wanna--?
No! I'm not--
I'm not.
Coffee Bean
It's just the principle of the thing, that's all.

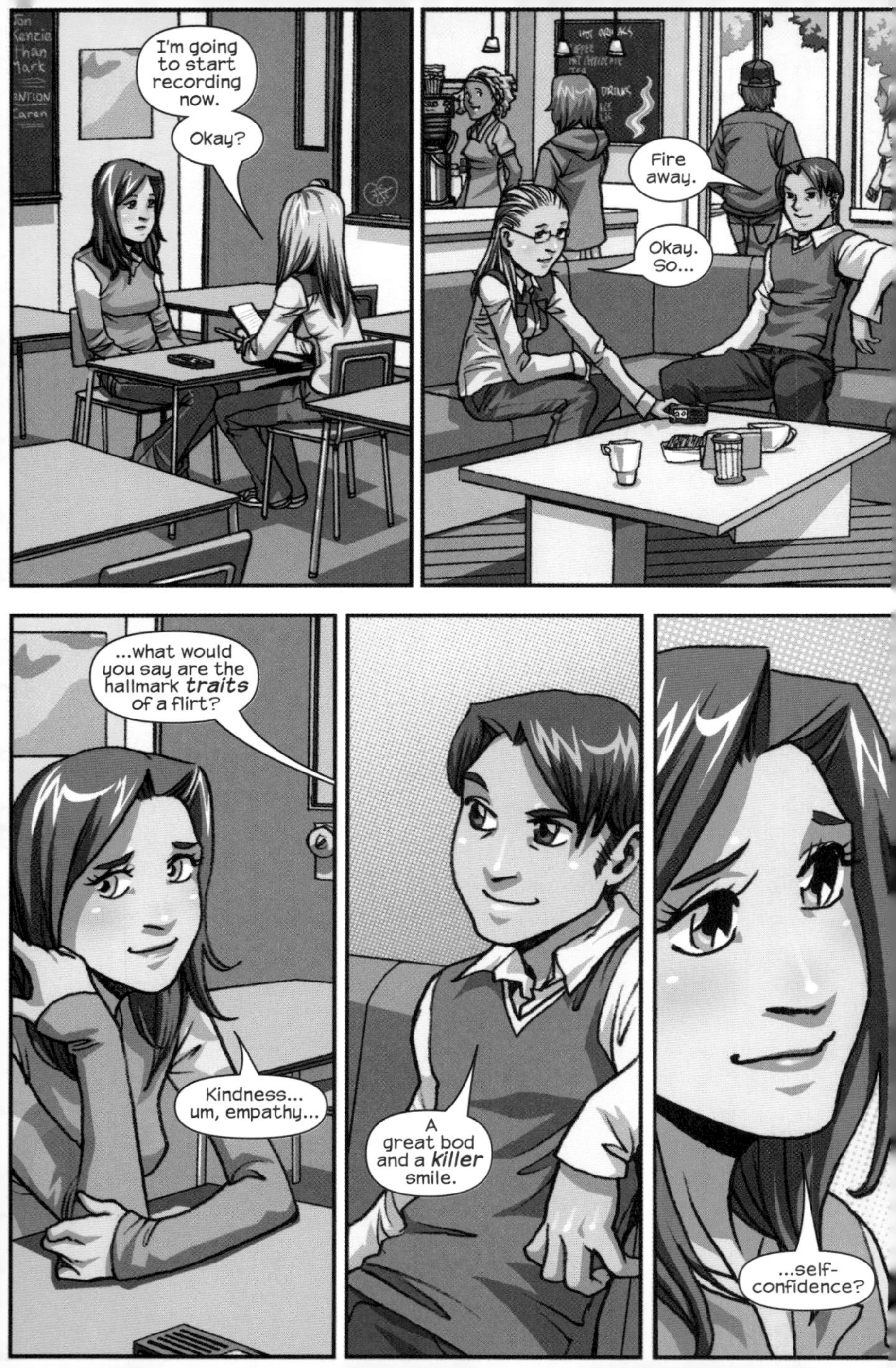
I'm going to start recording now.
Okay?
Fire away.
Okay. So...
...what would you say are the hallmark *traits* of a flirt?
Kindness... um, empathy...
A great bod and a *killer* smile.
...self-confidence?

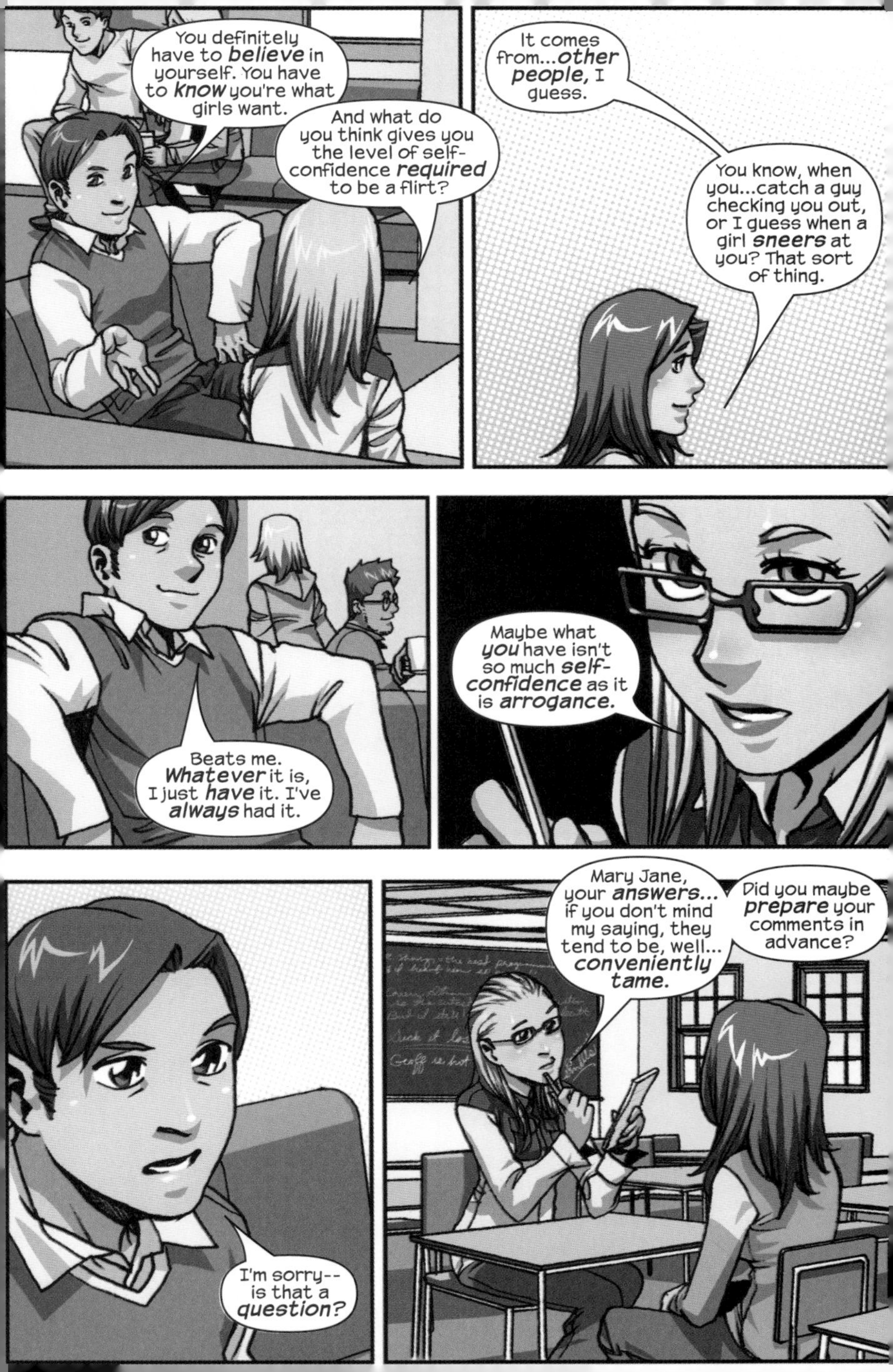

You definitely have to believe in yourself. You have to know you're what girls want.
And what do you think gives you the level of self-confidence required to be a flirt?
It comes from...other people, I guess.
You know, when you...catch a guy checking you out, or I guess when a girl sneers at you? That sort of thing.
Beats me. Whatever it is, I just have it. I've always had it.
Maybe what you have isn't so much self-confidence as it is arrogance.
I'm sorry-- is that a question?
Mary Jane, your answers... if you don't mind my saying, they tend to be, well... conveniently tame.
Did you maybe prepare your comments in advance?

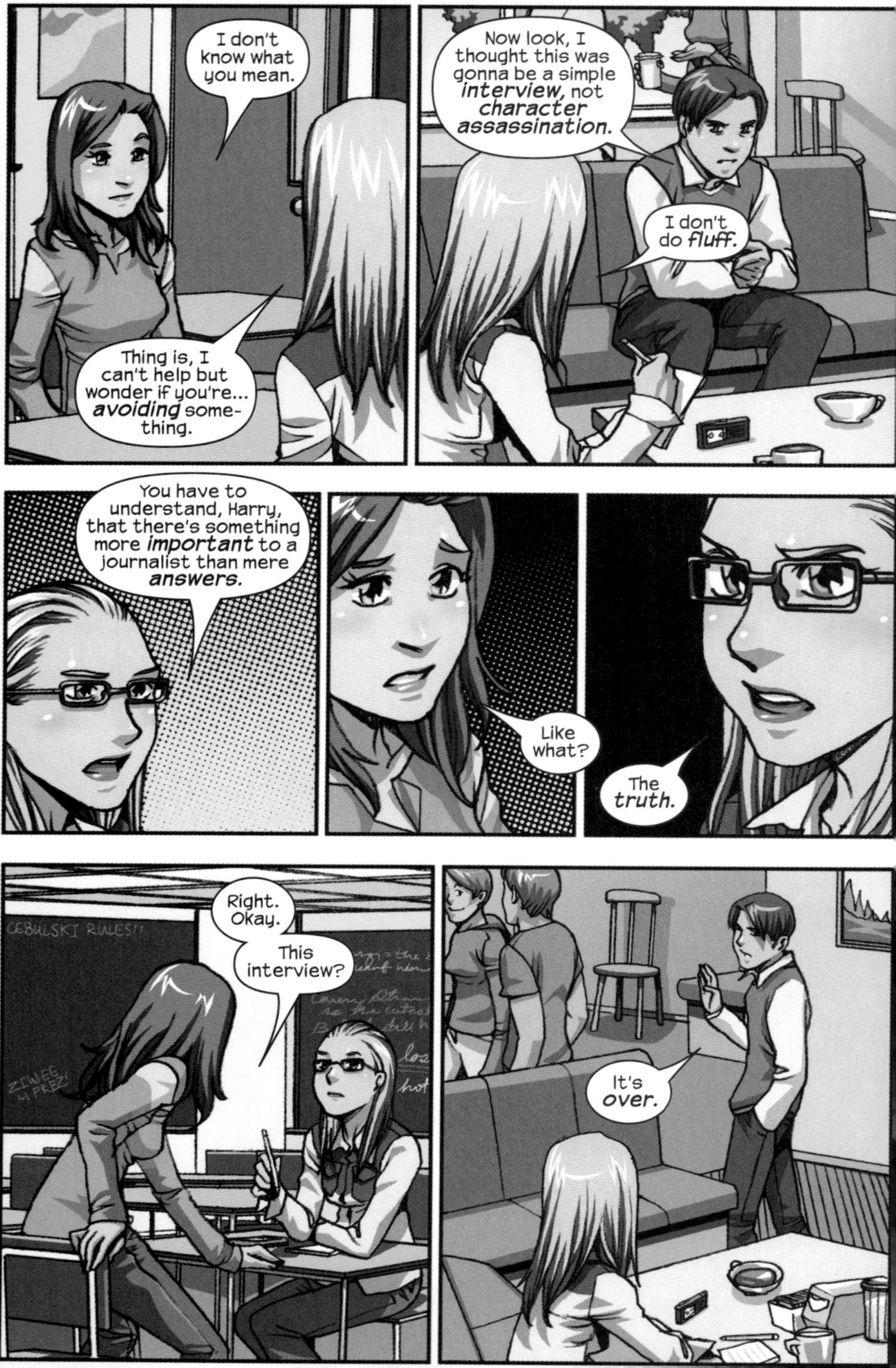
I don't know what you mean.
Thing is, I can't help but wonder if you're... *avoiding* some-thing.
Now look, I thought this was gonna be a simple *interview,* not *character assassination.*
I don't do *fluff.*
You have to understand, Harry, that there's something more *important* to a journalist than mere *answers.*
Like what?
The *truth.*
CEBULSKI RULES!!
Right. Okay.
This interview?
It's *over.*

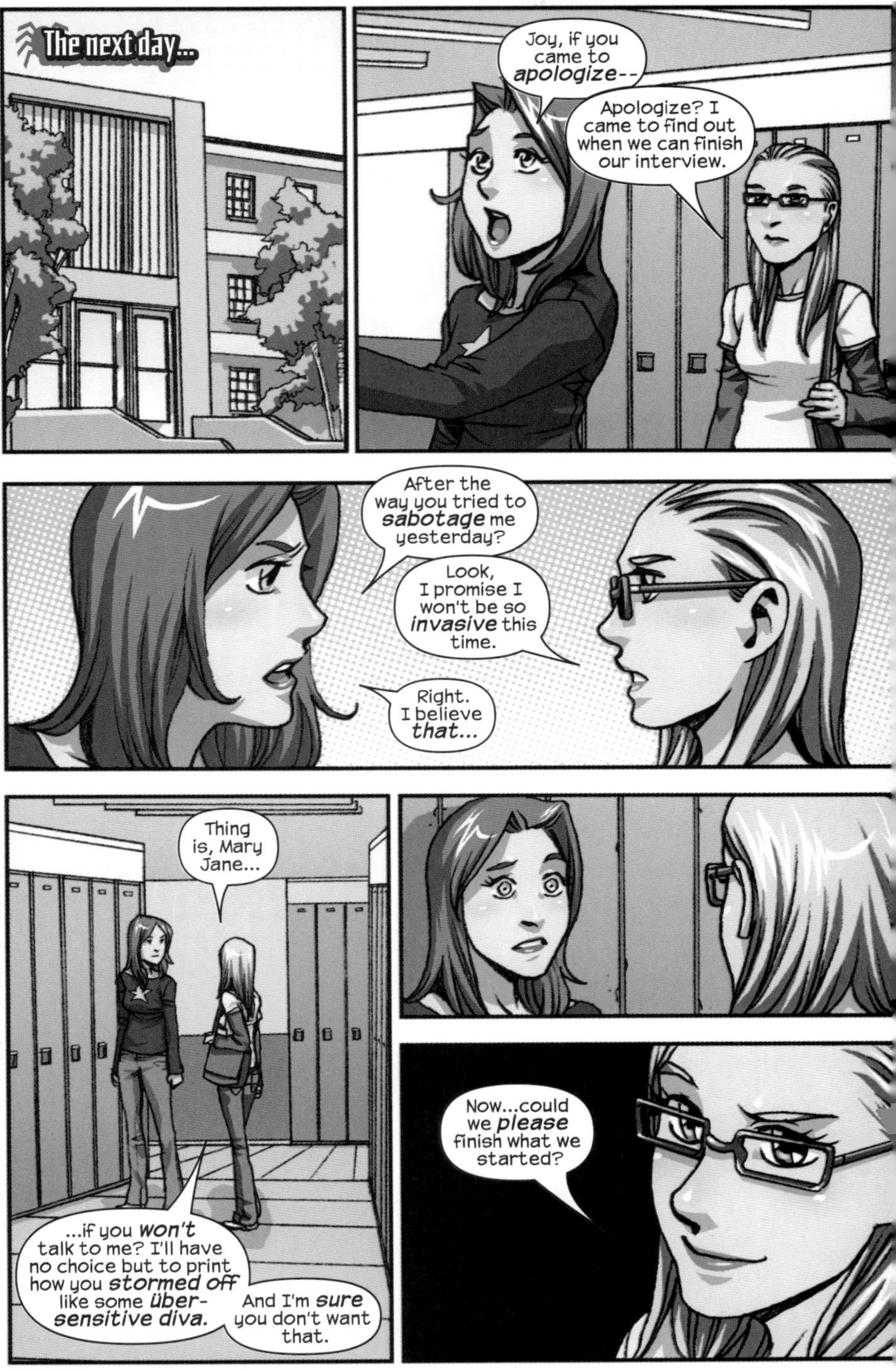
The next day...
Joy, if you came to apologize--
Apologize? I came to find out when we can finish our interview.
After the way you tried to sabotage me yesterday?
Look, I promise I won't be so invasive this time.
Right. I believe that...
Thing is, Mary Jane...
...if you won't talk to me? I'll have no choice but to print how you stormed off like some über-sensitive diva.
And I'm sure you don't want that.
Now...could we please finish what we started?

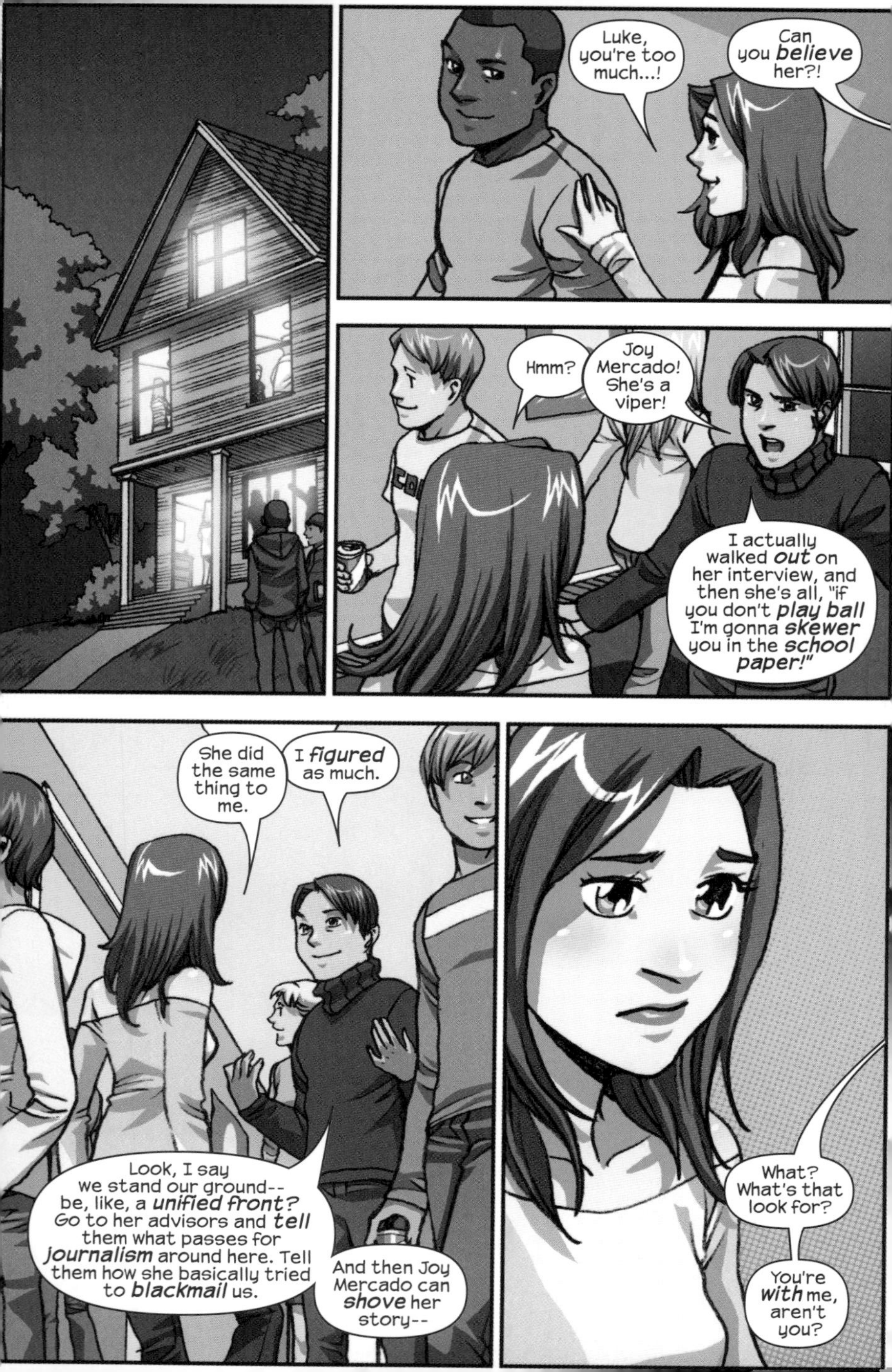

Luke, you're too much...!
Can you believe her?!
Hmm?
Joy Mercado! She's a viper!
I actually walked out on her interview, and then she's all, "if you don't play ball I'm gonna skewer you in the school paper!"
She did the same thing to me.
I figured as much.
Look, I say we stand our ground-- be, like, a unified front? Go to her advisors and tell them what passes for journalism around here. Tell them how she basically tried to blackmail us.
And then Joy Mercado can shove her story--
What? What's that look for?
You're with me, aren't you?

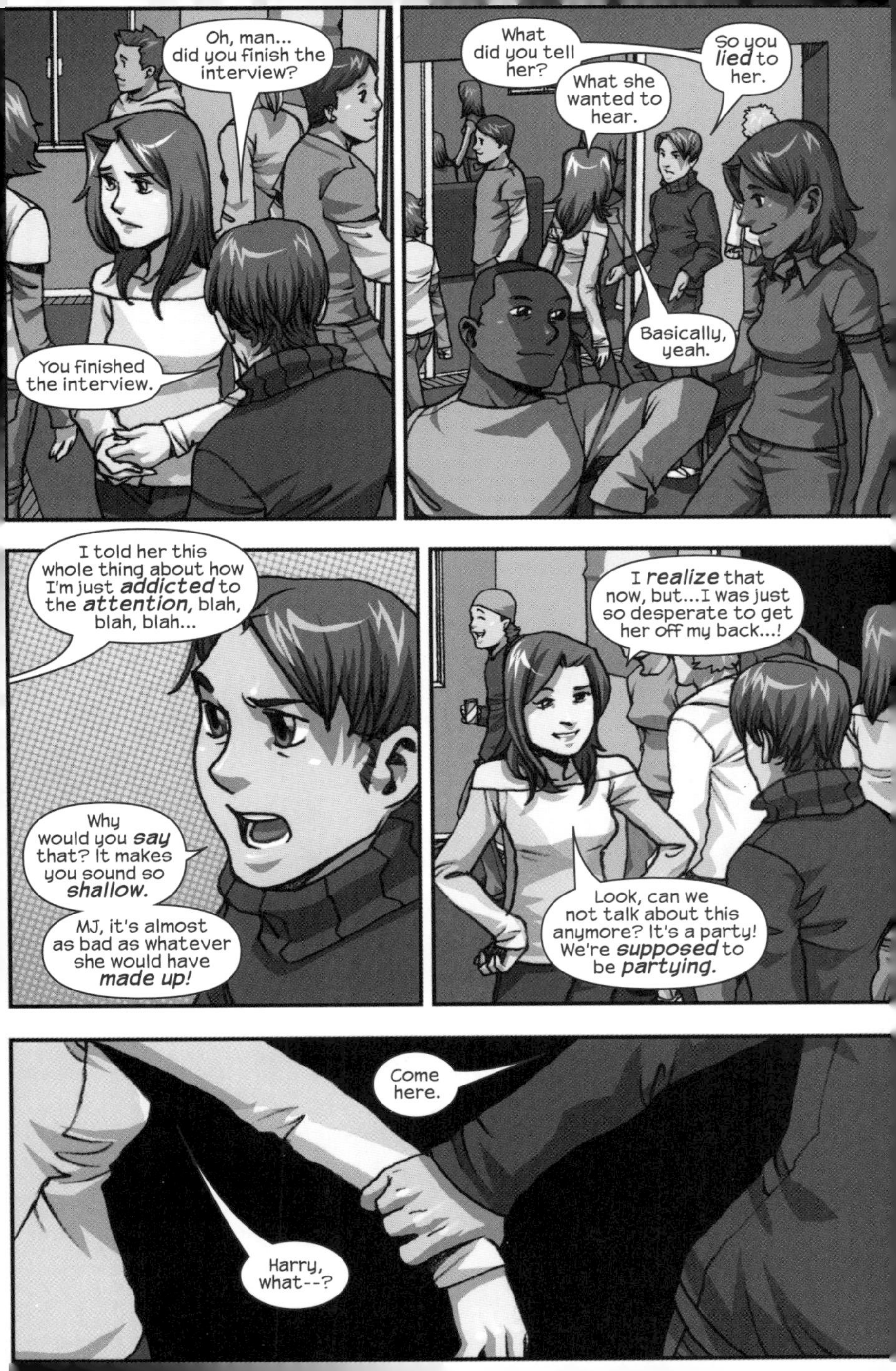
Oh, man... did you finish the interview?
You finished the interview.
What did you tell her?
What she wanted to hear.
So you *lied* to her.
Basically, yeah.
I told her this whole thing about how I'm just *addicted* to the *attention,* blah, blah, blah...
Why would you *say* that? It makes you sound so *shallow.*
MJ, it's almost as bad as whatever she would have *made up!*
I *realize* that now, but...I was just so desperate to get her off my back...!
Look, can we not talk about this anymore? It's a party! We're *supposed* to be *partying.*
Come here.
Harry, what--?

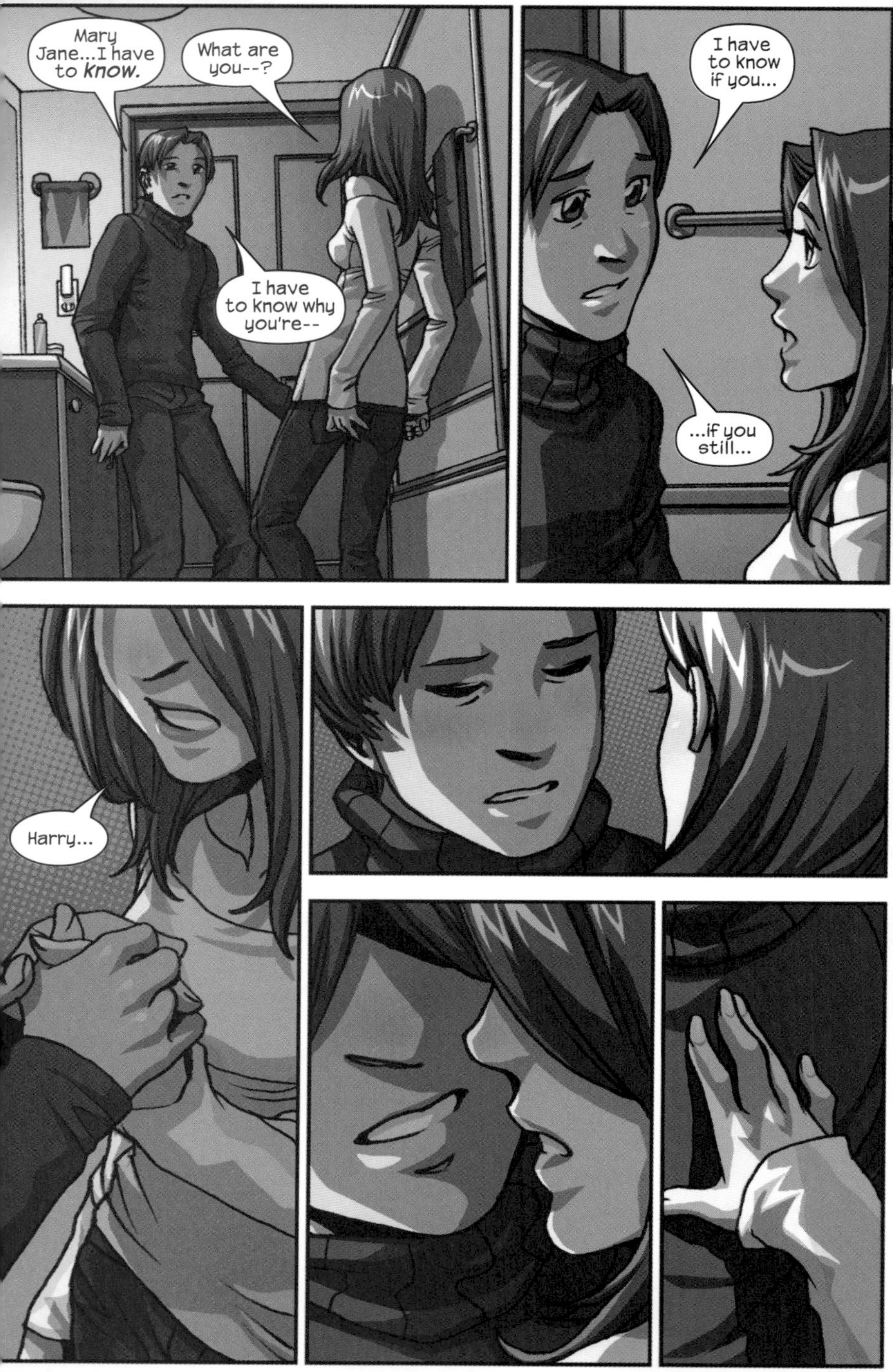
Mary Jane...I have to *know.*
What are you--?
I have to know why you're--
I have to know if you...
...if you still...
Harry...

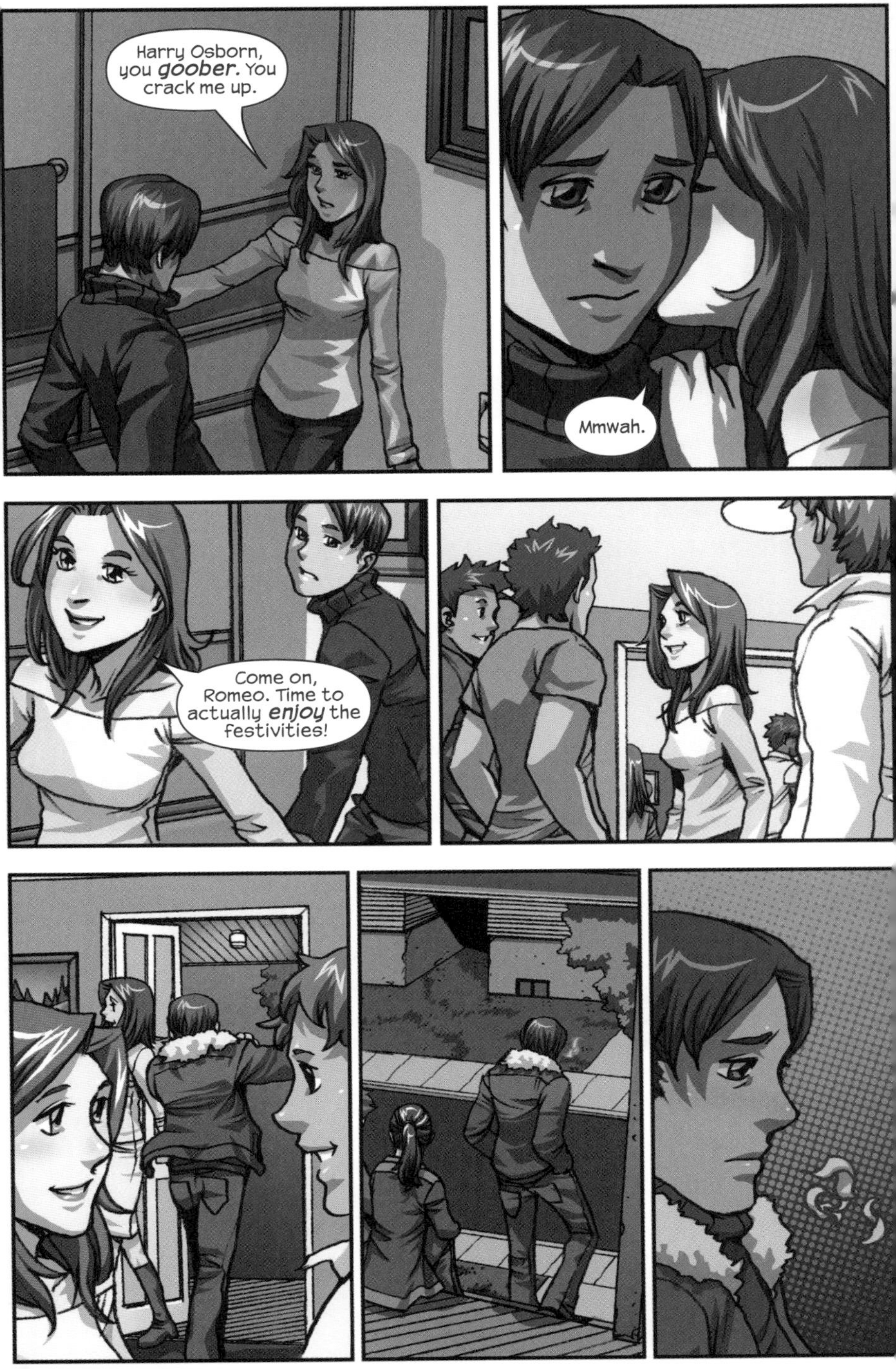
Harry Osborn, you **goober.** You crack me up.
Mmwah.
Come on, Romeo. Time to actually ***enjoy*** the festivities!

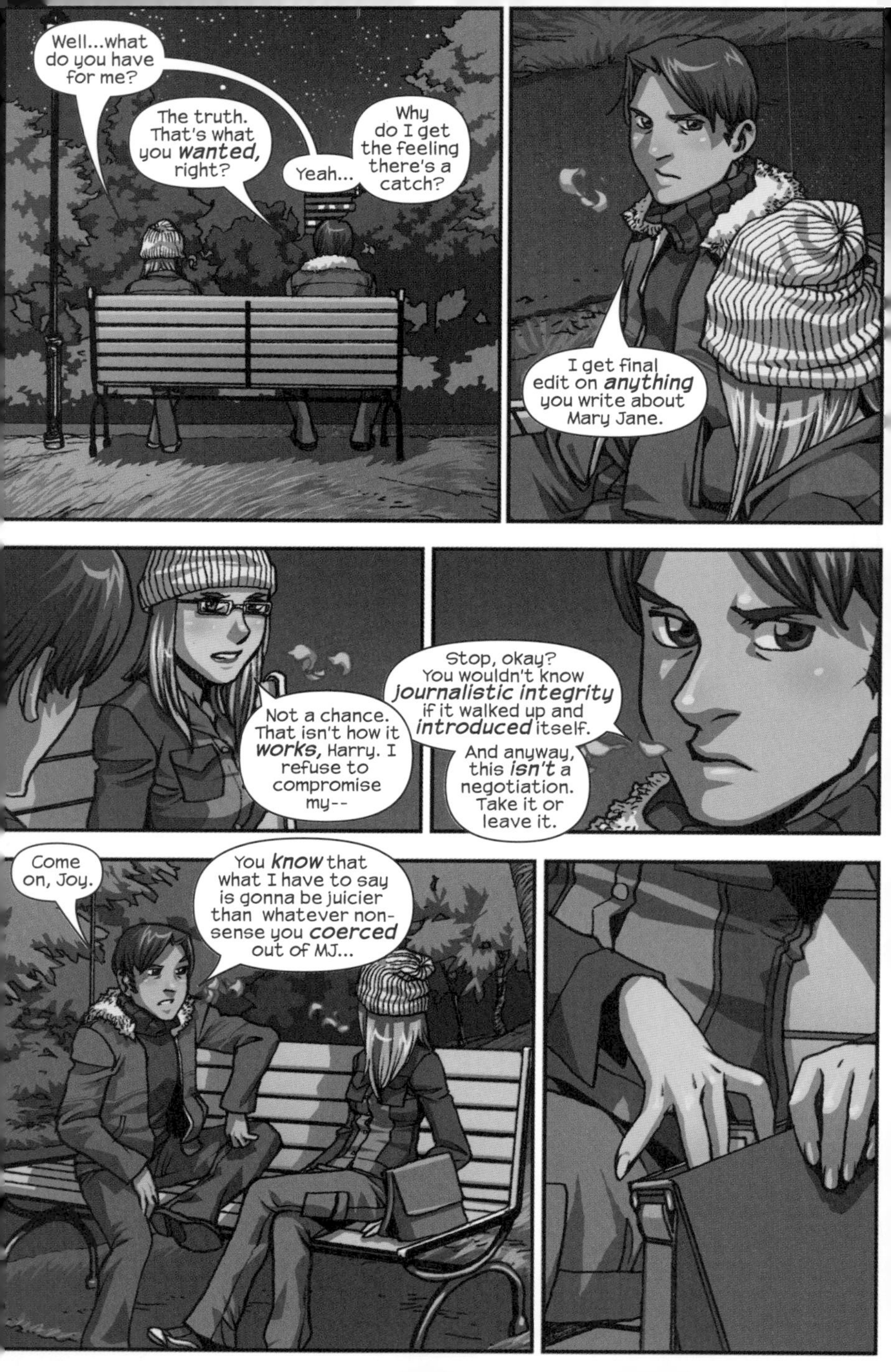

Well...what do you have for me?
The truth. That's what you *wanted,* right?
Yeah...
Why do I get the feeling there's a catch?
I get final edit on *anything* you write about Mary Jane.
Not a chance. That isn't how it *works,* Harry. I refuse to compromise my--
Stop, okay? You wouldn't know *journalistic integrity* if it walked up and *introduced* itself.
And anyway, this *isn't* a negotiation. Take it or leave it.
Come on, Joy.
You *know* that what I have to say is gonna be juicier than whatever nonsense you *coerced* out of MJ...

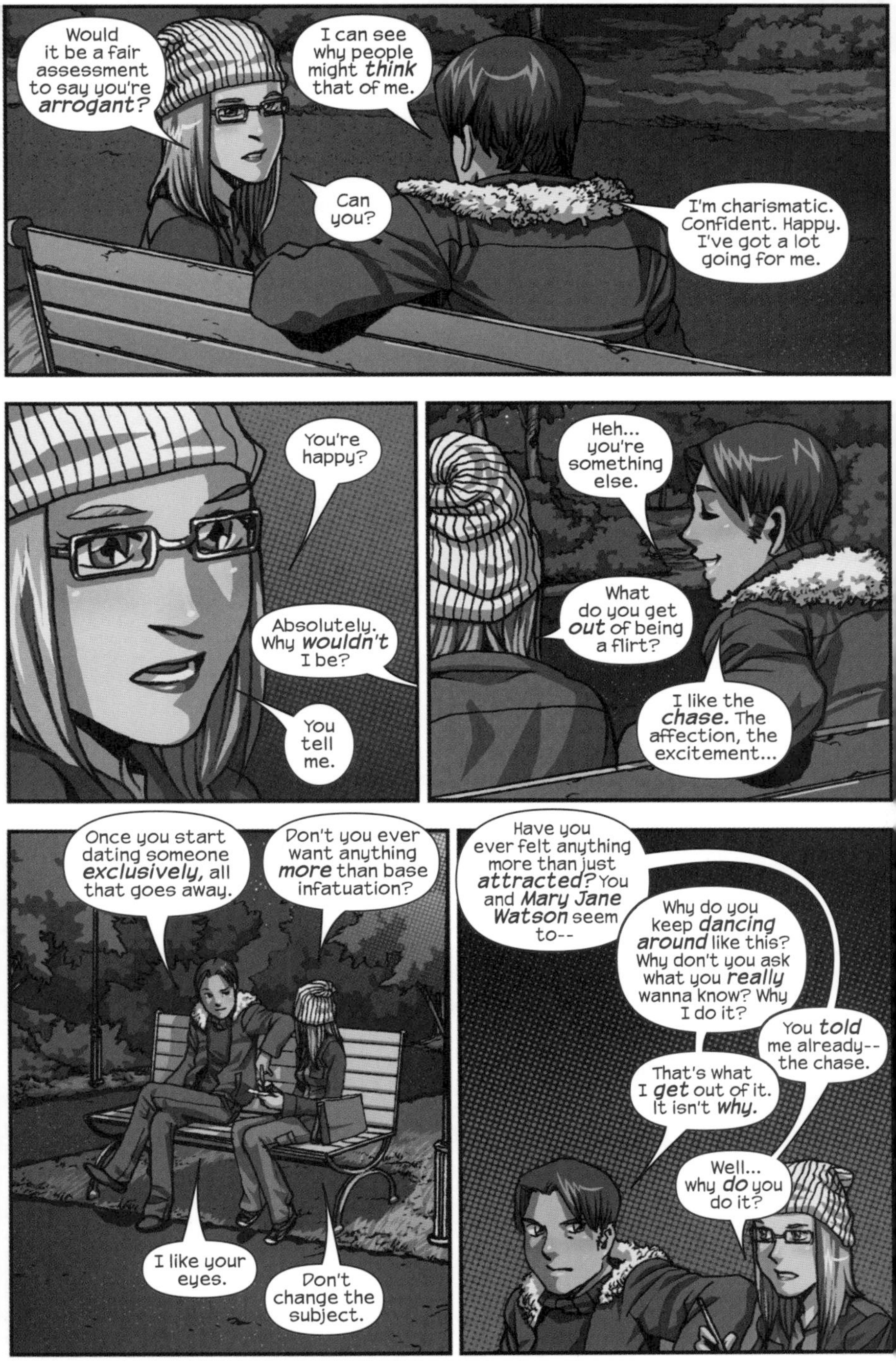
Would it be a fair assessment to say you're *arrogant?*
I can see why people might *think* that of me.
Can you?
I'm charismatic. Confident. Happy. I've got a lot going for me.
You're happy?
Absolutely. Why *wouldn't* I be?
You tell me.
Heh... you're something else.
What do you get *out* of being a flirt?
I like the *chase.* The affection, the excitement...
Once you start dating someone *exclusively,* all that goes away.
Don't you ever want anything *more* than base infatuation?
I like your eyes.
Don't change the subject.
Have you ever felt anything more than just *attracted?* You and *Mary Jane Watson* seem to--
Why do you keep *dancing around* like this? Why don't you ask what you *really* wanna know? Why I do it?
You *told* me already-- the chase.
That's what I *get* out of it. It isn't *why.*
Well... why *do* you do it?

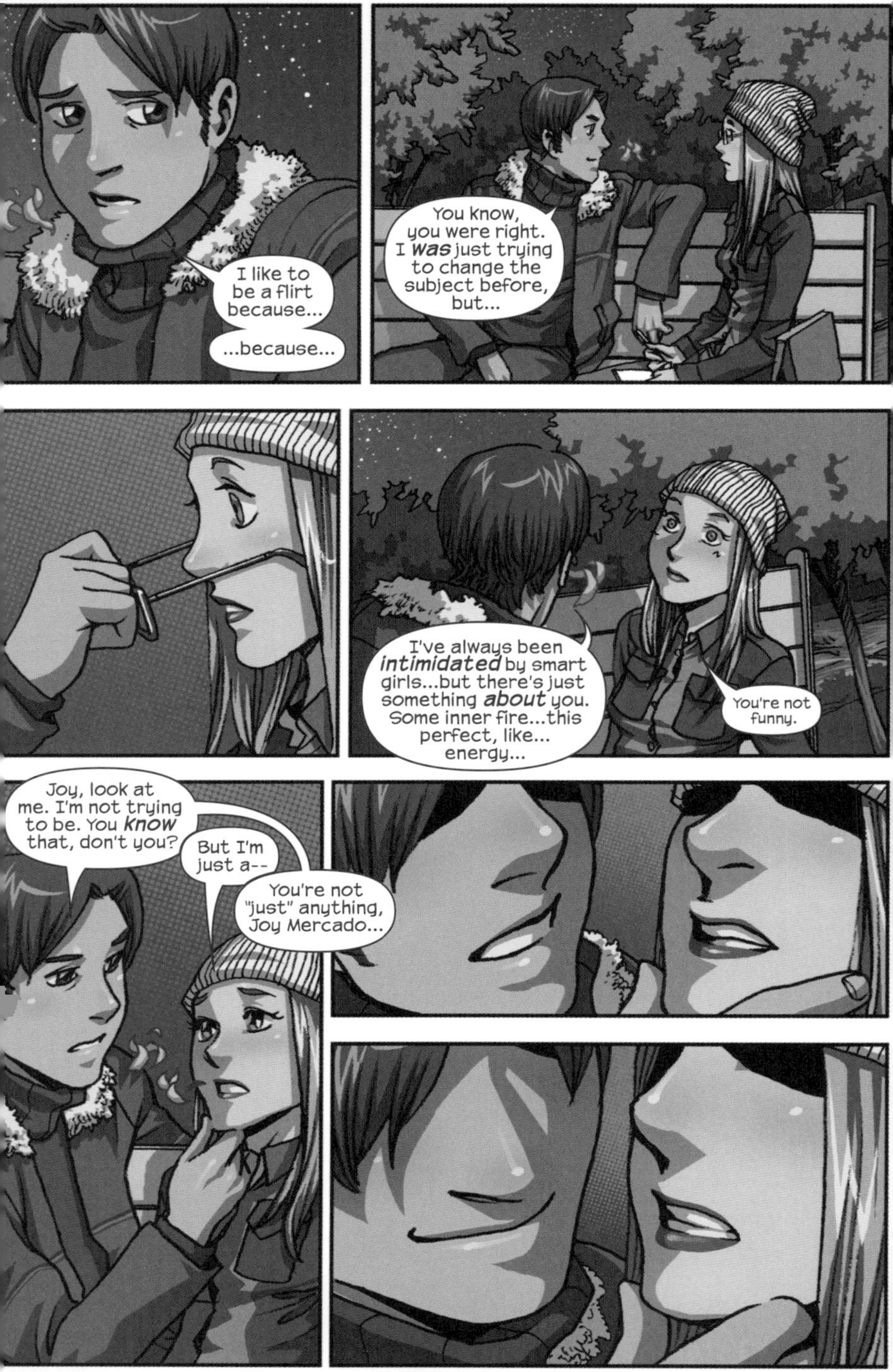
I like to be a flirt because...
...because...
You know, you were right. I *was* just trying to change the subject before, but...
I've always been *intimidated* by smart girls...but there's just something *about* you. Some inner fire...this perfect, like... energy...
You're not funny.
Joy, look at me. I'm not trying to be. You *know* that, don't you?
But I'm just a--
You're not "just" anything, Joy Mercado...

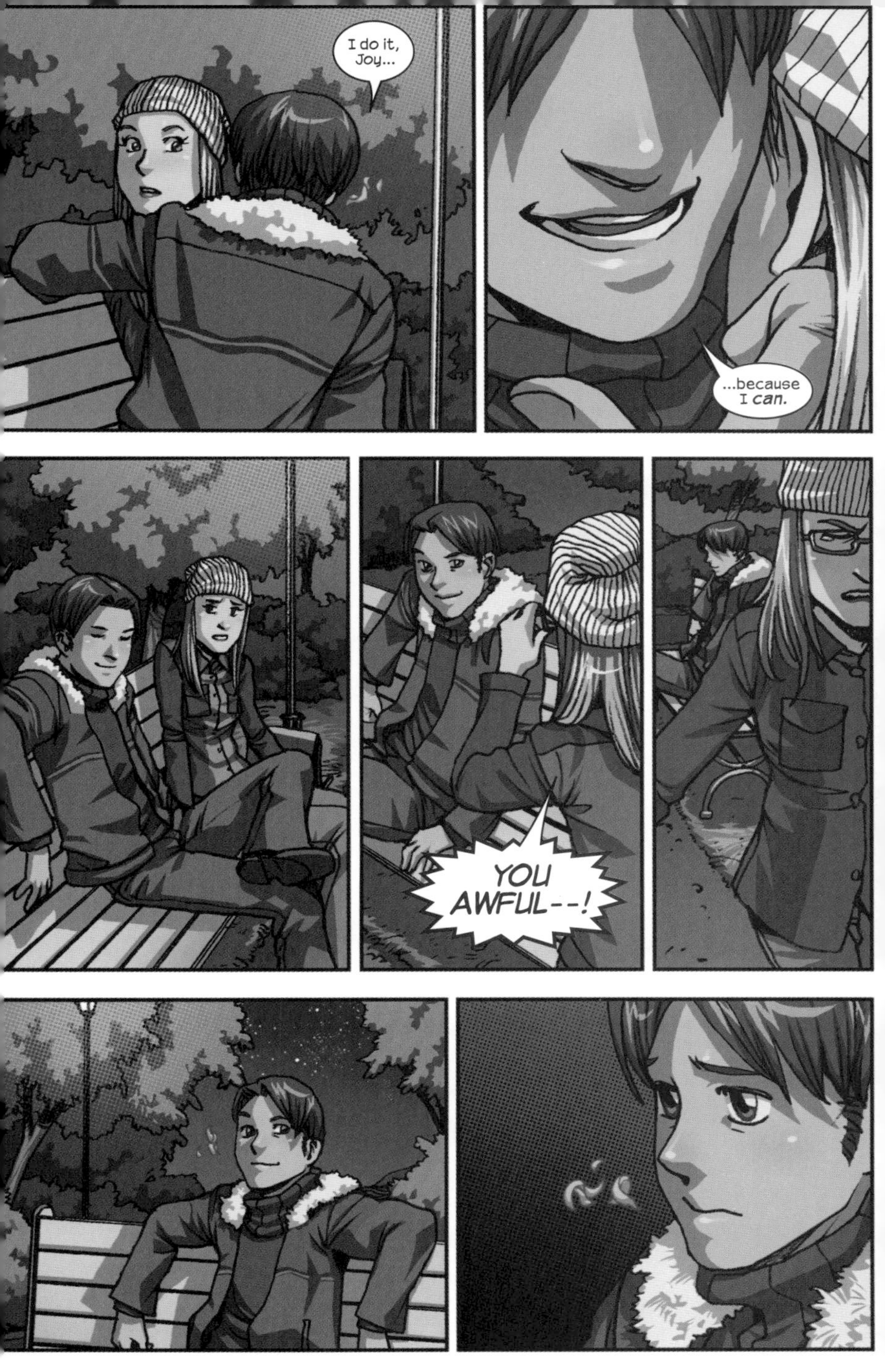
I do it, Joy...
...because I *can.*
YOU AWFUL--!

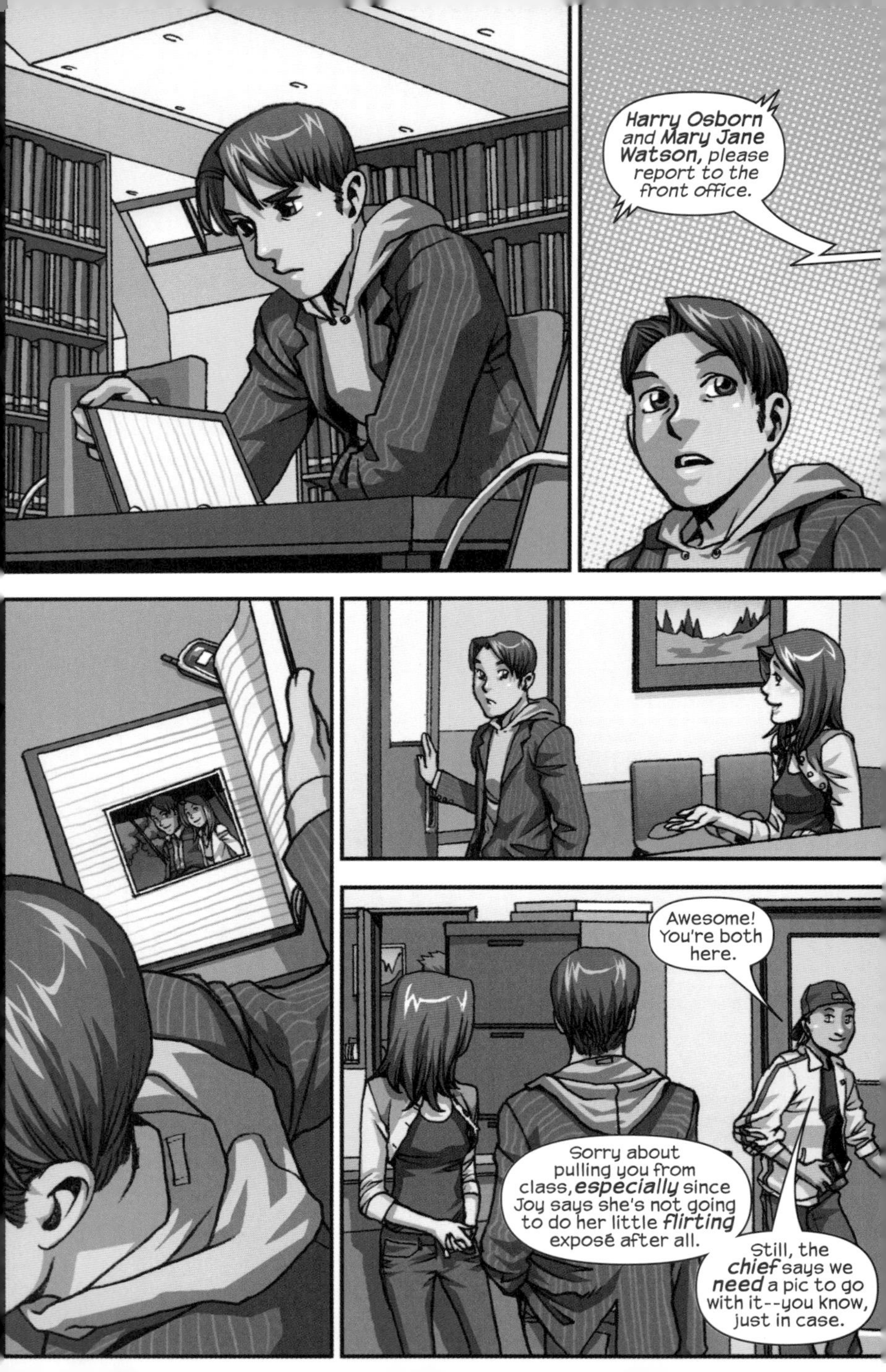
Harry Osborn and Mary Jane Watson, please report to the front office.
Awesome! You're both here.
Sorry about pulling you from class, especially since Joy says she's not going to do her little flirting exposé after all.
Still, the chief says we need a pic to go with it--you know, just in case.

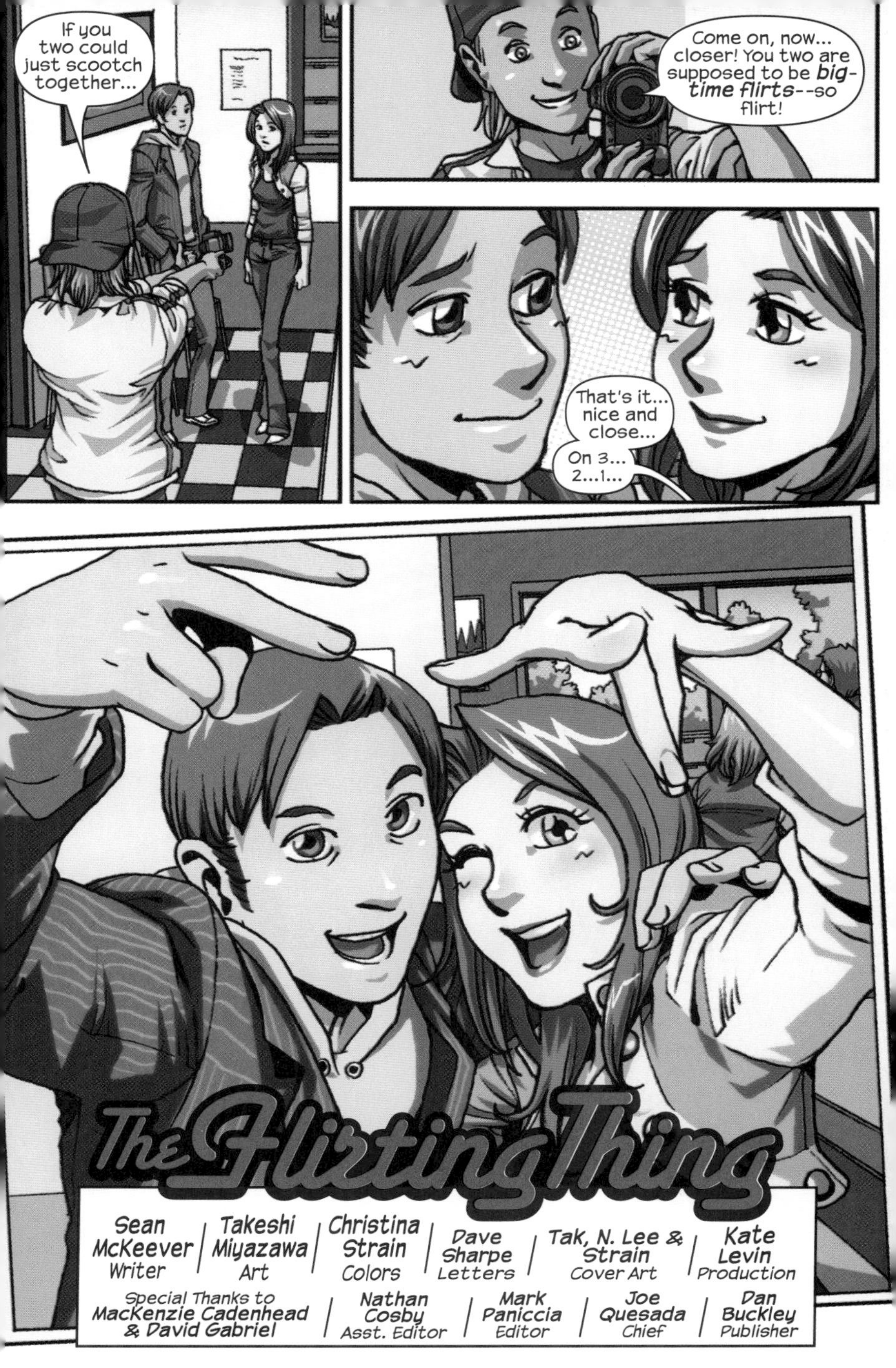
If you two could just scootch together...
Come on, now... closer! You two are supposed to be *big-time flirts*--so flirt!
That's it... nice and close...
On 3... 2...1...
The Flirting Thing
Sean McKeever Writer
Takeshi Miyazawa Art
Christina Strain Colors
Dave Sharpe Letters
Tak, N. Lee & Strain Cover Art
Kate Levin Production
Special Thanks to MacKenzie Cadenhead & David Gabriel
Nathan Cosby Asst. Editor
Mark Paniccia Editor
Joe Quesada Chief
Dan Buckley Publisher

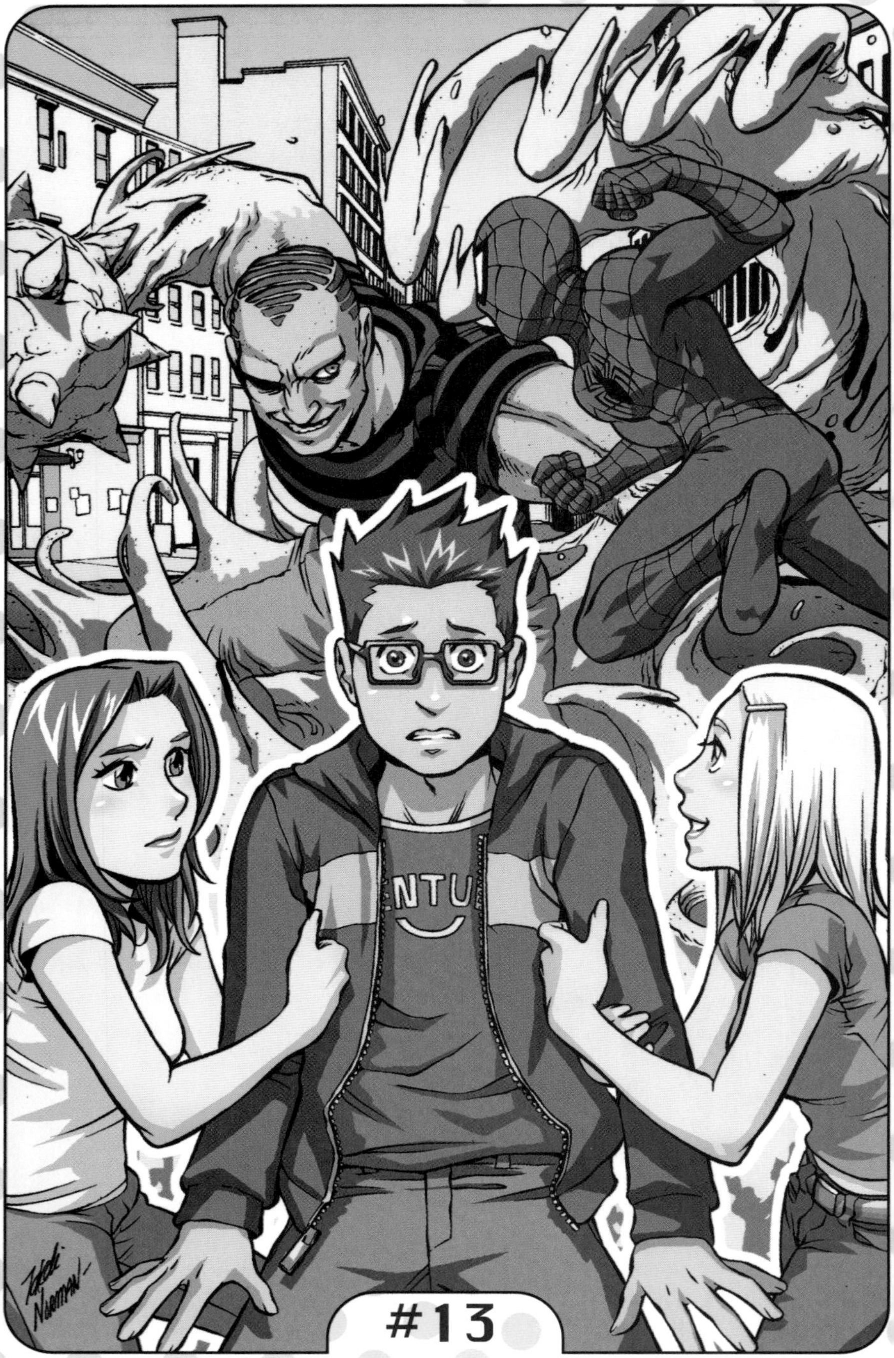
#13

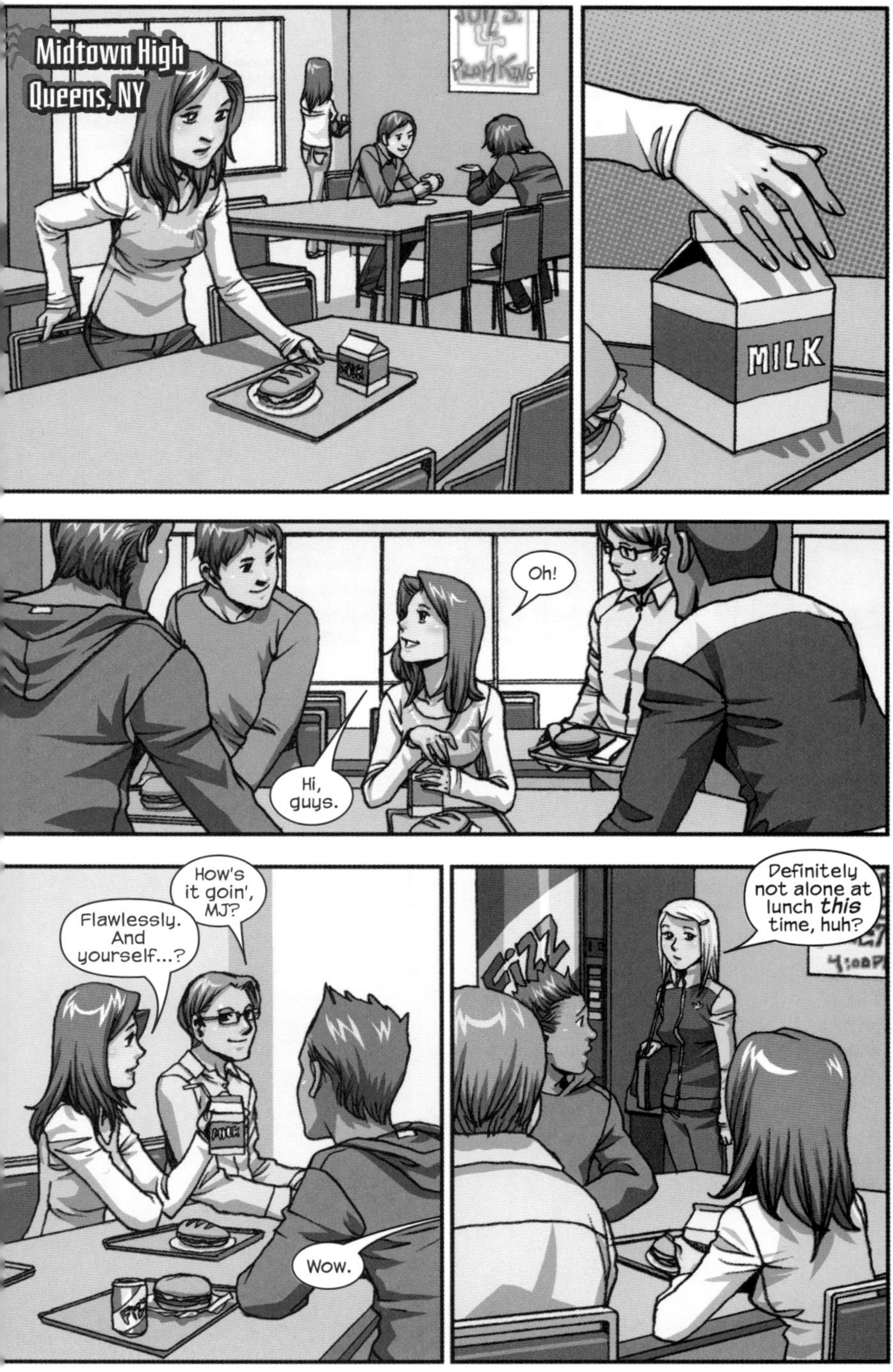
Midtown High
Queens, NY
MILK
Oh!
Hi, guys.
How's it goin', MJ?
Flawlessly. And yourself...?
Wow.
Definitely not alone at lunch *this* time, huh?

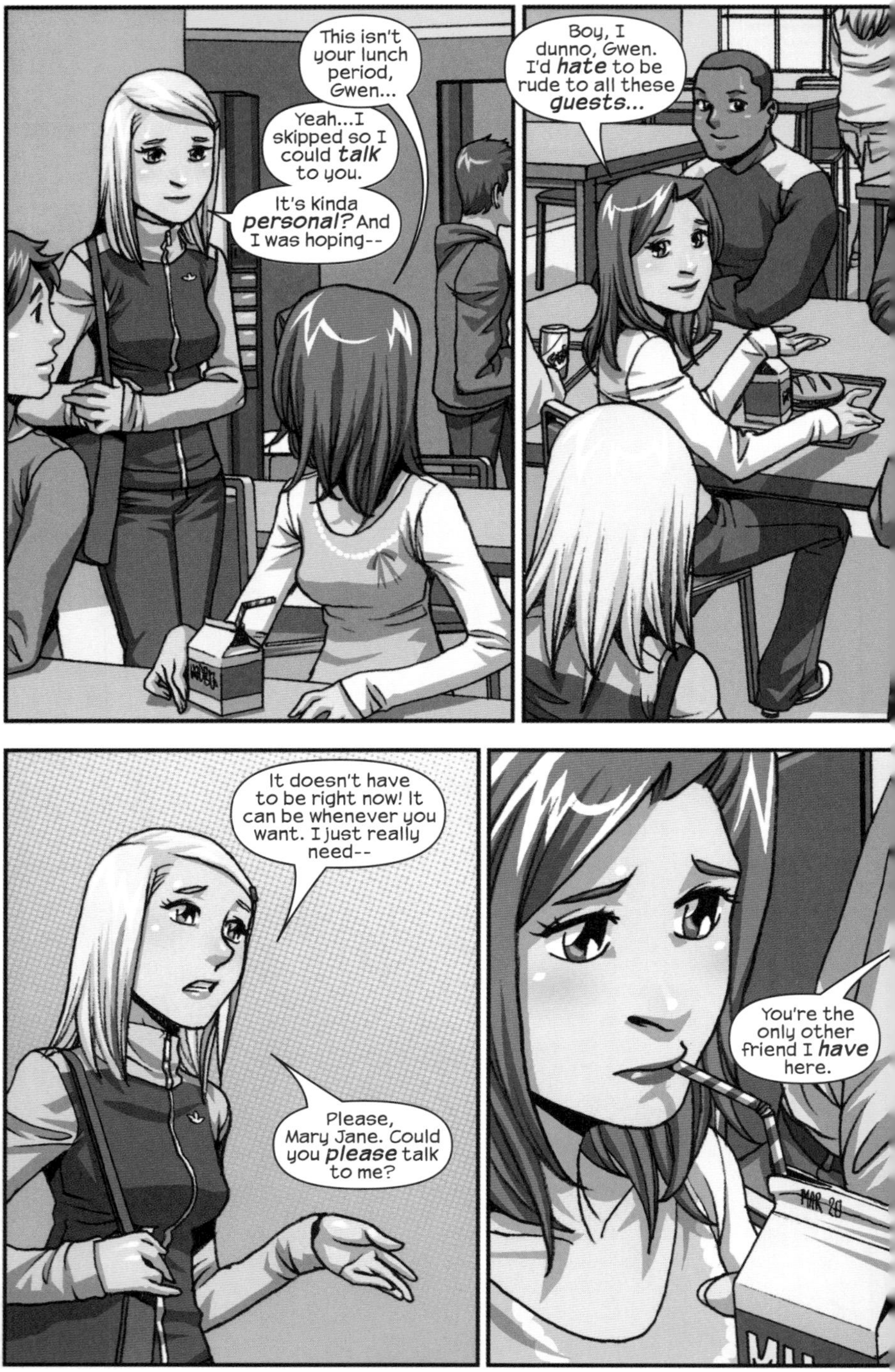
This isn't your lunch period, Gwen...
Yeah...I skipped so I could *talk* to you.
It's kinda *personal?* And I was hoping--
Boy, I dunno, Gwen. I'd *hate* to be rude to all these *guests...*
It doesn't have to be right now! It can be whenever you want. I just really need--
Please, Mary Jane. Could you *please* talk to me?
You're the only other friend I *have* here.

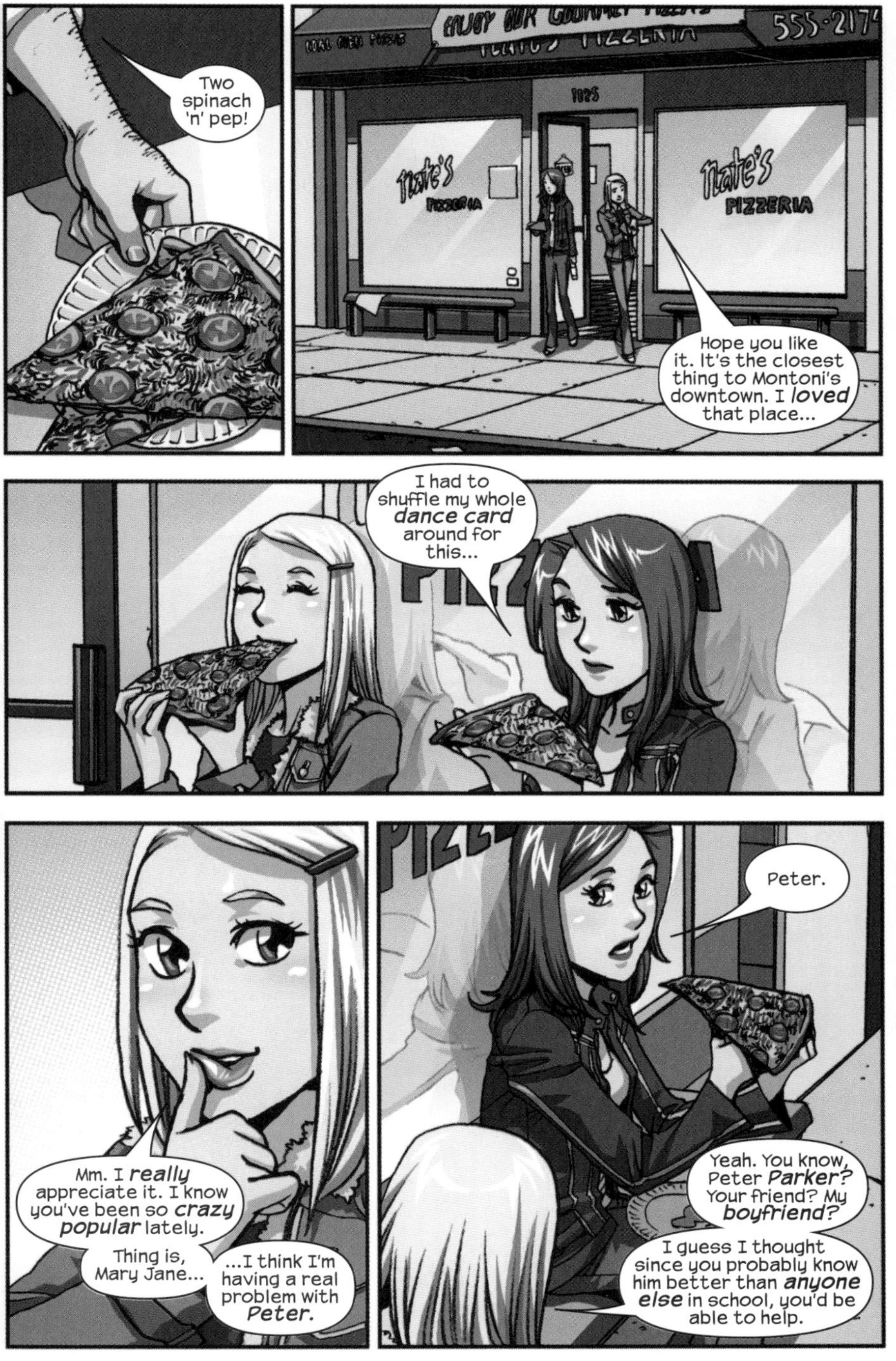
Two spinach 'n' pep!
Nate's PIZZERIA
Nate's PIZZERIA
Hope you like it. It's the closest thing to Montoni's downtown. I *loved* that place...
I had to shuffle my whole *dance card* around for this...
Mm. I *really* appreciate it. I know you've been so *crazy popular* lately.
Thing is, Mary Jane...
...I think I'm having a real problem with *Peter.*
Peter.
Yeah. You know, Peter *Parker?* Your friend? My *boyfriend?*
I guess I thought since you probably know him better than *anyone else* in school, you'd be able to help.

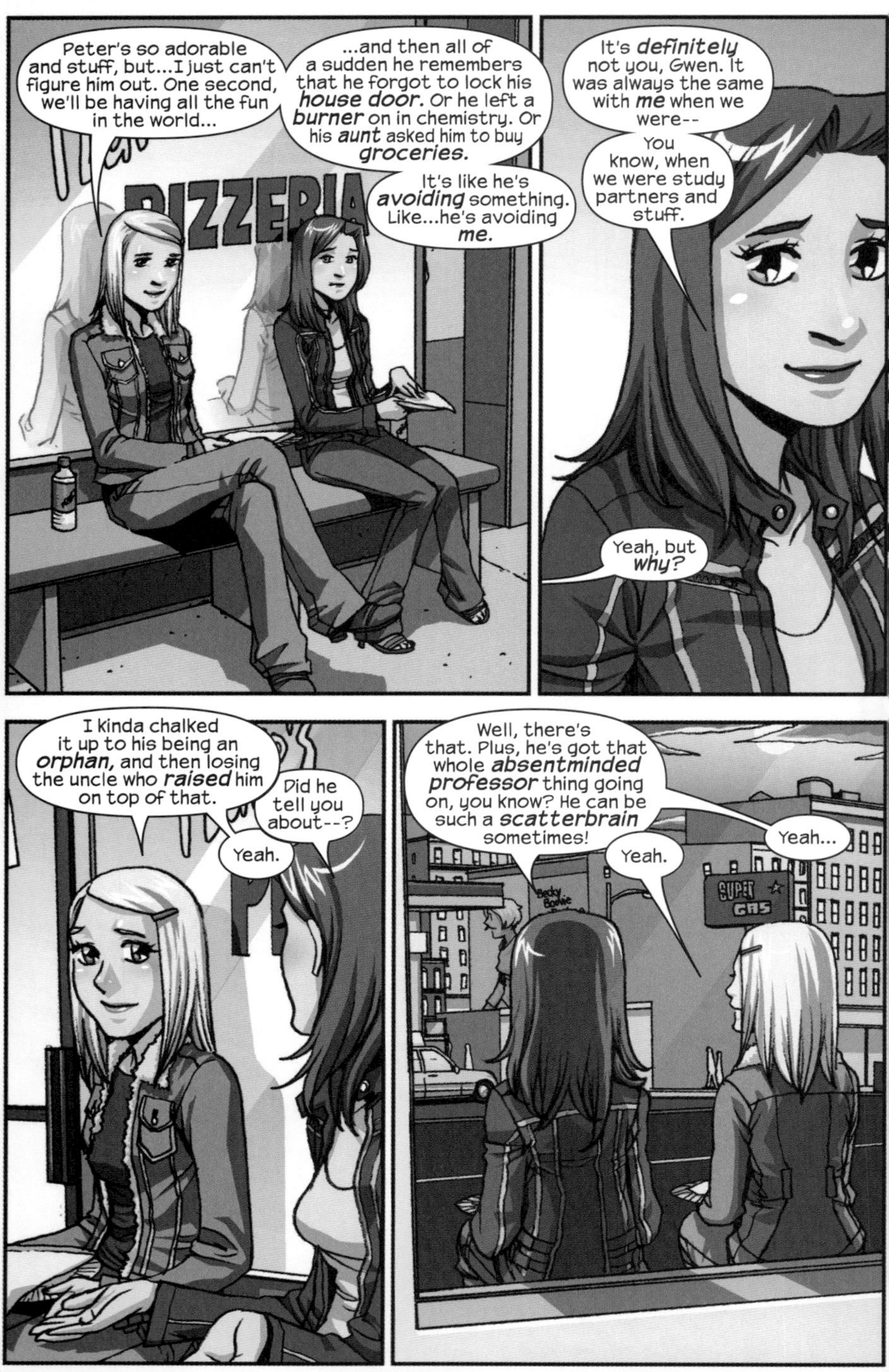
Peter's so adorable and stuff, but...I just can't figure him out. One second, we'll be having all the fun in the world...
...and then all of a sudden he remembers that he forgot to lock his house door. Or he left a burner on in chemistry. Or his aunt asked him to buy groceries.
It's like he's avoiding something. Like...he's avoiding me.
PIZZERIA
It's definitely not you, Gwen. It was always the same with me when we were--
You know, when we were study partners and stuff.
Yeah, but why?
I kinda chalked it up to his being an orphan, and then losing the uncle who raised him on top of that.
Did he tell you about--?
Yeah.
Well, there's that. Plus, he's got that whole absentminded professor thing going on, you know? He can be such a scatterbrain sometimes!
Yeah.
Yeah...
SUPER GAS

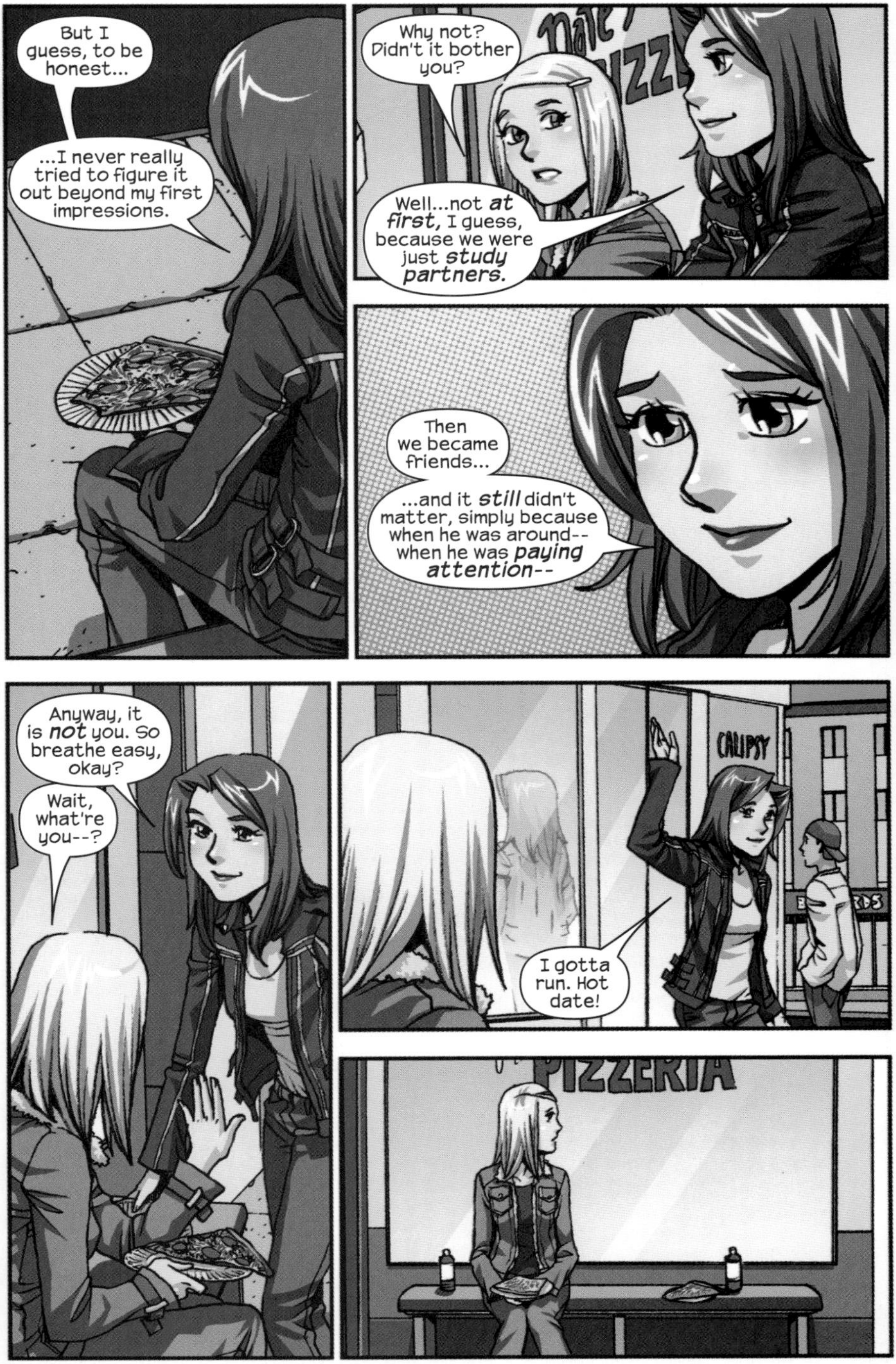
But I guess, to be honest...
...I never really tried to figure it out beyond my first impressions.
Why not? Didn't it bother you?
Well...not at first, I guess, because we were just study partners.
Then we became friends...
...and it still didn't matter, simply because when he was around-- when he was paying attention--
Anyway, it is not you. So breathe easy, okay?
Wait, what're you--?
CALIPSY
I gotta run. Hot date!
PIZZERIA

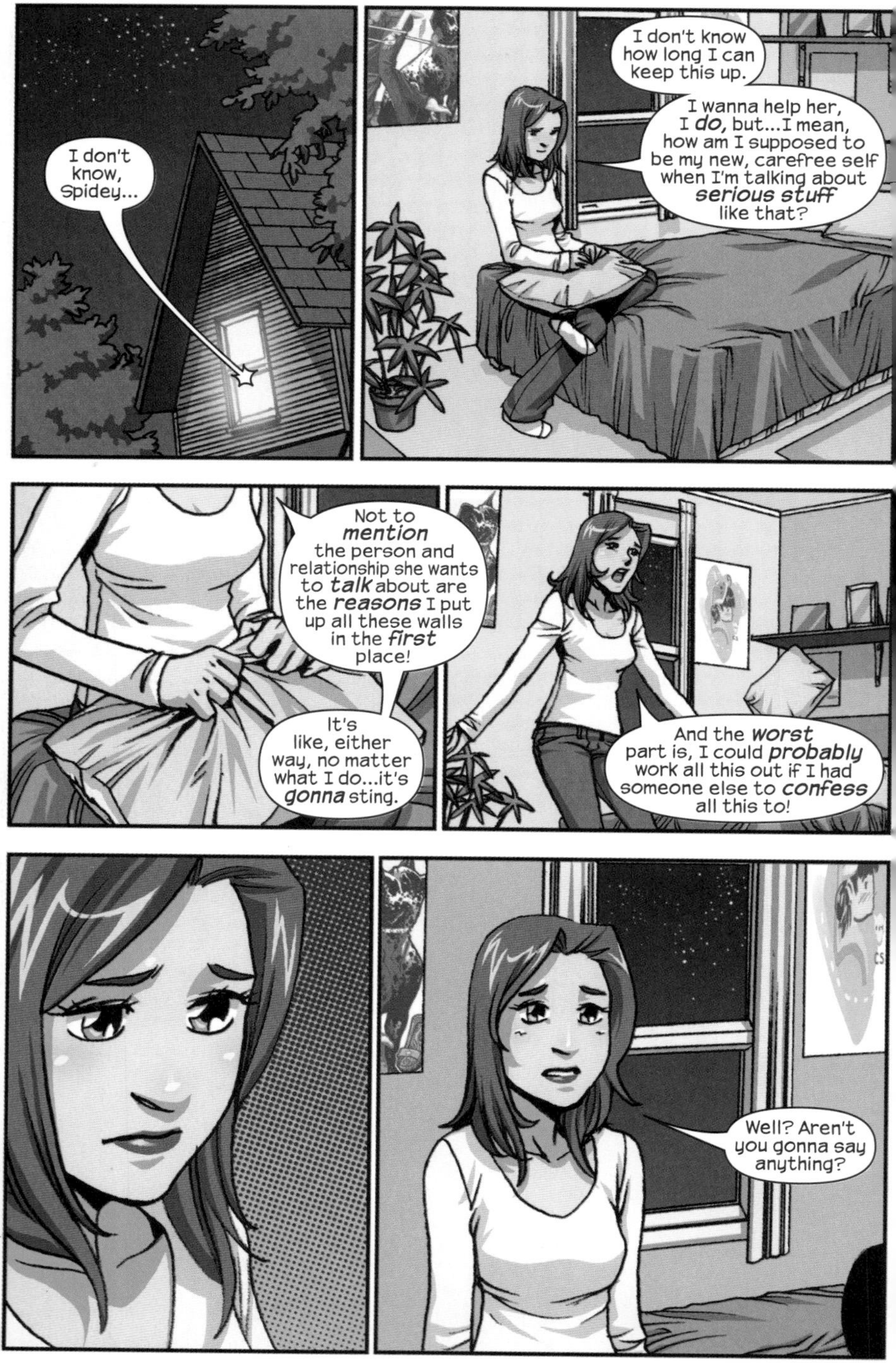
I don't know, Spidey...
I don't know how long I can keep this up.
I wanna help her, I do, but...I mean, how am I supposed to be my new, carefree self when I'm talking about serious stuff like that?
Not to mention the person and relationship she wants to talk about are the reasons I put up all these walls in the first place!
It's like, either way, no matter what I do...it's gonna sting.
And the worst part is, I could probably work all this out if I had someone else to confess all this to!
Well? Aren't you gonna say anything?

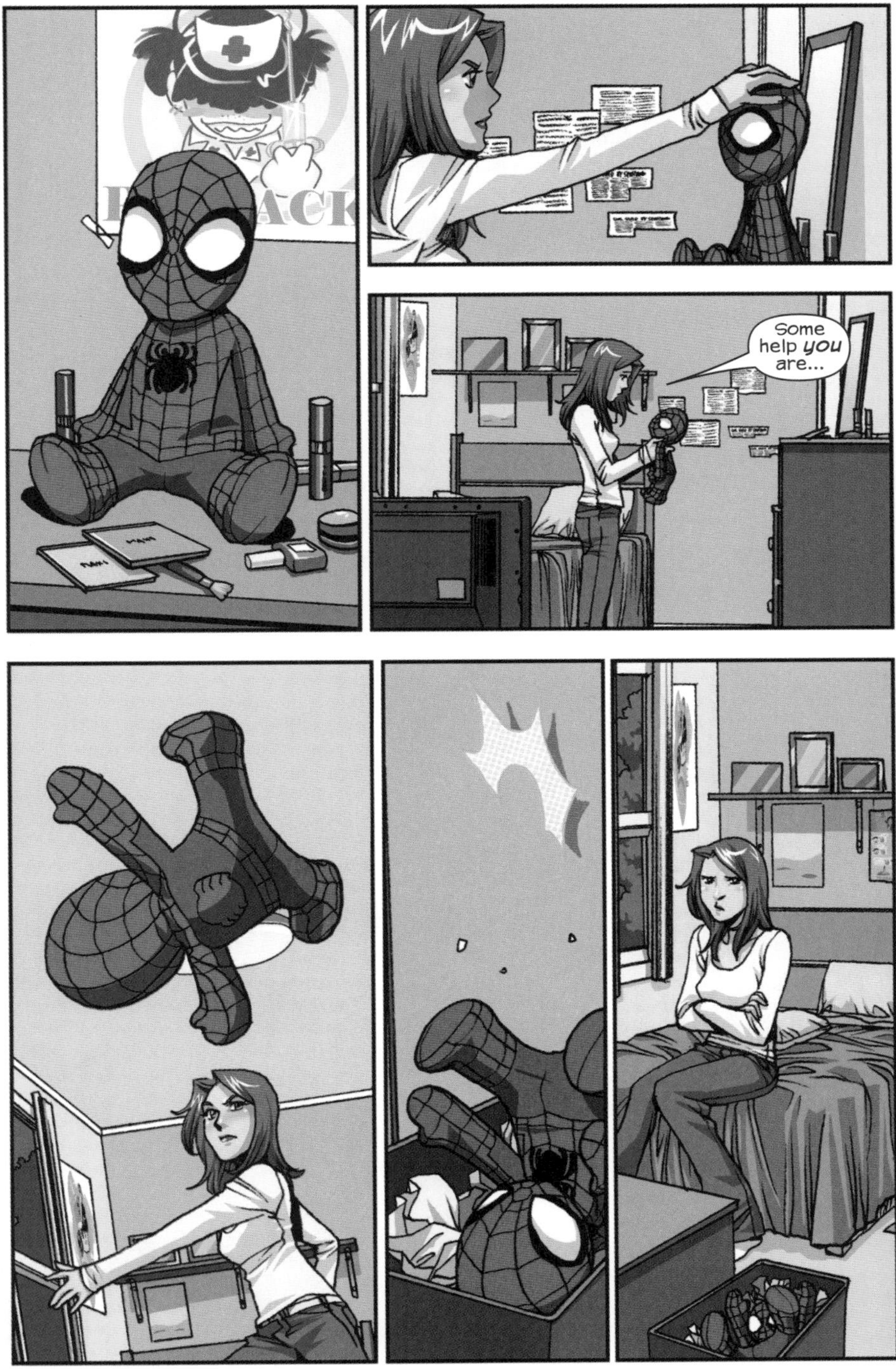
Some help *you* are...

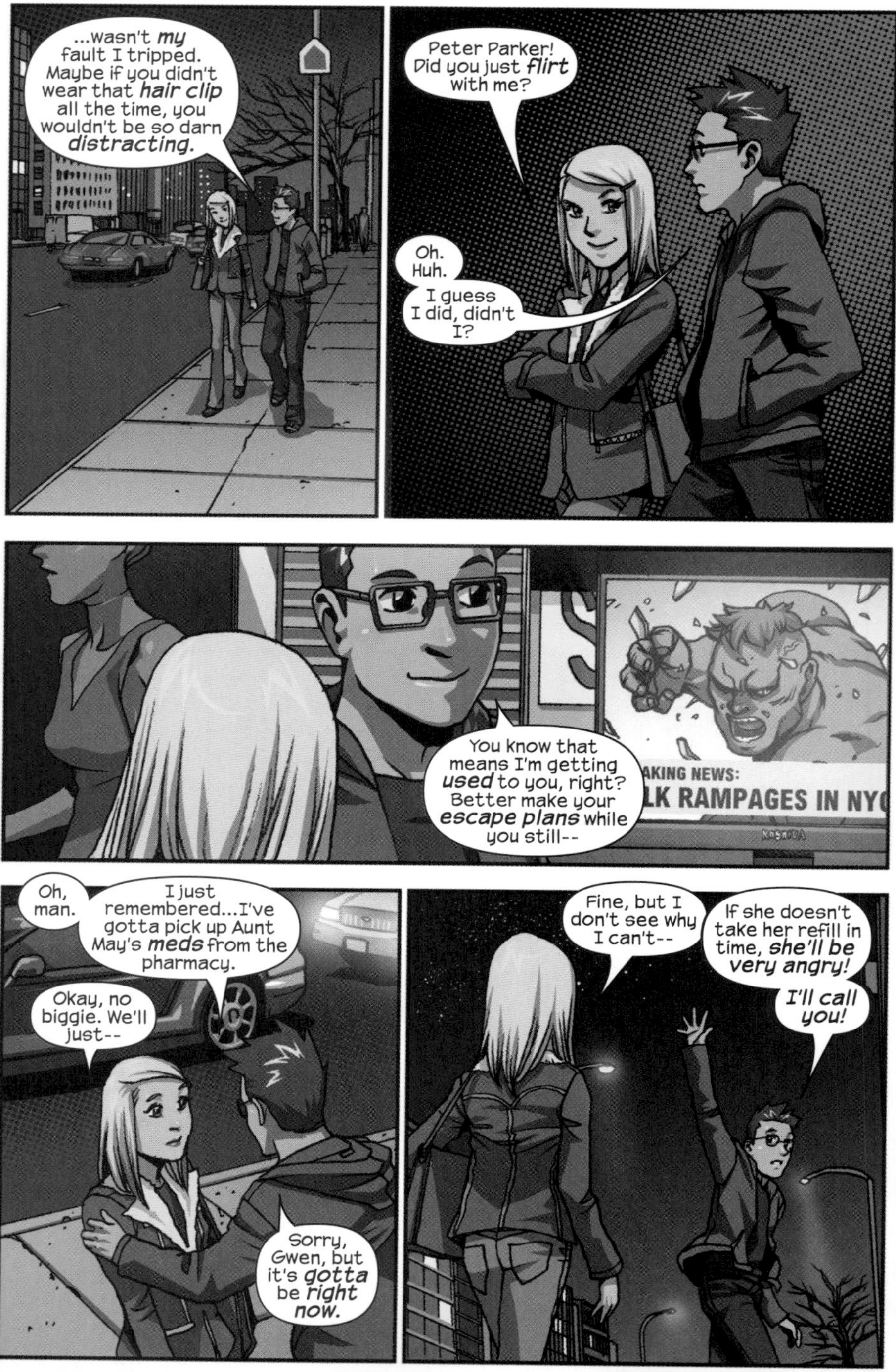

...wasn't *my* fault I tripped. Maybe if you didn't wear that *hair clip* all the time, you wouldn't be so darn *distracting.*
Peter Parker! Did you just *flirt* with me?
Oh. Huh.
I guess I did, didn't I?
You know that means I'm getting *used* to you, right? Better make your *escape plans* while you still--
AKING NEWS:
LK RAMPAGES IN NY
Oh, man.
I just remembered...I've gotta pick up Aunt May's *meds* from the pharmacy.
Okay, no biggie. We'll just--
Sorry, Gwen, but it's *gotta* be *right now.*
Fine, but I don't see why I can't--
If she doesn't take her refill in time, *she'll be very angry!*
I'll call you!

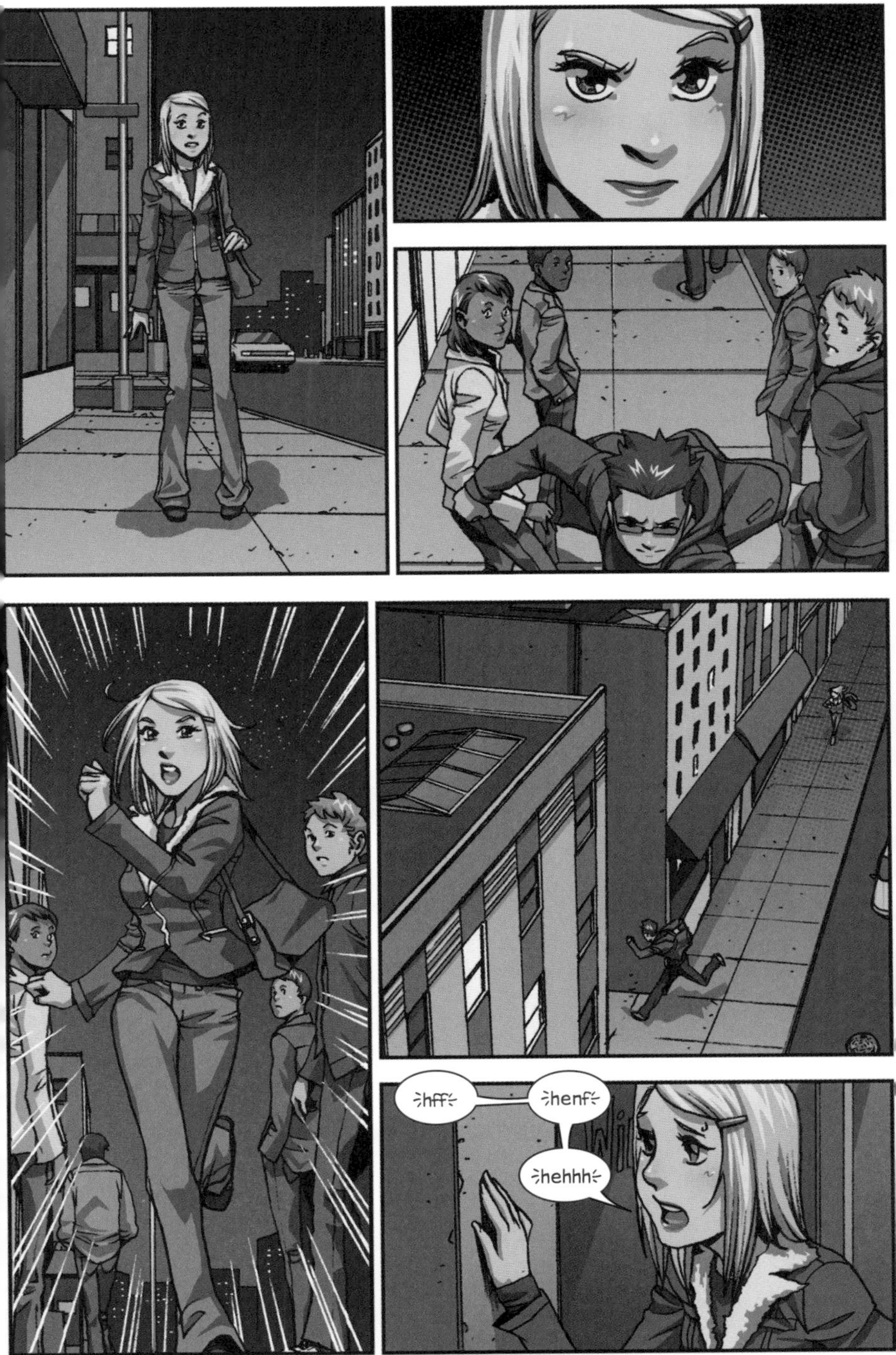
hff
henf
hehhh

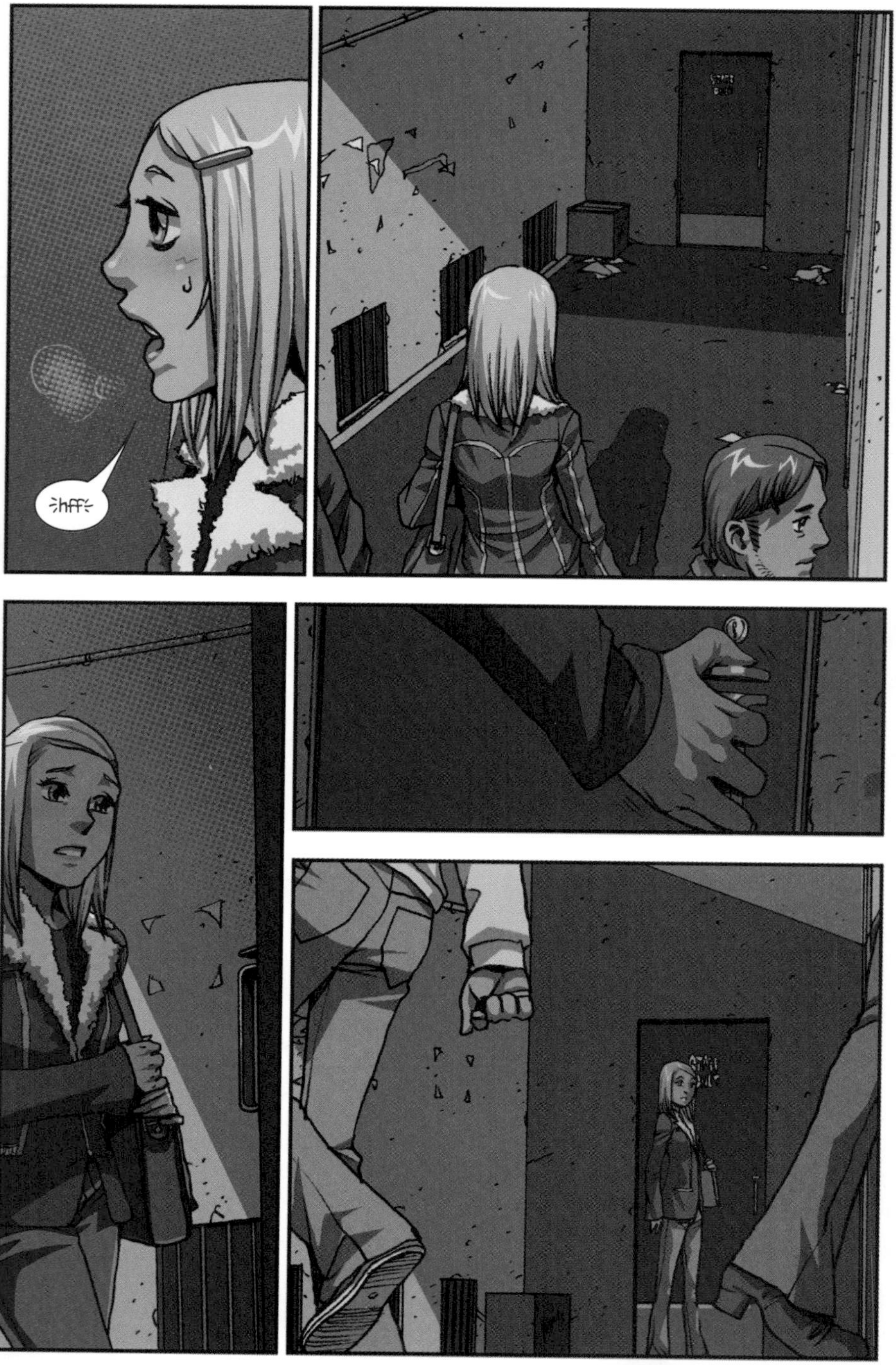

hff

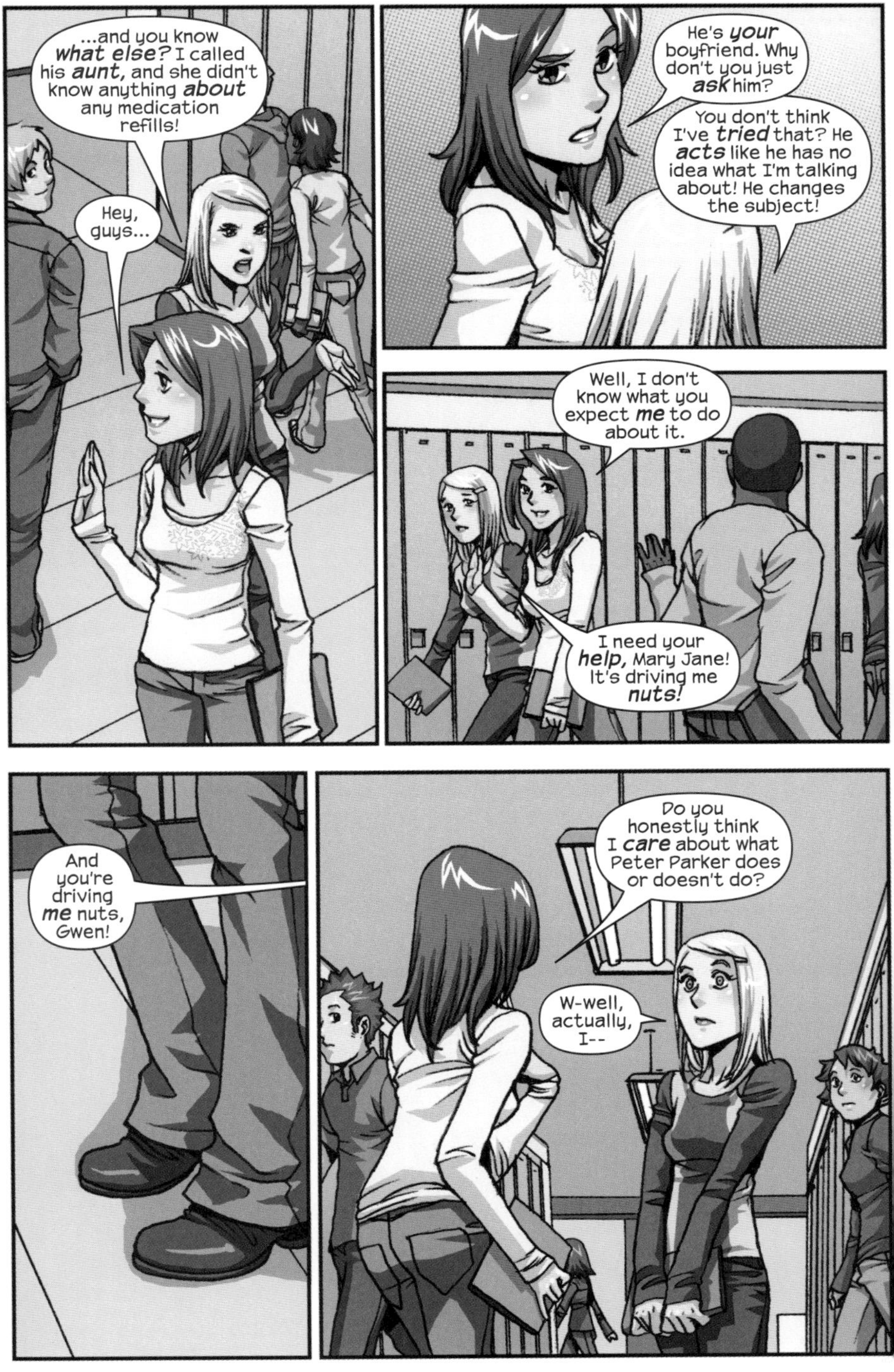
...and you know what else? I called his aunt, and she didn't know anything about any medication refills!
Hey, guys...
He's your boyfriend. Why don't you just ask him?
You don't think I've tried that? He acts like he has no idea what I'm talking about! He changes the subject!
Well, I don't know what you expect me to do about it.
I need your help, Mary Jane! It's driving me nuts!
And you're driving me nuts, Gwen!
Do you honestly think I care about what Peter Parker does or doesn't do?
W-well, actually, I--

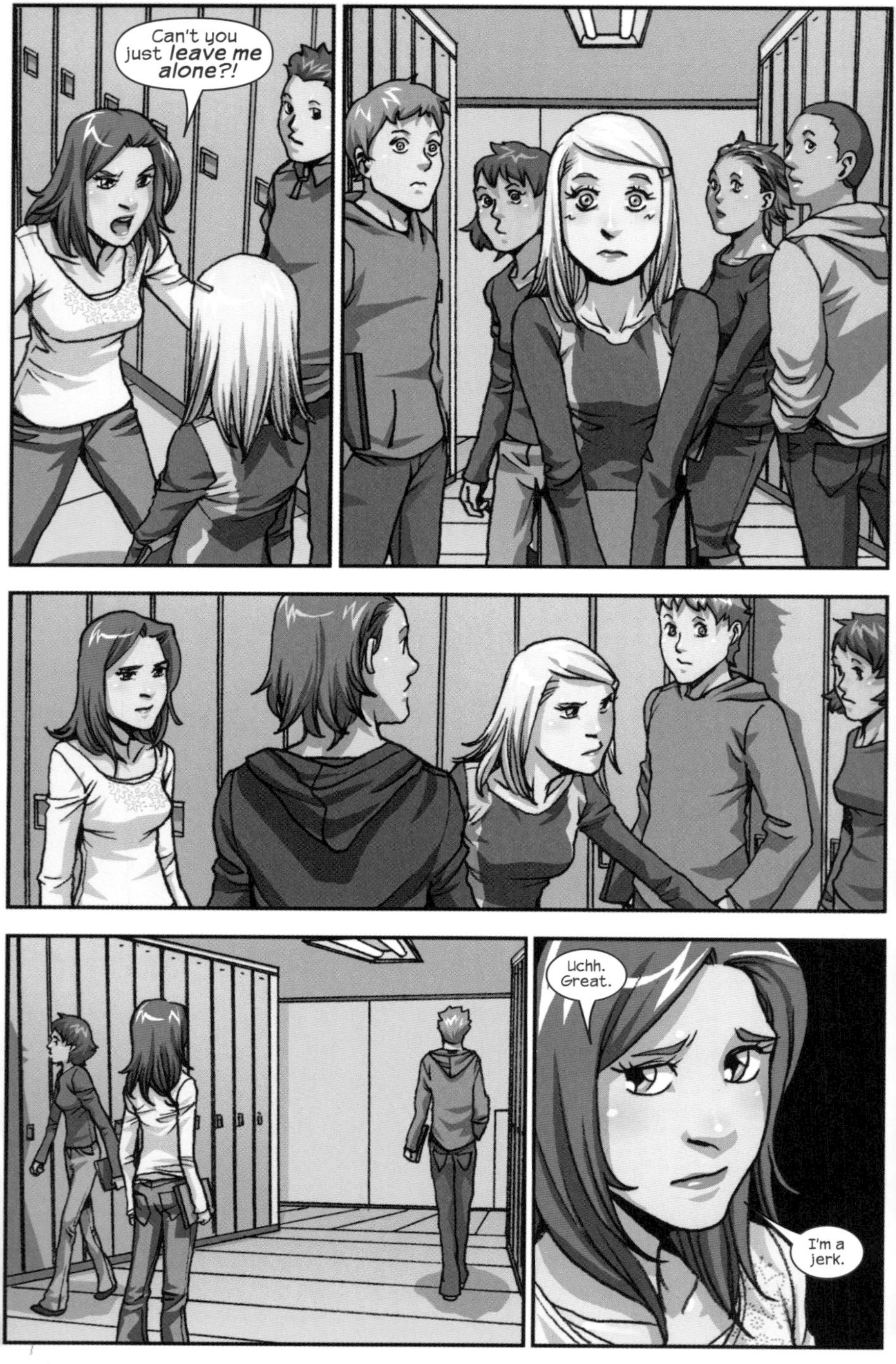
Can't you just *leave me alone?!*
Uchh. Great.
I'm a jerk.

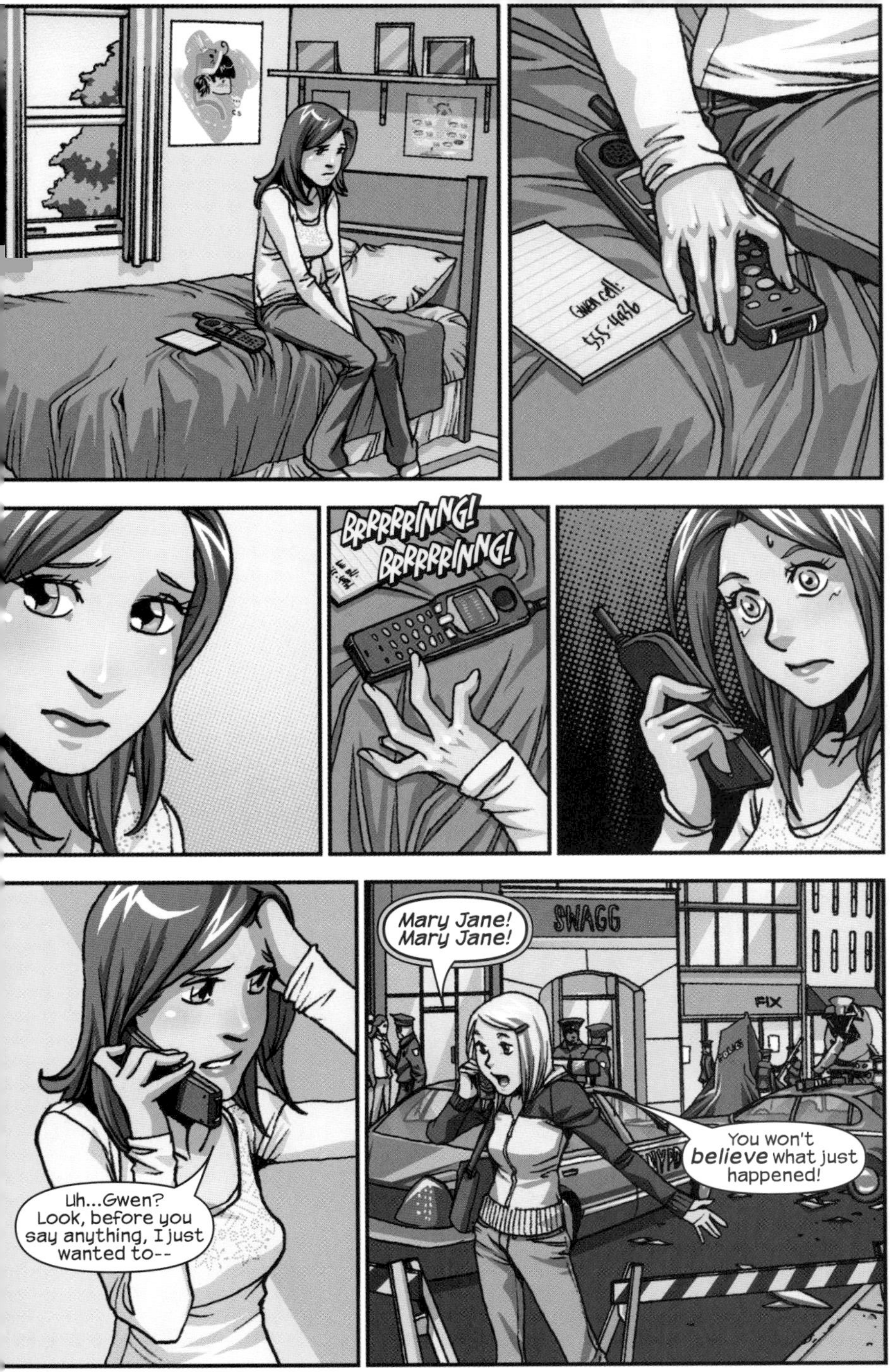
Gwen cell:
555-4836
BRRRRRING!
BRRRRRING!
Uh...Gwen? Look, before you say anything, I just wanted to--
SWAGG
Mary Jane! Mary Jane!
FIX
You won't *believe* what just happened!

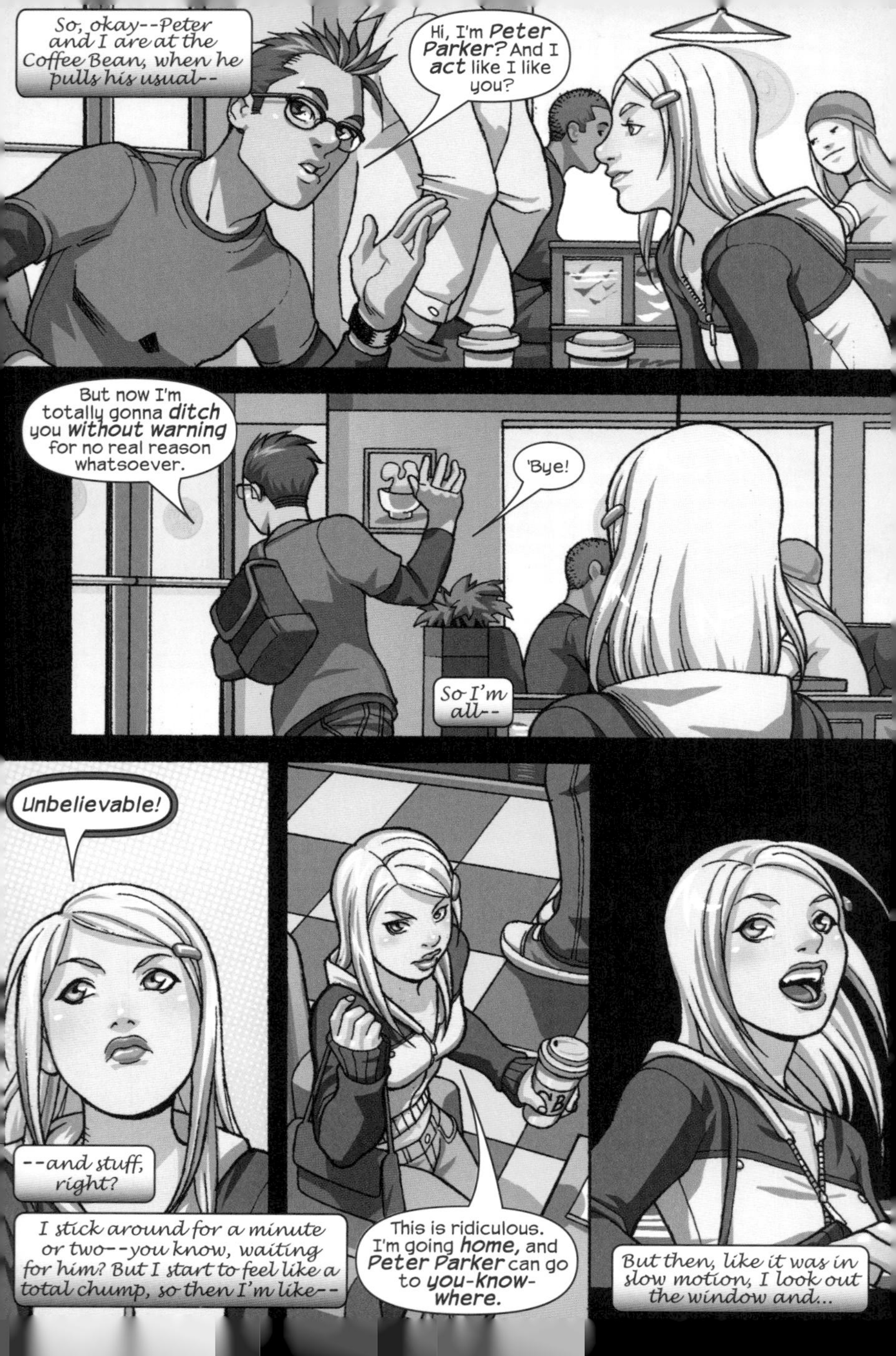
So, okay--Peter and I are at the Coffee Bean, when he pulls his usual--
Hi, I'm Peter Parker? And I act like I like you?
But now I'm totally gonna ditch you without warning for no real reason whatsoever.
'Bye!
So I'm all--
Unbelievable!
--and stuff, right?
I stick around for a minute or two--you know, waiting for him? But I start to feel like a total chump, so then I'm like--
This is ridiculous. I'm going home, and Peter Parker can go to you-know-where.
But then, like it was in slow motion, I look out the window and...

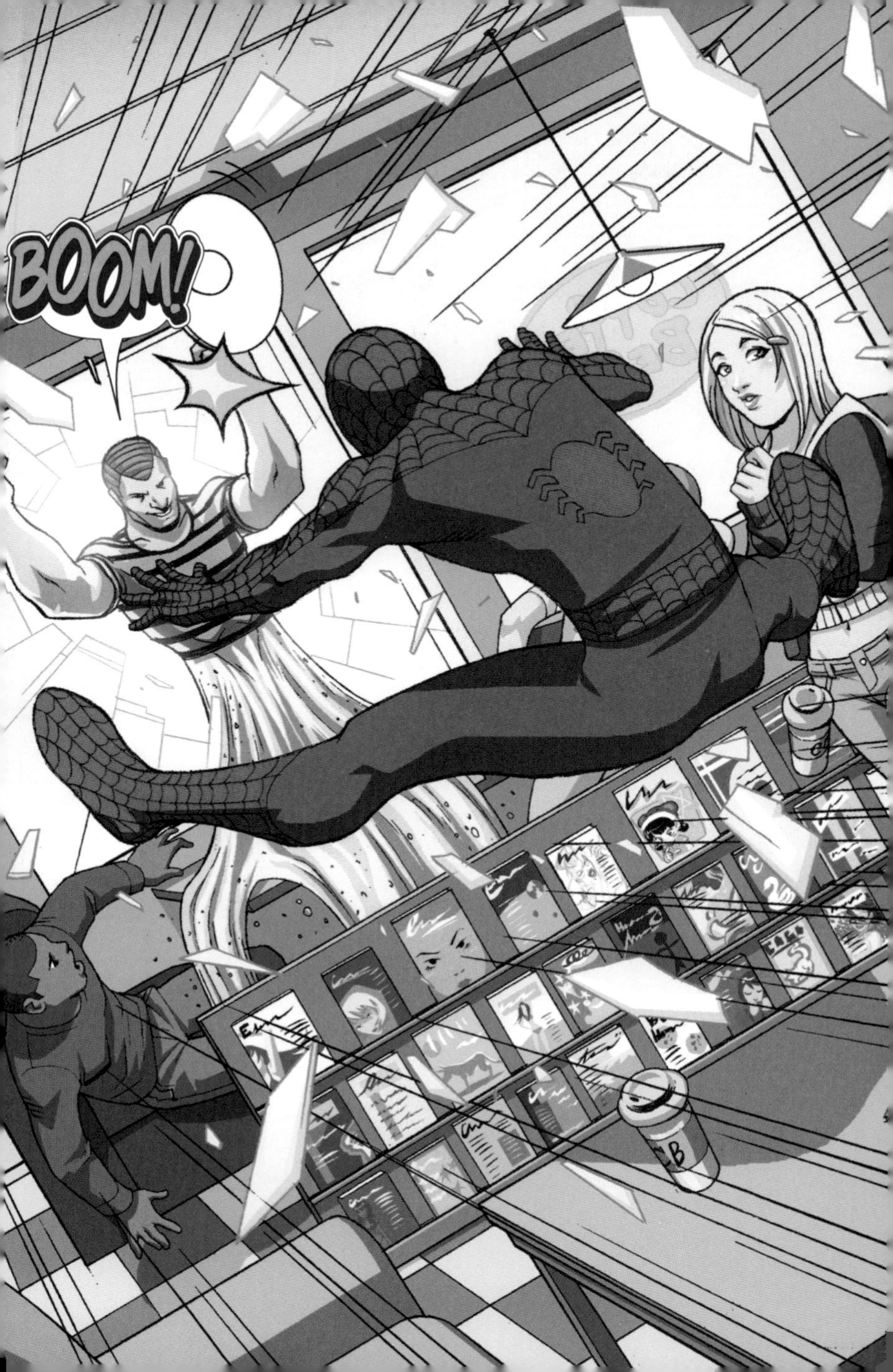
BOOM!

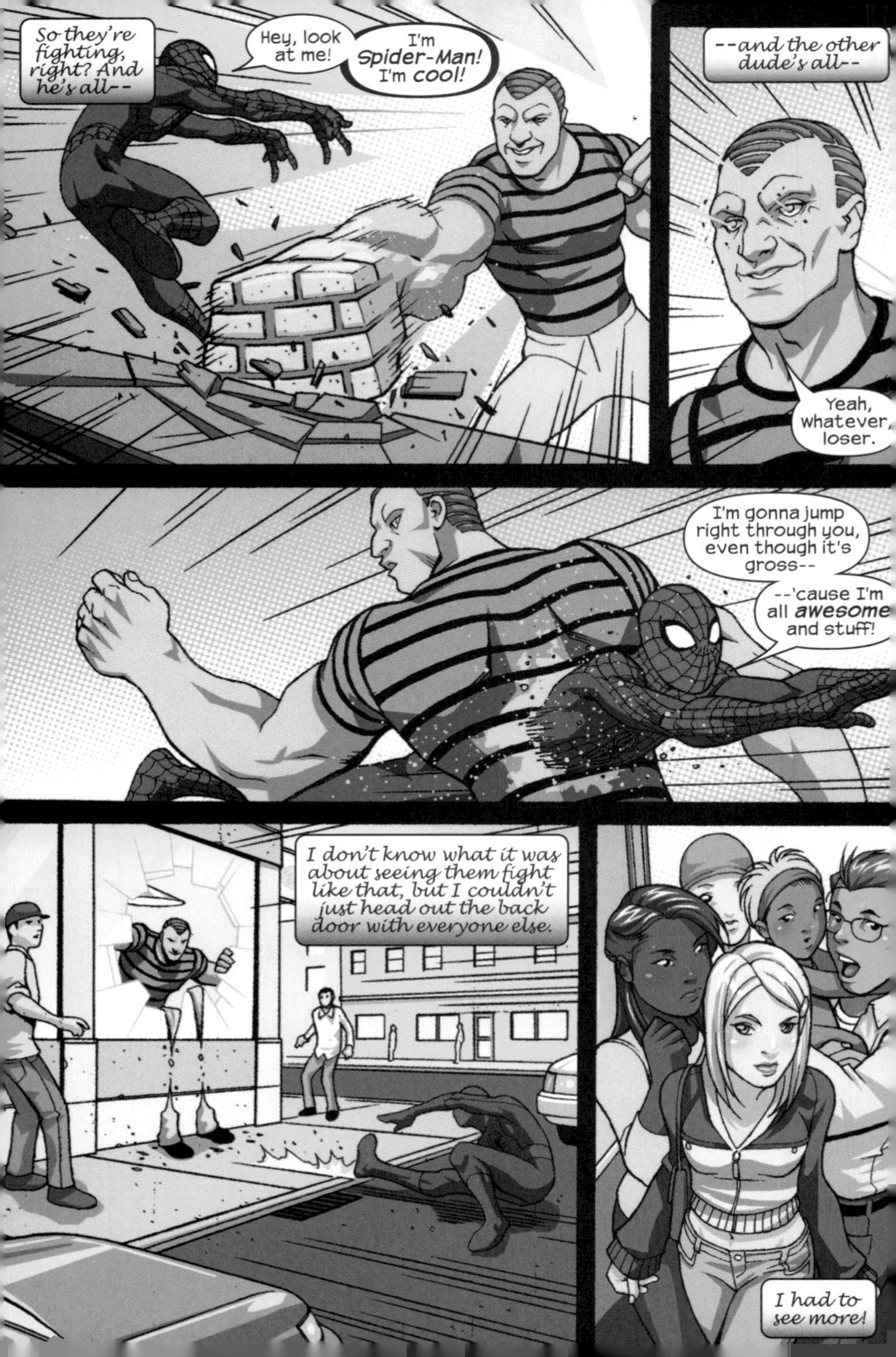
So they're fighting, right? And he's all--
Hey, look at me!
I'm Spider-Man! I'm cool!
--and the other dude's all--
Yeah, whatever, loser.
I'm gonna jump right through you, even though it's gross--
--'cause I'm all awesome and stuff!
I don't know what it was about seeing them fight like that, but I couldn't just head out the back door with everyone else.
I had to see more!

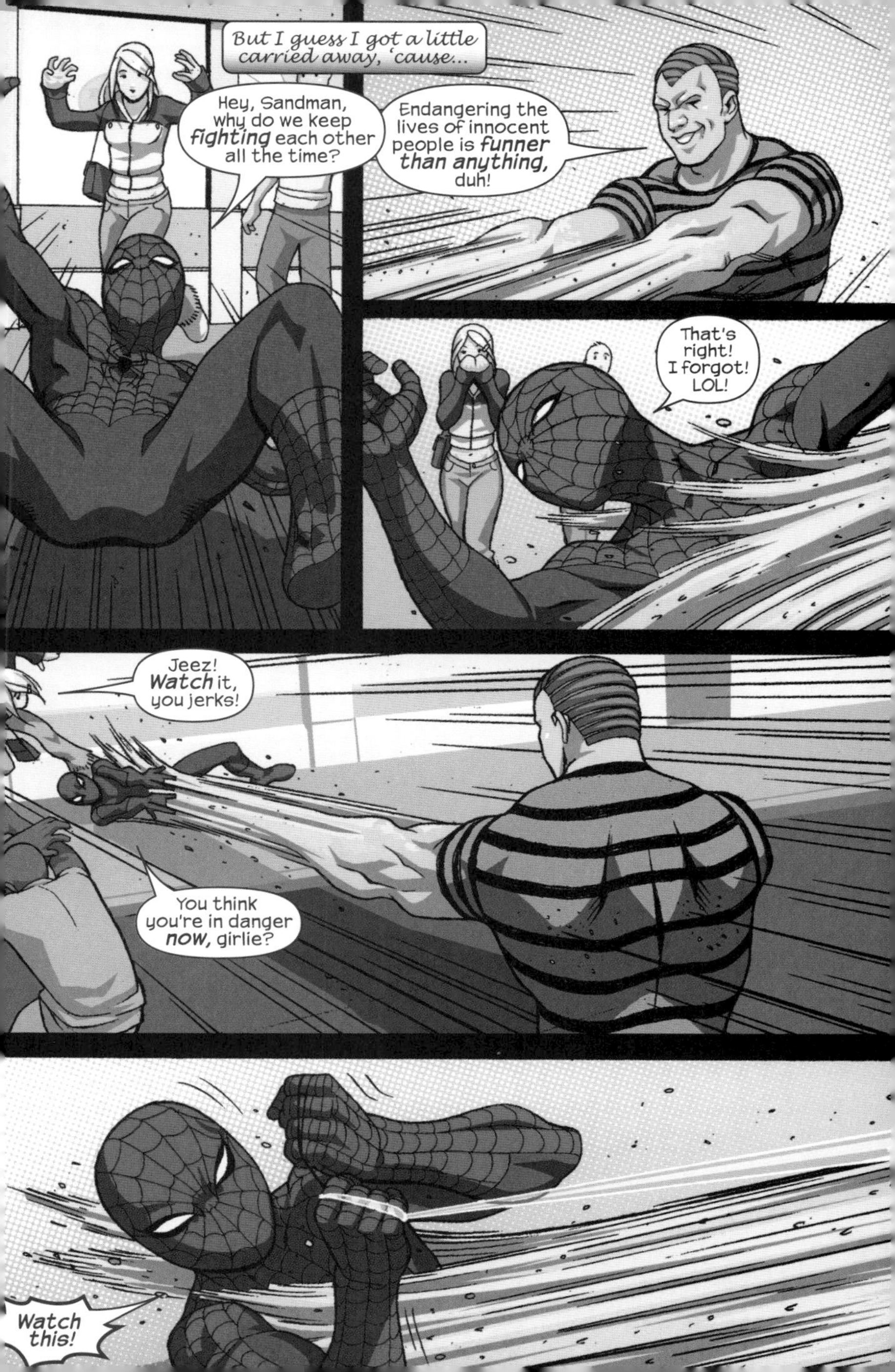
But I guess I got a little carried away, 'cause...
Hey, Sandman, why do we keep fighting each other all the time?
Endangering the lives of innocent people is funner than anything, duh!
That's right! I forgot! LOL!
Jeez! Watch it, you jerks!
You think you're in danger now, girlie?
Watch this!

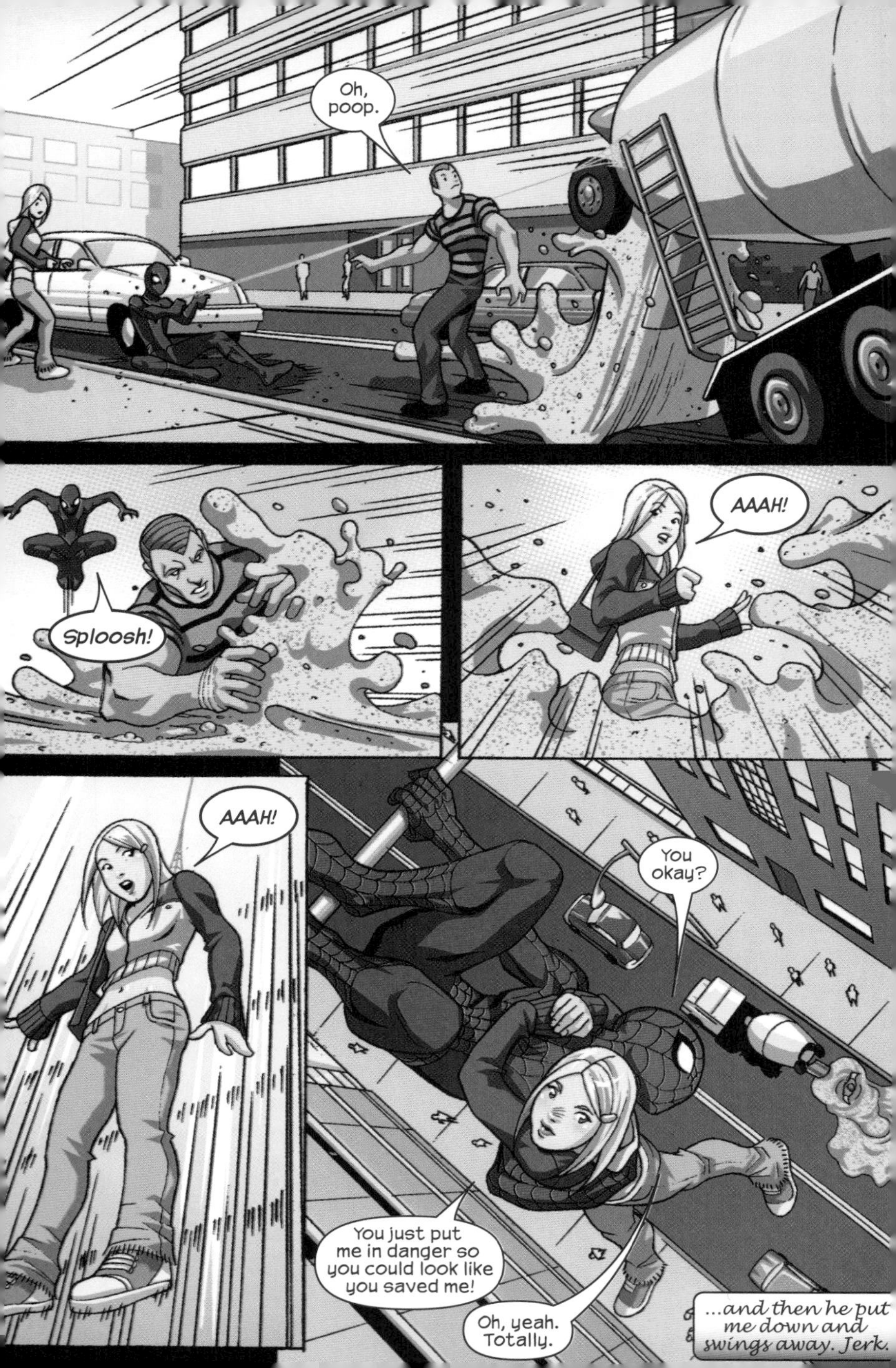
Oh, poop.
Sploosh!
AAAH!
AAAH!
You okay?
You just put me in danger so you could look like you saved me!
Oh, yeah. Totally.
...and then he put me down and swings away. Jerk.

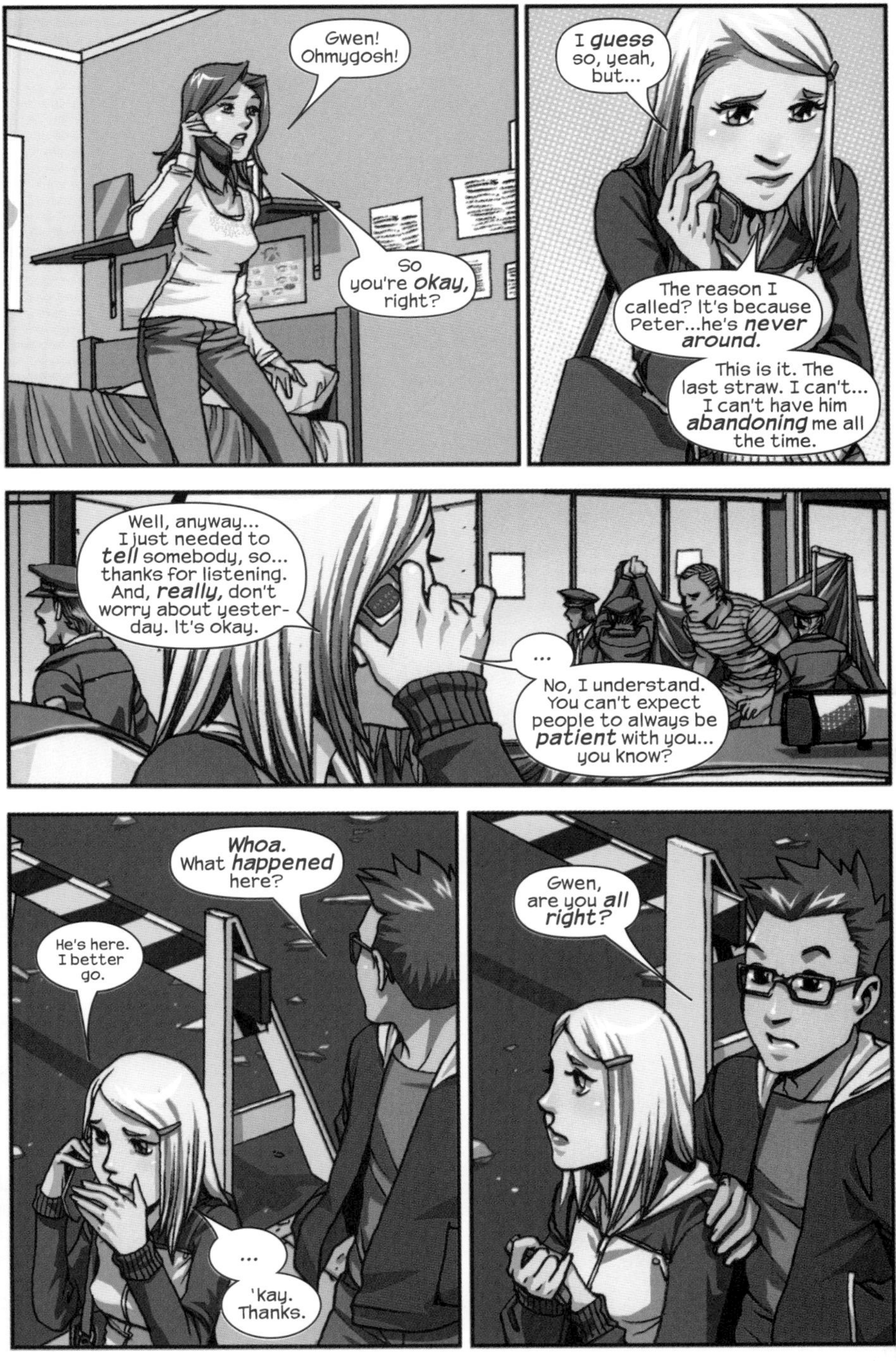

Gwen! Ohmygosh!
So you're okay, right?
I guess so, yeah, but...
The reason I called? It's because Peter...he's never around.
This is it. The last straw. I can't... I can't have him abandoning me all the time.
Well, anyway... I just needed to tell somebody, so... thanks for listening. And, really, don't worry about yesterday. It's okay.
...
No, I understand. You can't expect people to always be patient with you... you know?
Whoa. What happened here?
He's here. I better go.
...
'kay. Thanks.
Gwen, are you all right?

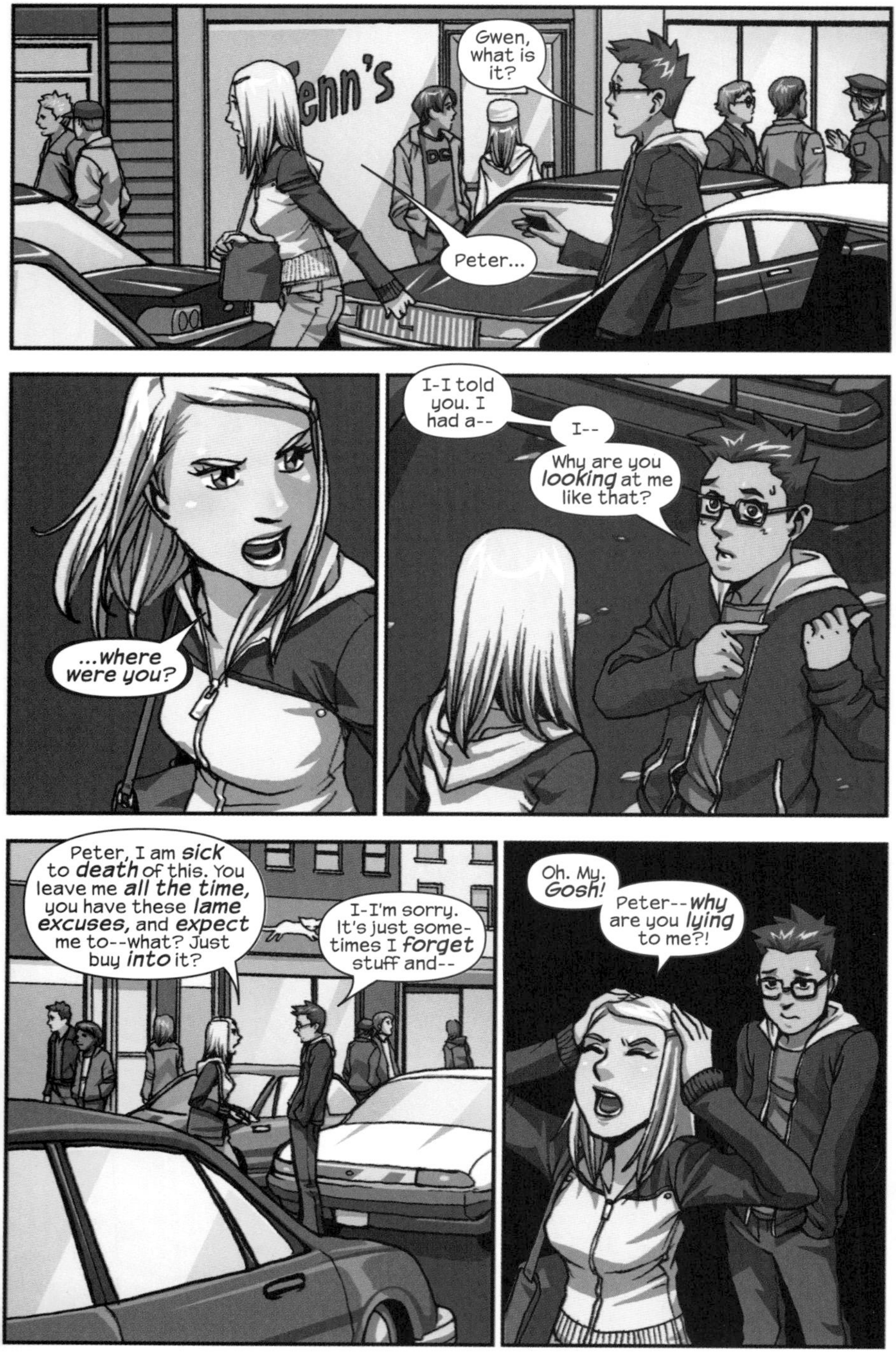
Gwen, what is it?
Peter...
...where were you?
I-I told you. I had a--
I--
Why are you *looking* at me like that?
Peter, I am *sick* to *death* of this. You leave me *all the time,* you have these *lame excuses,* and *expect* me to--what? Just buy *into* it?
I-I'm sorry. It's just some-times I *forget* stuff and--
Oh. My. *Gosh!*
Peter--*why* are you *lying* to me?!

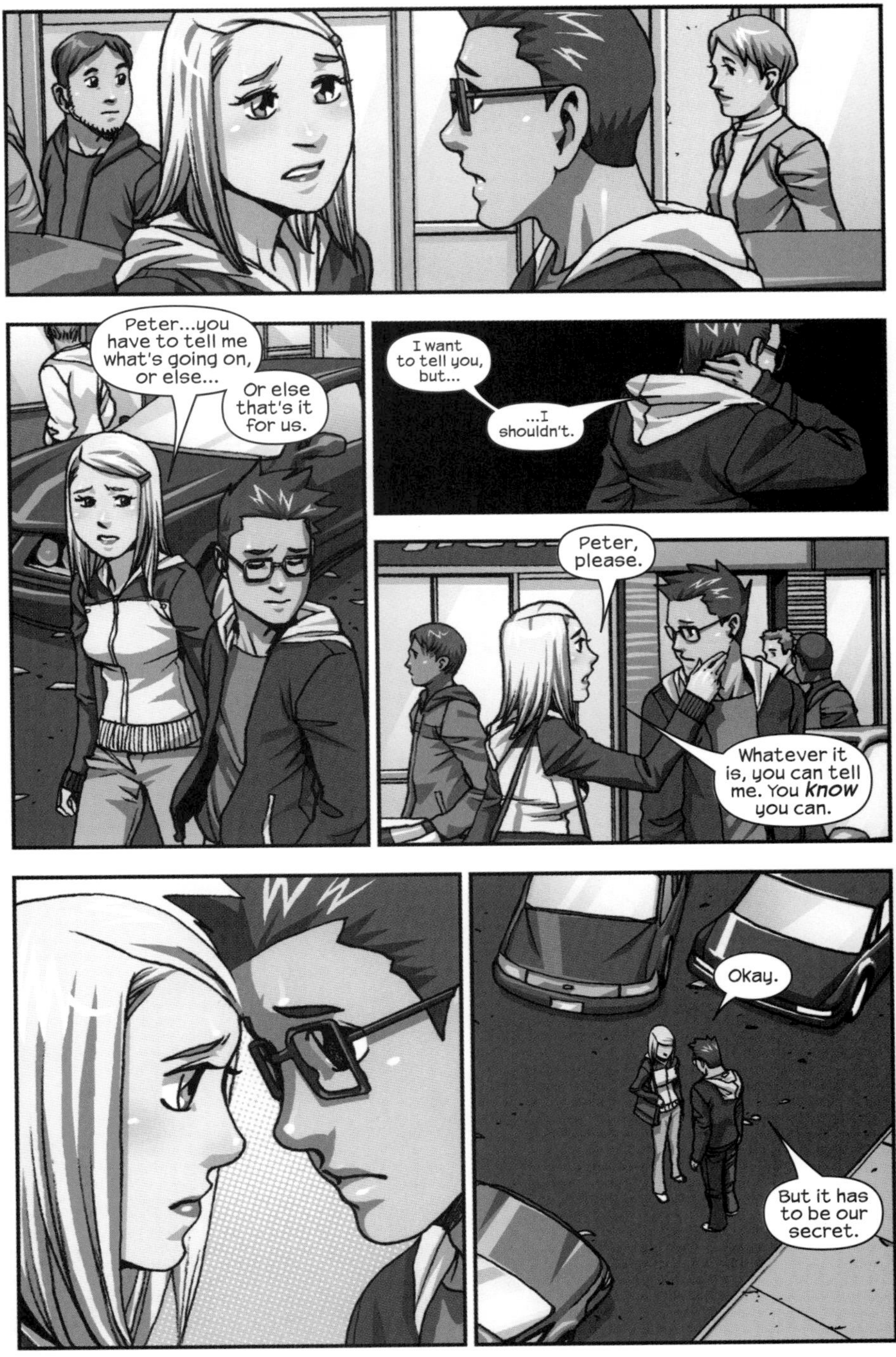
Peter...you have to tell me what's going on, or else...
Or else that's it for us.
I want to tell you, but...
...I shouldn't.
Peter, please.
Whatever it is, you can tell me. You **KNOW** you can.
Okay.
But it has to be our secret.

The Parker Thing

Sean McKeever Writer | Takeshi Miyazawa with Rick Mays Art | Christina Strain Colors | Dave Sharpe Letters | Tak, N. Lee & Strain Cover Art | Kate Levin Production | Special Thanks to MacKenzie Cadenhead & David Gabriel

Nathan Cosby Asst. Editor | Mark Paniccia Editor | Joe Quesada Chief | Dan Buckley Publisher

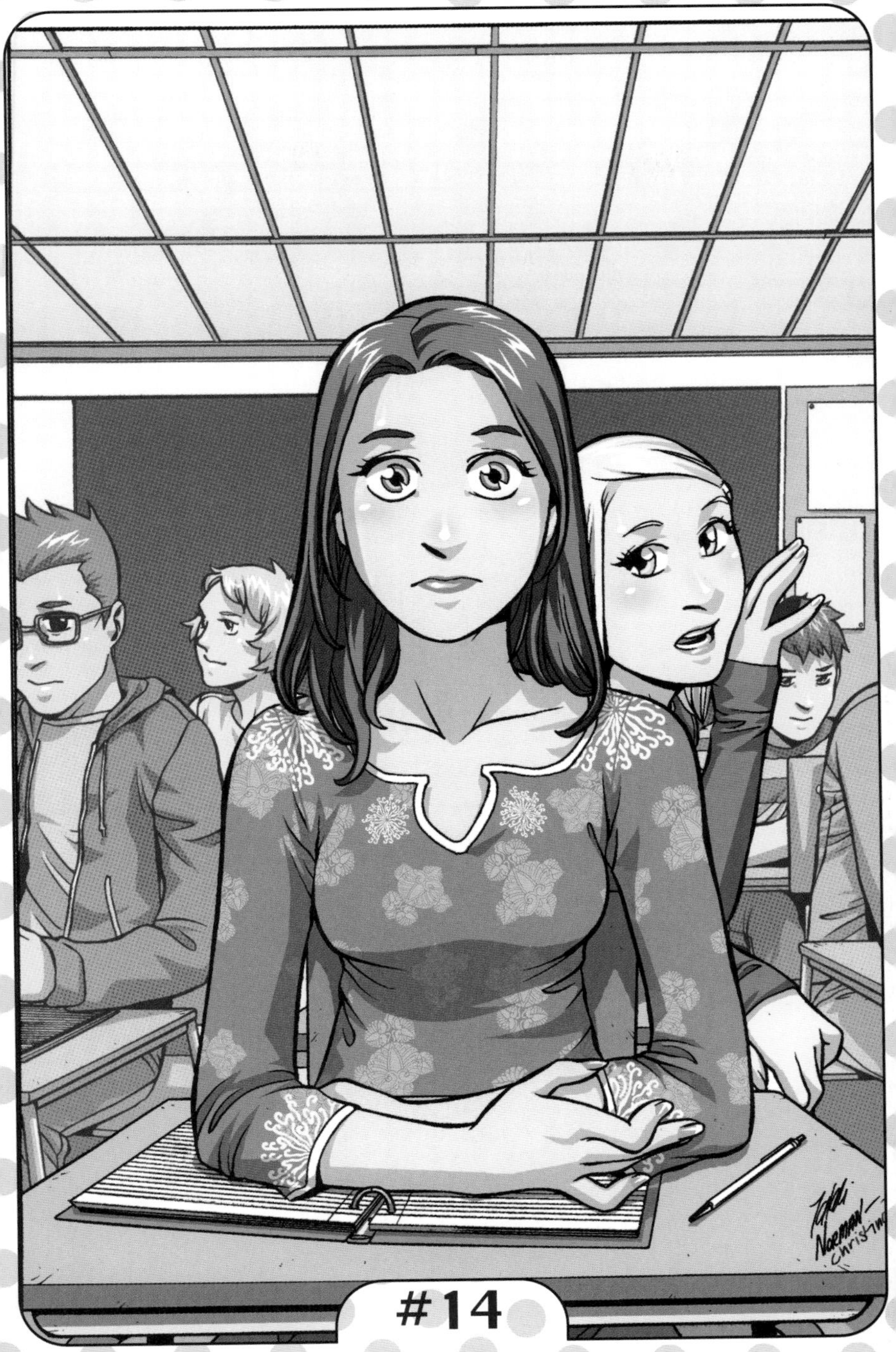
#14

Queens, NY

WAKE UP, SLEEPY–HEAD!

WAKE UP! WAKE UP!

WAUGH!

WAKE UP, SLEEPY–HEAD!

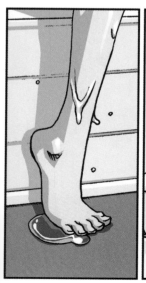

This is it, girl.

No more running. No more party-girl façade.

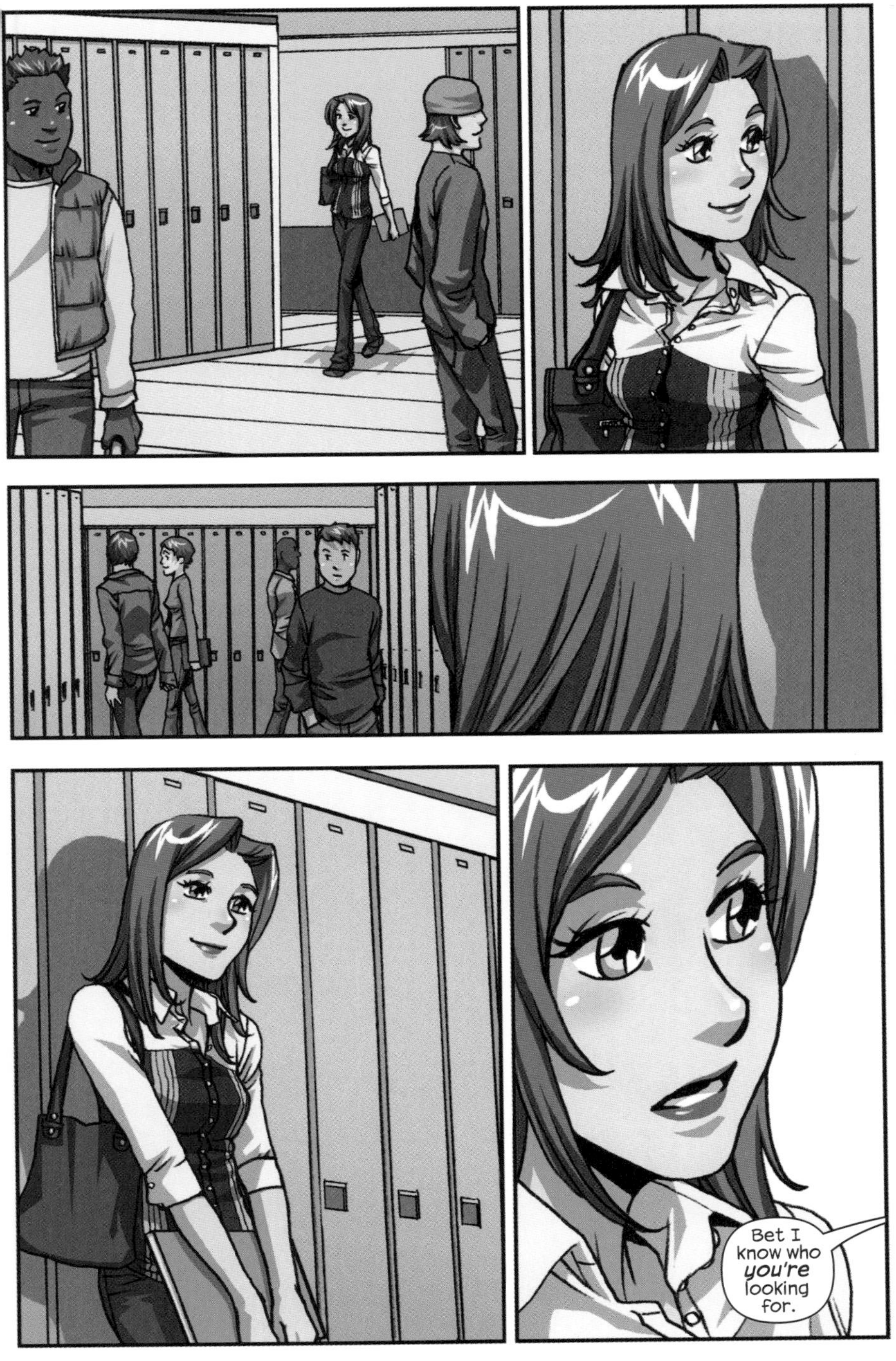
Bet I know who *you're* looking for.

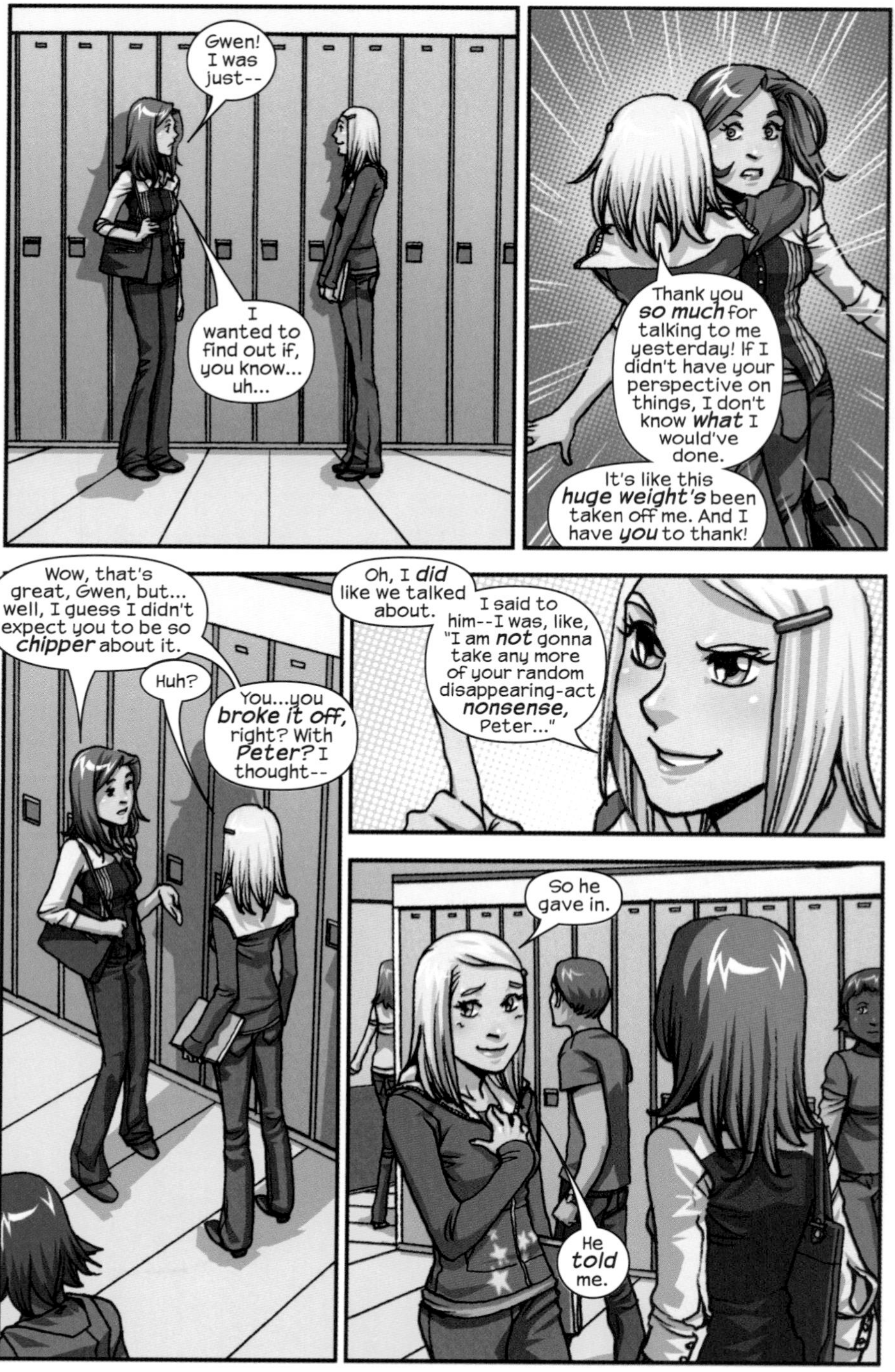
Gwen! I was just--
I wanted to find out if, you know... uh...
Thank you *so much* for talking to me yesterday! If I didn't have your perspective on things, I don't know *what* I would've done.
It's like this *huge weight's* been taken off me. And I have *you* to thank!
Wow, that's great, Gwen, but... well, I guess I didn't expect you to be so *chipper* about it.
Huh?
You...you *broke it off,* right? With *Peter?* I thought--
Oh, I *did* like we talked about.
I said to him--I was, like, "I am *not* gonna take any more of your random disappearing-act *nonsense,* Peter..."
So he gave in.
He *told* me.

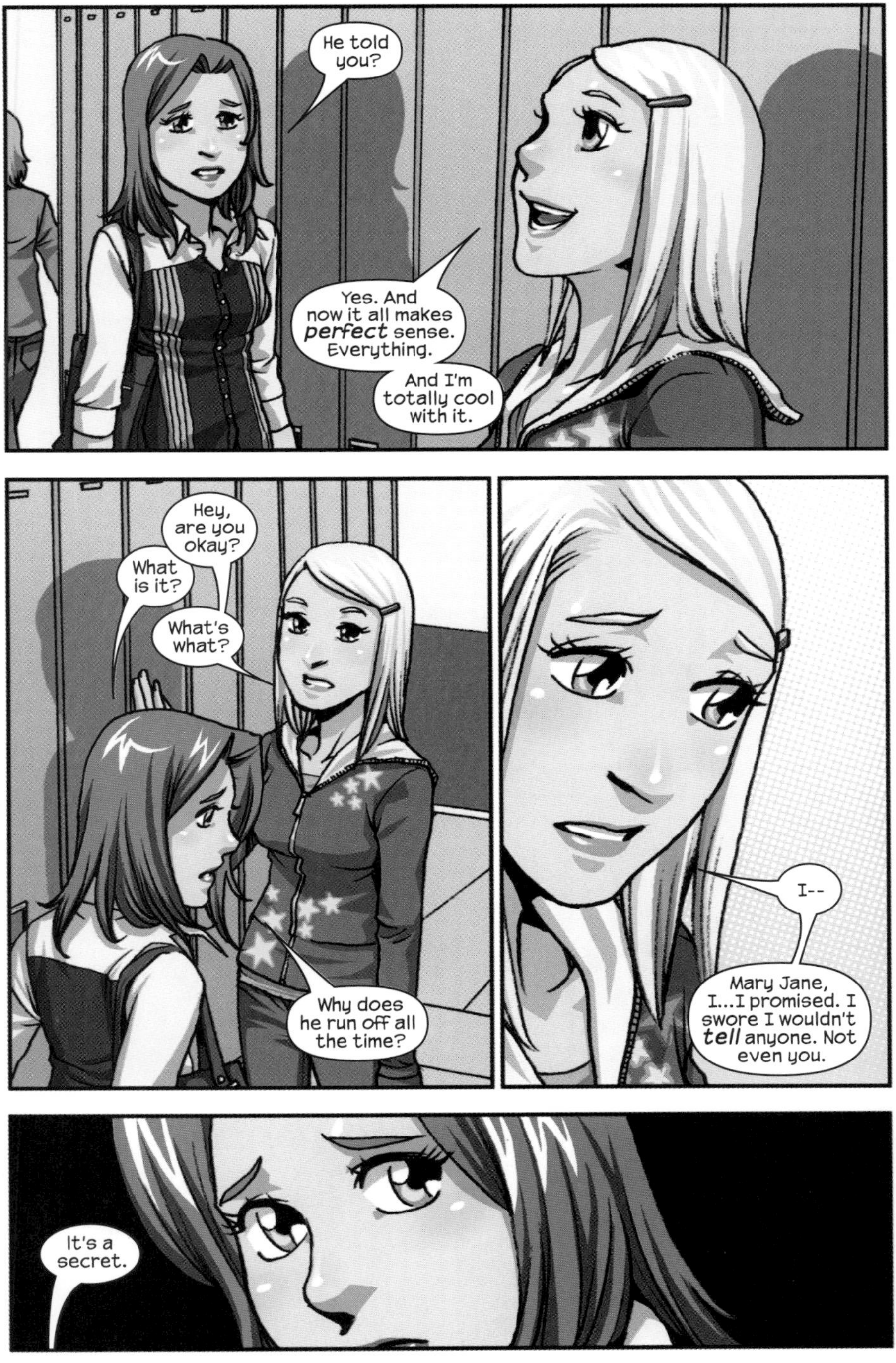
He told you?
Yes. And now it all makes perfect sense. Everything.
And I'm totally cool with it.
Hey, are you okay?
What is it?
What's what?
Why does he run off all the time?
I--
Mary Jane, I...I promised. I swore I wouldn't tell anyone. Not even you.
It's a secret.

MJ?

MJ...

I thought they were going to break up and then I could drop this whole *pretense* and tell Peter how I feel and everything would be--well, not *perfect*, nothing's ever perfect, is it--but I thought I could be *myself* again and it felt *so good*, I just--

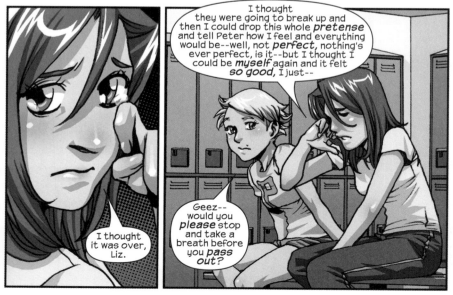

Geez-- would you *please* stop and take a breath before you *pass out?*

I thought it was over, Liz.

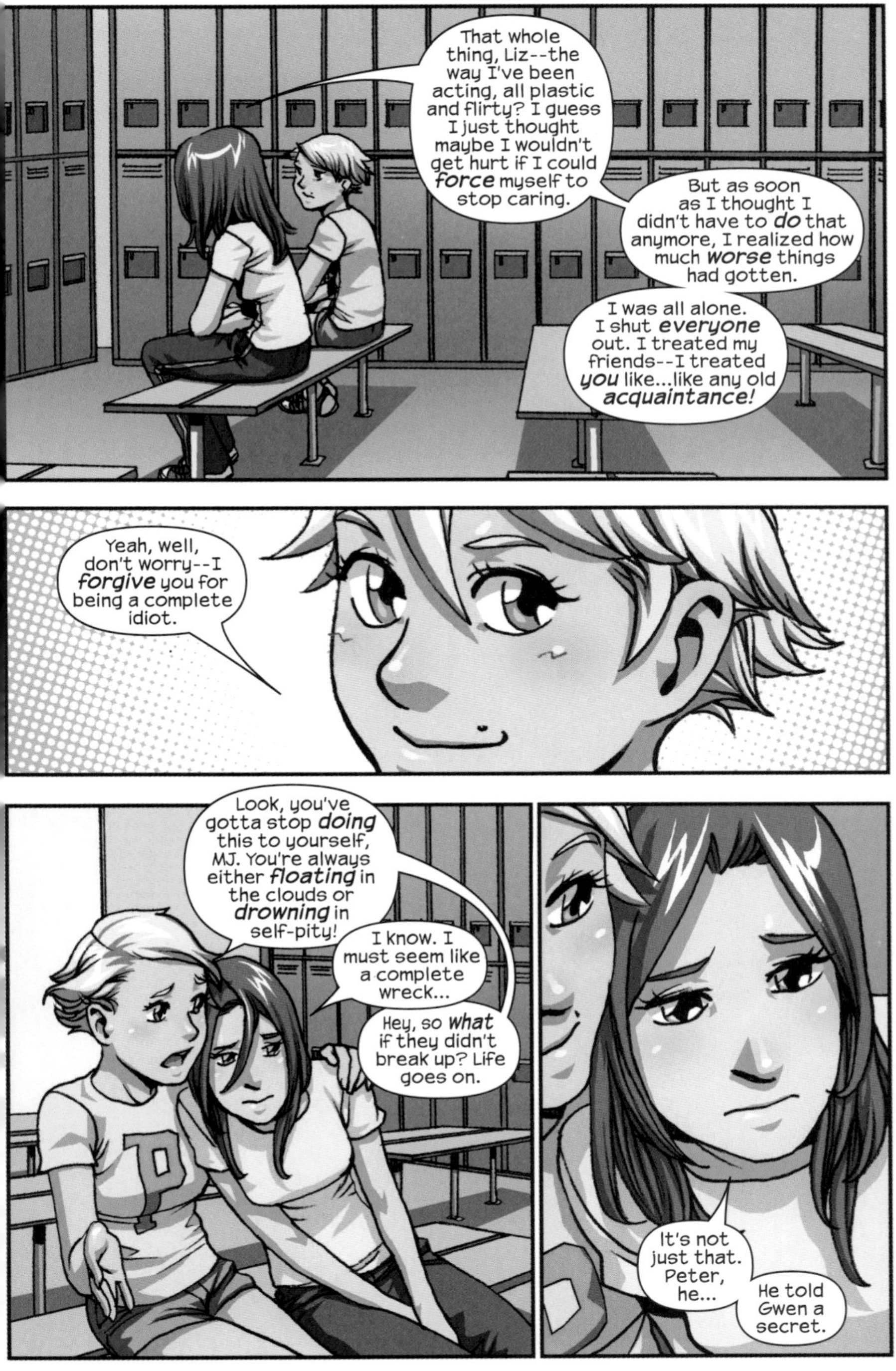
That whole thing, Liz--the way I've been acting, all plastic and flirty? I guess I just thought maybe I wouldn't get hurt if I could *force* myself to stop caring.
But as soon as I thought I didn't have to *do* that anymore, I realized how much *worse* things had gotten.
I was all alone. I shut *everyone* out. I treated my friends--I treated *you* like...like any old *acquaintance!*
Yeah, well, don't worry--I *forgive* you for being a complete idiot.
Look, you've gotta stop *doing* this to yourself, MJ. You're always either *floating* in the clouds or *drowning* in self-pity!
I know. I must seem like a complete wreck...
Hey, so *what* if they didn't break up? Life goes on.
It's not just that. Peter, he...
He told Gwen a secret.

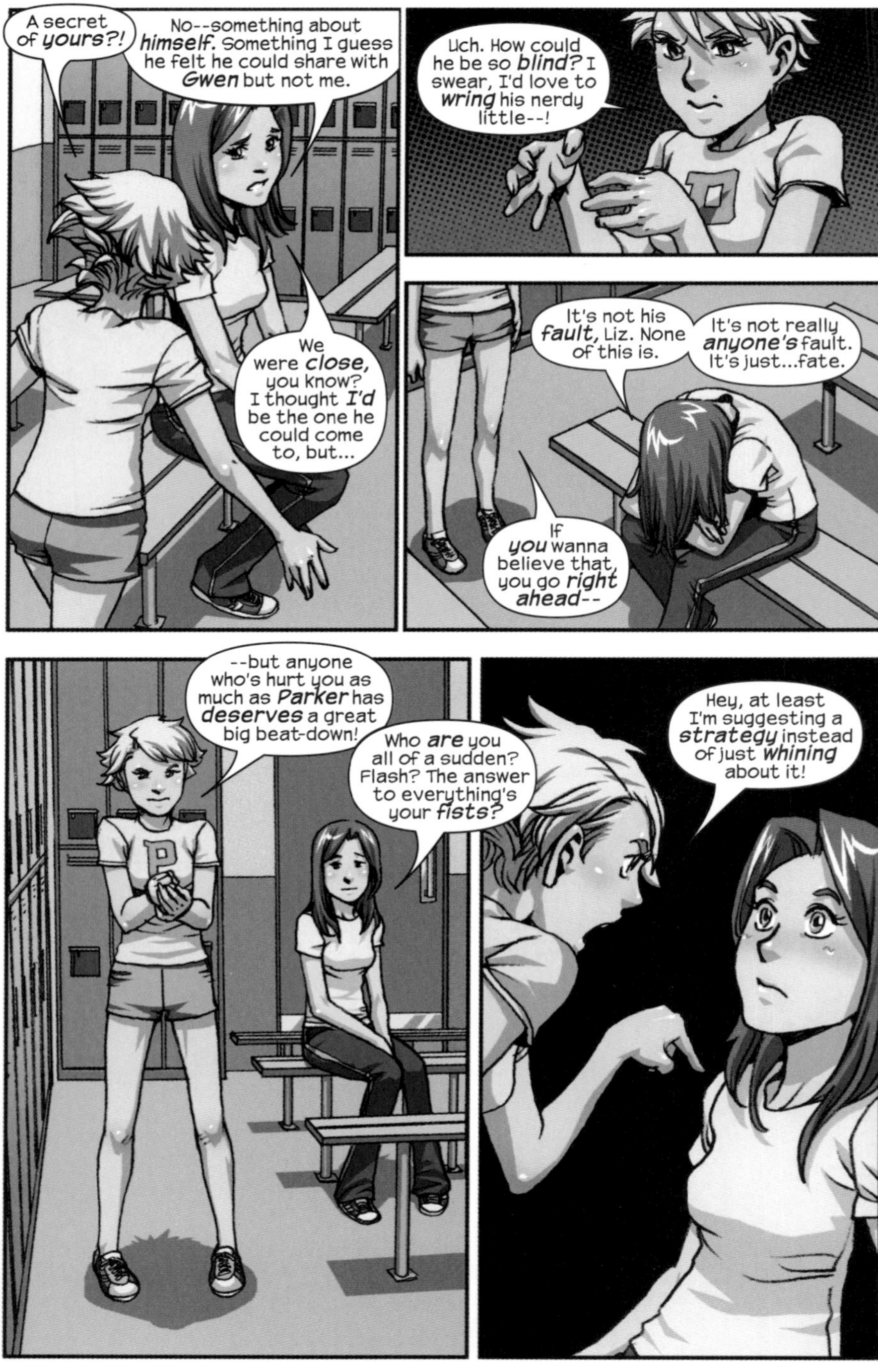
A secret of yours?!
No--something about himself. Something I guess he felt he could share with Gwen but not me.
We were close, you know? I thought I'd be the one he could come to, but...
Uch. How could he be so blind? I swear, I'd love to wring his nerdy little--!
It's not his fault, Liz. None of this is.
It's not really anyone's fault. It's just...fate.
If you wanna believe that, you go right ahead--
--but anyone who's hurt you as much as Parker has deserves a great big beat-down!
Who are you all of a sudden? Flash? The answer to everything's your fists?
Hey, at least I'm suggesting a strategy instead of just whining about it!

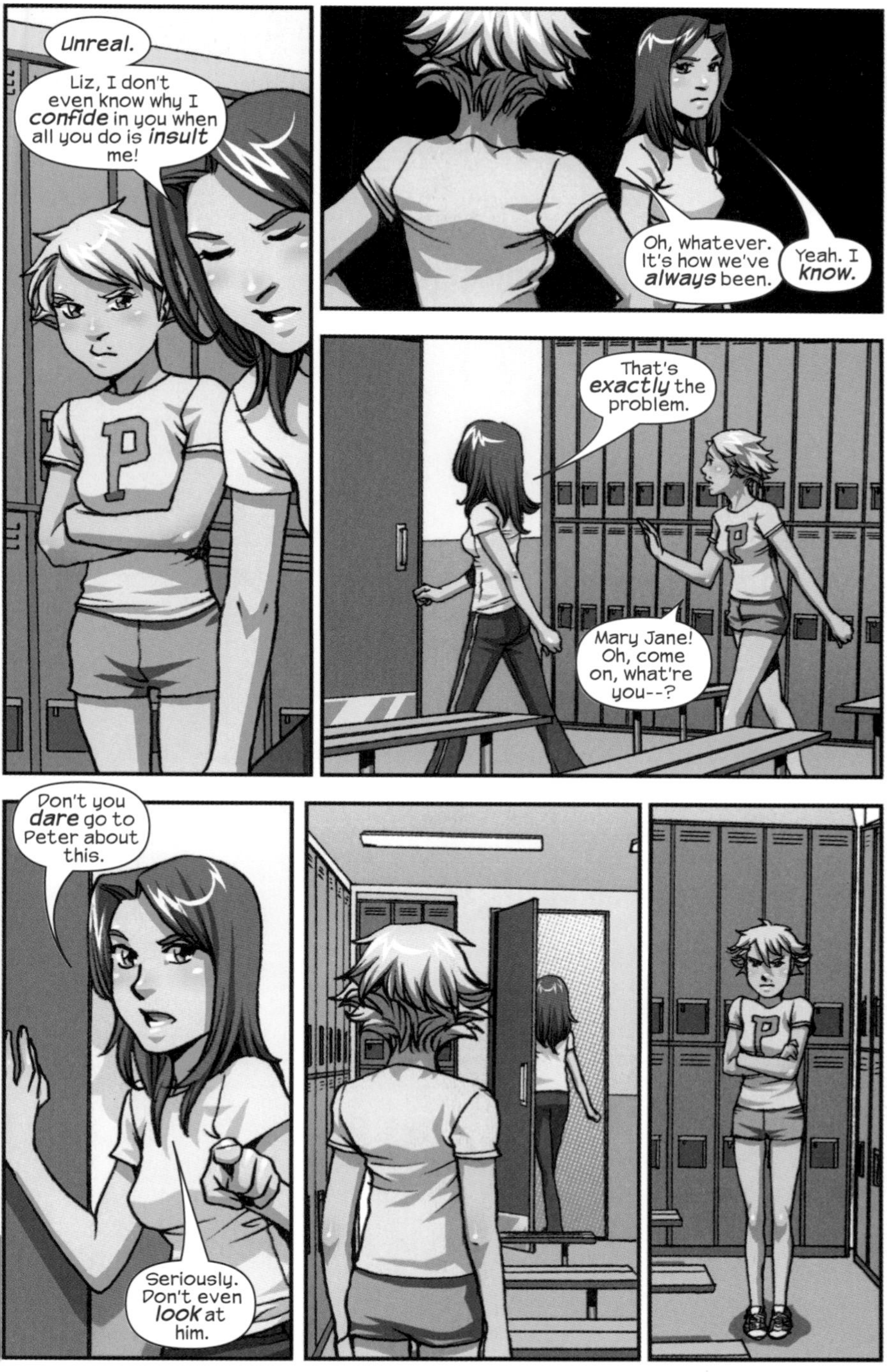
Unreal.
Liz, I don't even know why I *confide* in you when all you do is *insult* me!
Oh, whatever. It's how we've *always* been.
Yeah. I *know.*
That's *exactly* the problem.
Mary Jane! Oh, come on, what're you--?
Don't you *dare* go to Peter about this.
Seriously. Don't even *look* at him.

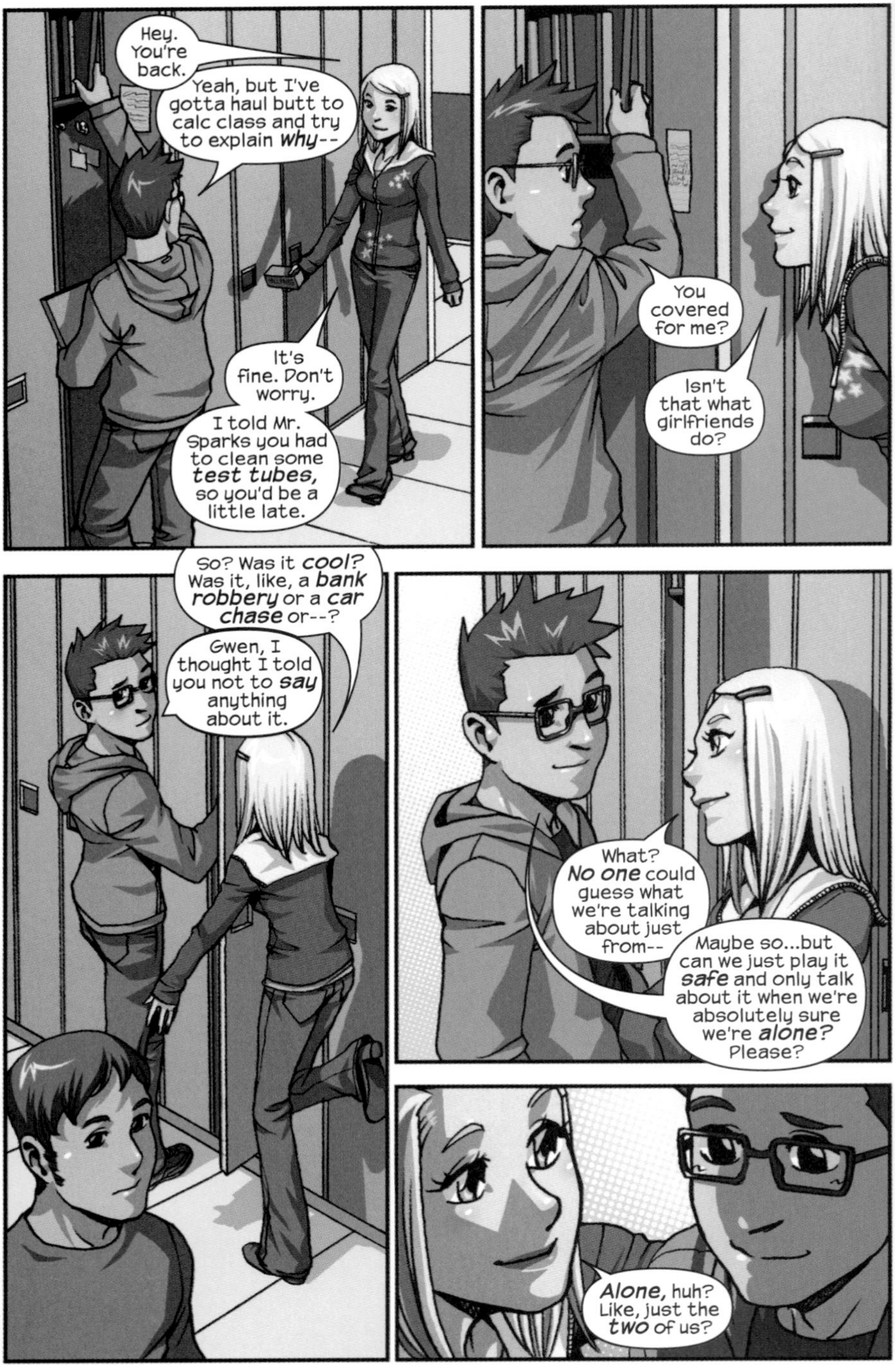
Hey. You're back.
Yeah, but I've gotta haul butt to calc class and try to explain *why*--
It's fine. Don't worry.
I told Mr. Sparks you had to clean some *test tubes,* so you'd be a little late.
You covered for me?
Isn't that what girlfriends do?
So? Was it *cool?* Was it, like, a *bank robbery* or a *car chase* or--?
Gwen, I thought I told you not to *say* anything about it.
What? *No one* could guess what we're talking about just from--
Maybe so...but can we just play it *safe* and only talk about it when we're absolutely sure we're *alone?* Please?
Alone, huh? Like, just the *two* of us?

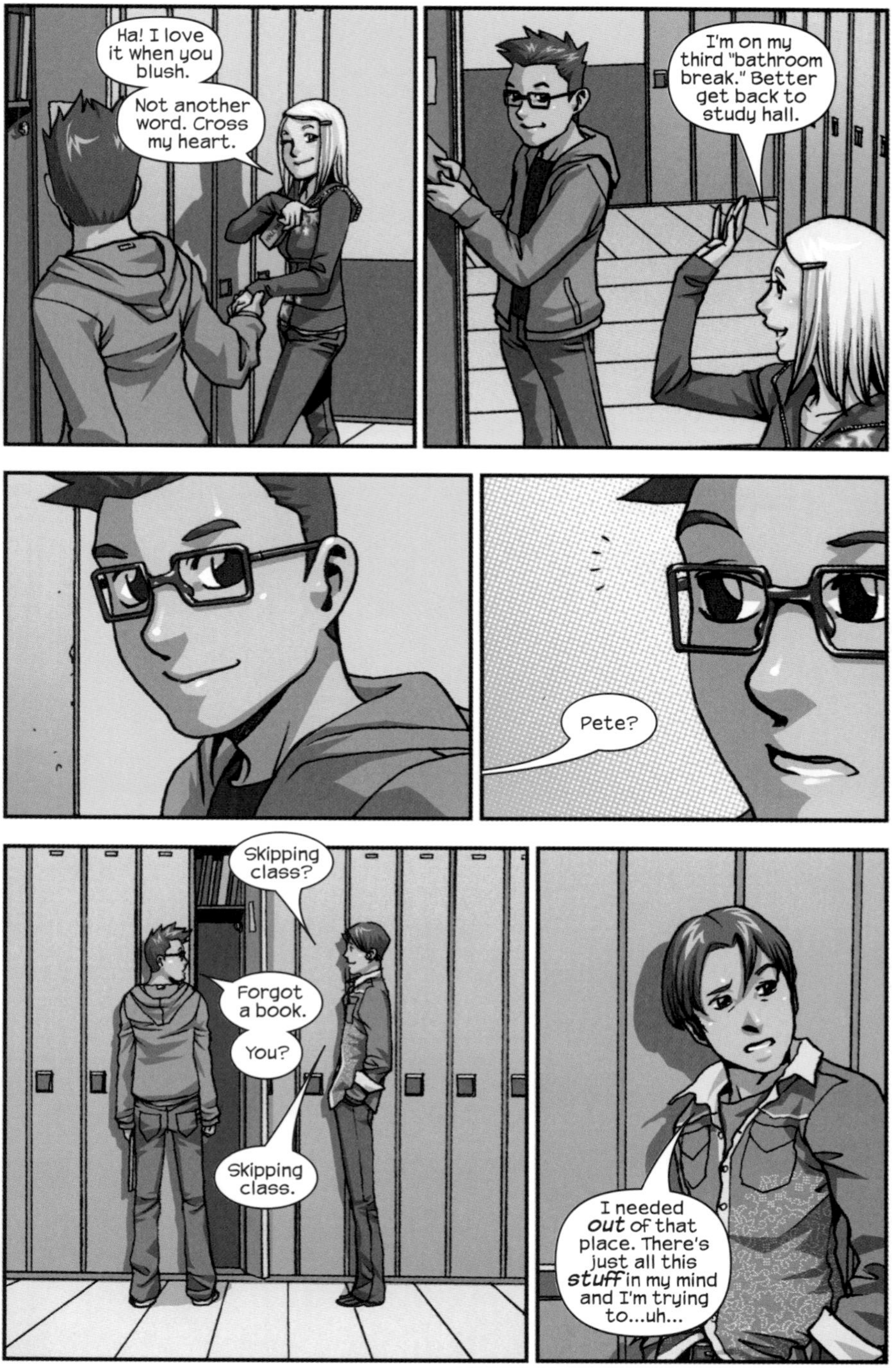
Ha! I love it when you blush.
Not another word. Cross my heart.
I'm on my third "bathroom break." Better get back to study hall.
Pete?
Skipping class?
Forgot a book.
You?
Skipping class.
I needed *out* of that place. There's just all this *stuff* in my mind and I'm trying to...uh...

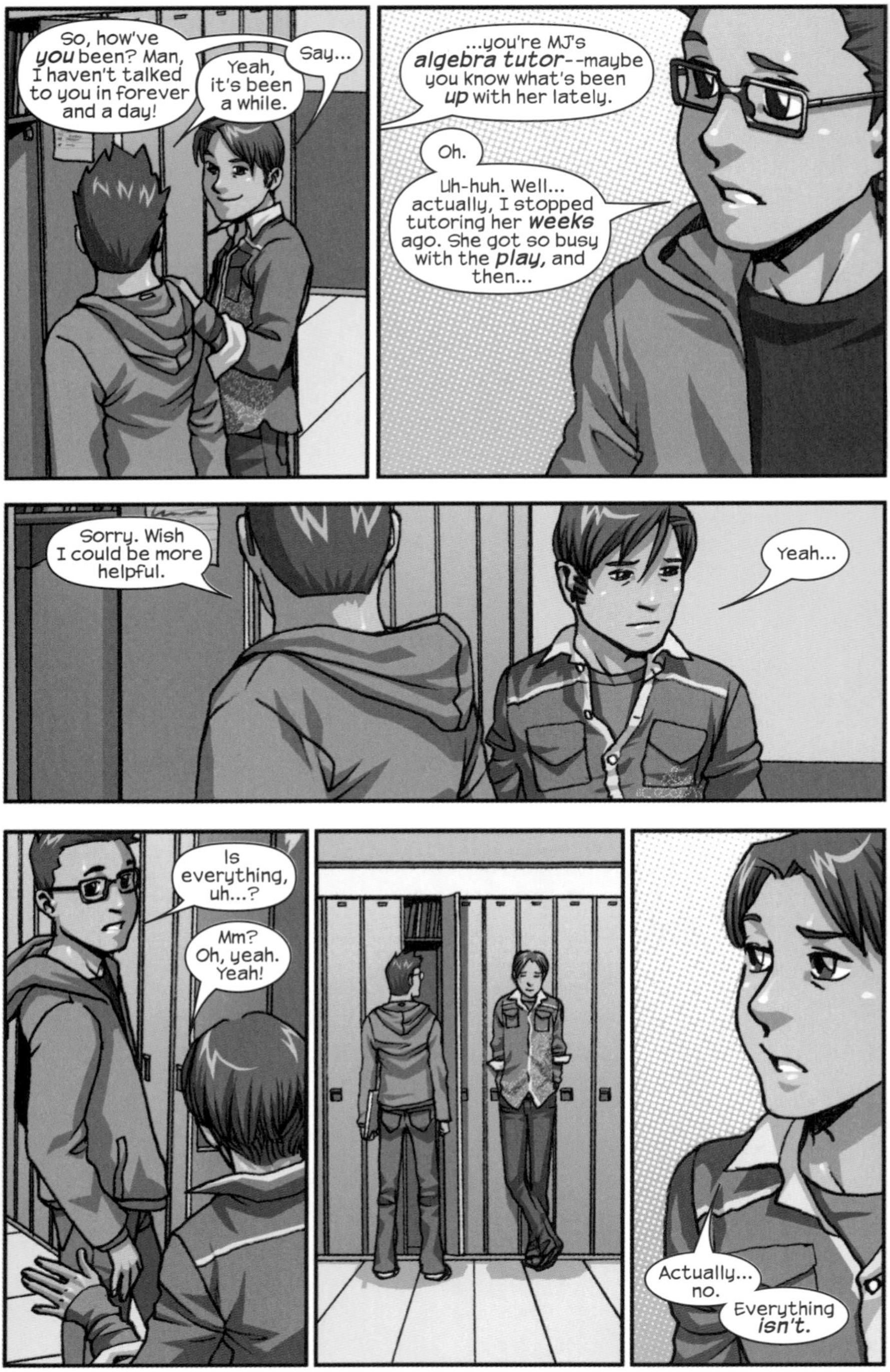
So, how've *you* been? Man, I haven't talked to you in forever and a day!
Yeah, it's been a while.
Say...
...you're MJ's *algebra tutor*--maybe you know what's been *up* with her lately.
Oh.
Uh-huh. Well... actually, I stopped tutoring her *weeks* ago. She got so busy with the *play,* and then...
Sorry. Wish I could be more helpful.
Yeah...
Is everything, uh...?
Mm? Oh, yeah. Yeah!
Actually... no.
Everything *isn't.*

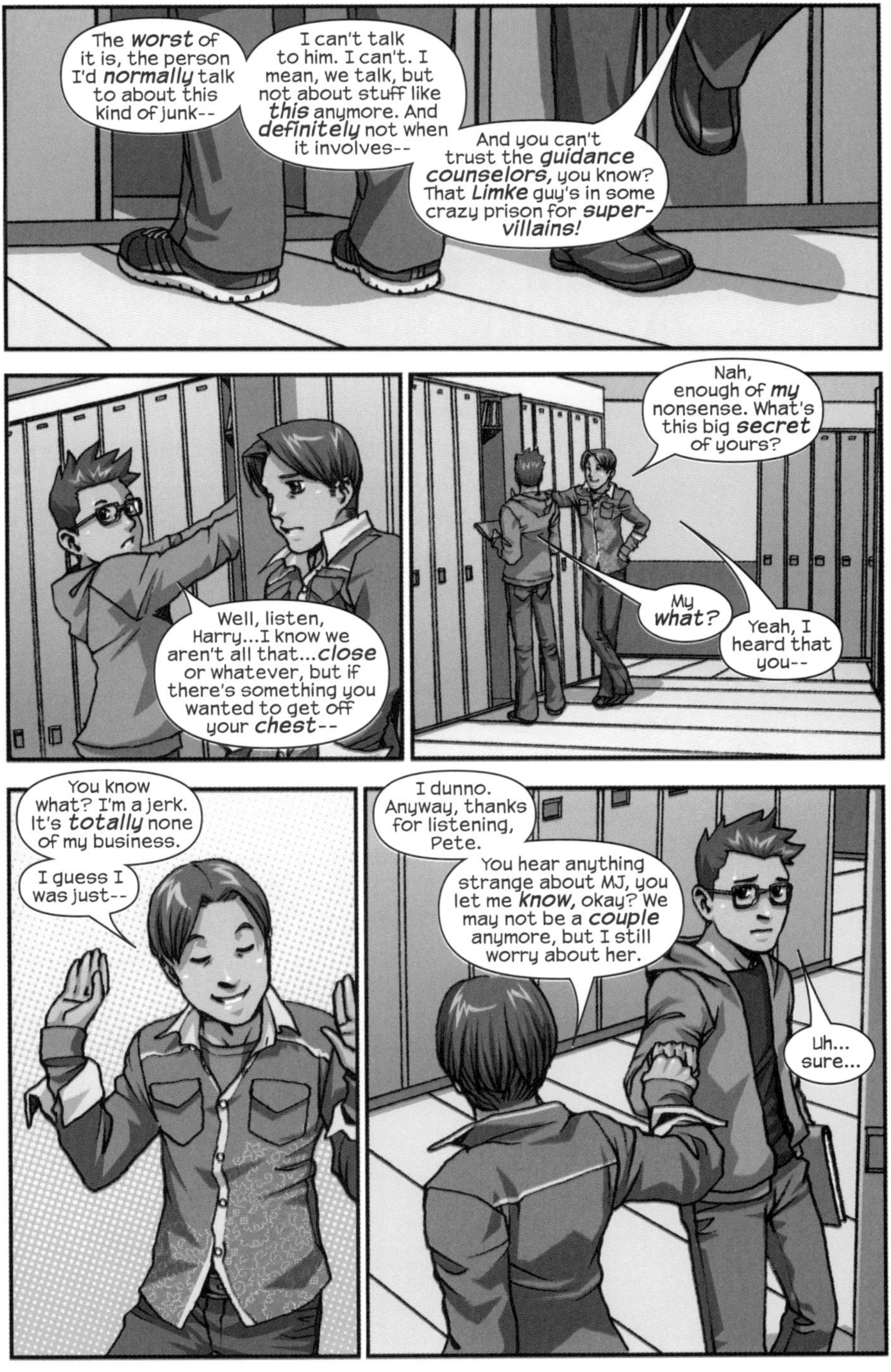
The worst of it is, the person I'd normally talk to about this kind of junk--
I can't talk to him. I can't. I mean, we talk, but not about stuff like this anymore. And definitely not when it involves--
And you can't trust the guidance counselors, you know? That Limke guy's in some crazy prison for super-villains!
Well, listen, Harry...I know we aren't all that...close or whatever, but if there's something you wanted to get off your chest--
Nah, enough of my nonsense. What's this big secret of yours?
My what?
Yeah, I heard that you--
You know what? I'm a jerk. It's totally none of my business.
I guess I was just--
I dunno. Anyway, thanks for listening, Pete.
You hear anything strange about MJ, you let me know, okay? We may not be a couple anymore, but I still worry about her.
Uh... sure...

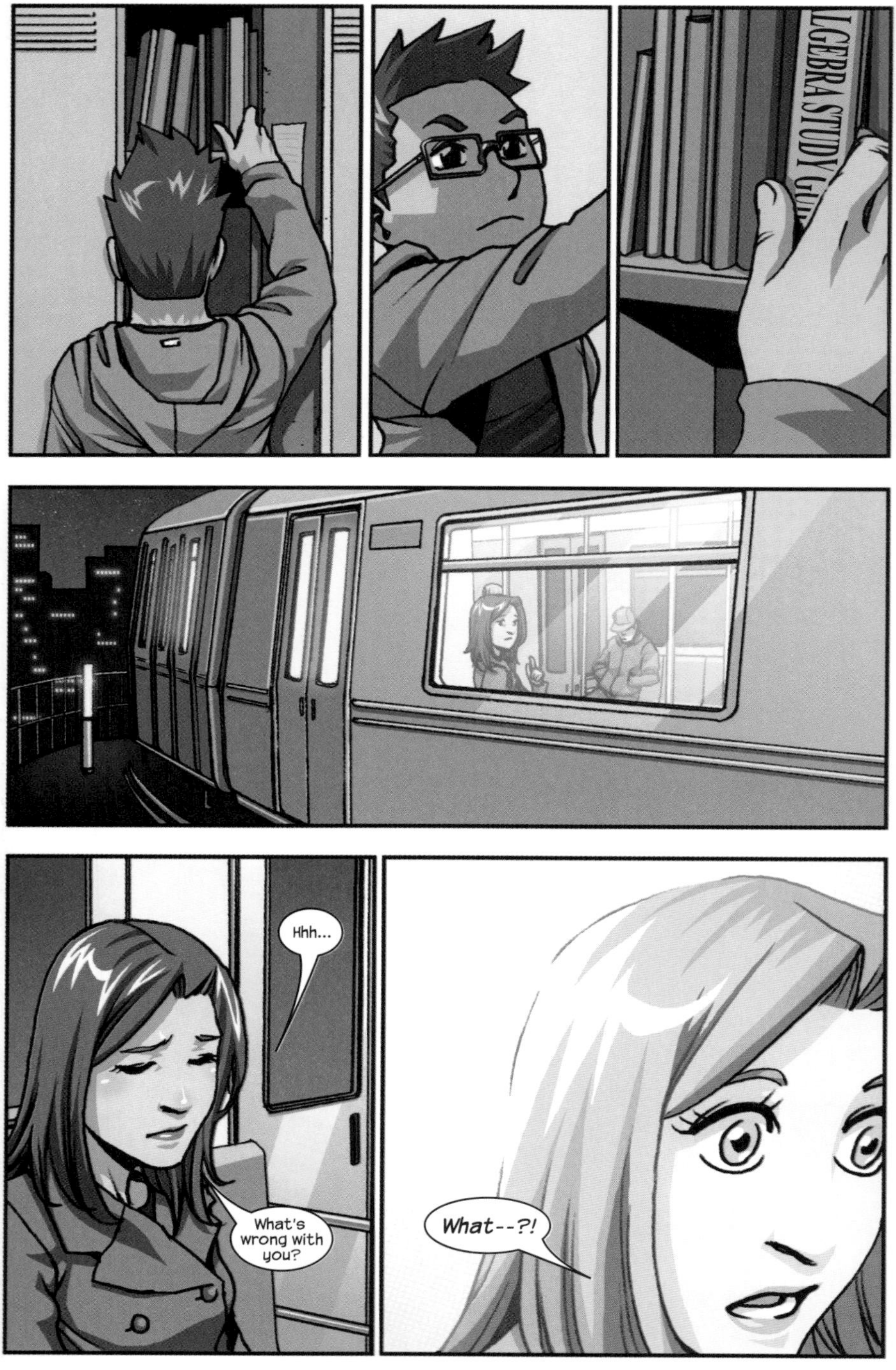
LGEBRA STUDY GUI
Hhh...
What's wrong with you?
What--?!

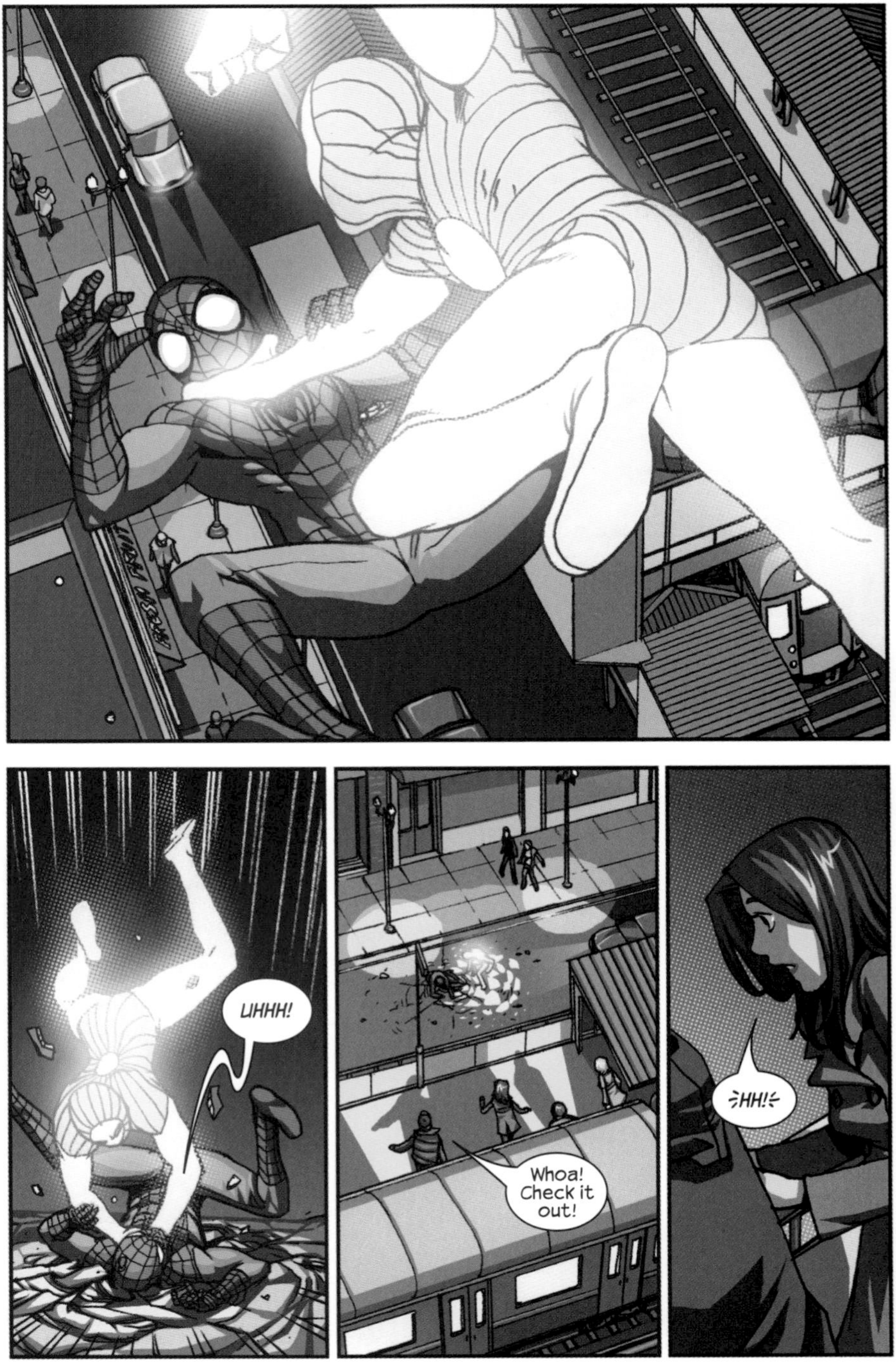
UHHH!
Whoa! Check it out!
HH!

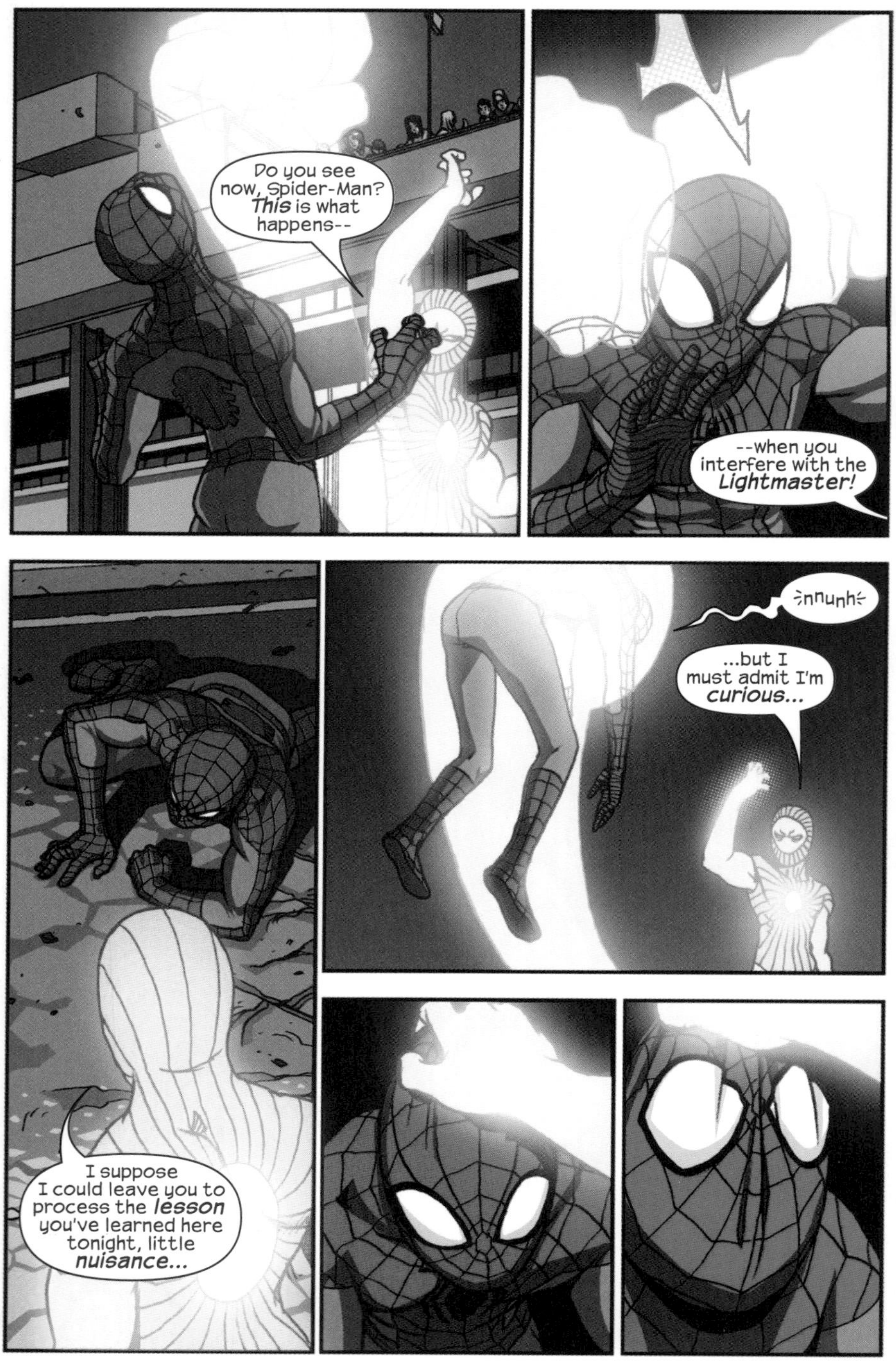
Do you see now, Spider-Man? *This* is what happens--
--when you interfere with the *Lightmaster!*
nnunh
...but I must admit I'm *curious...*
I suppose I could leave you to process the *lesson* you've learned here tonight, little *nuisance...*

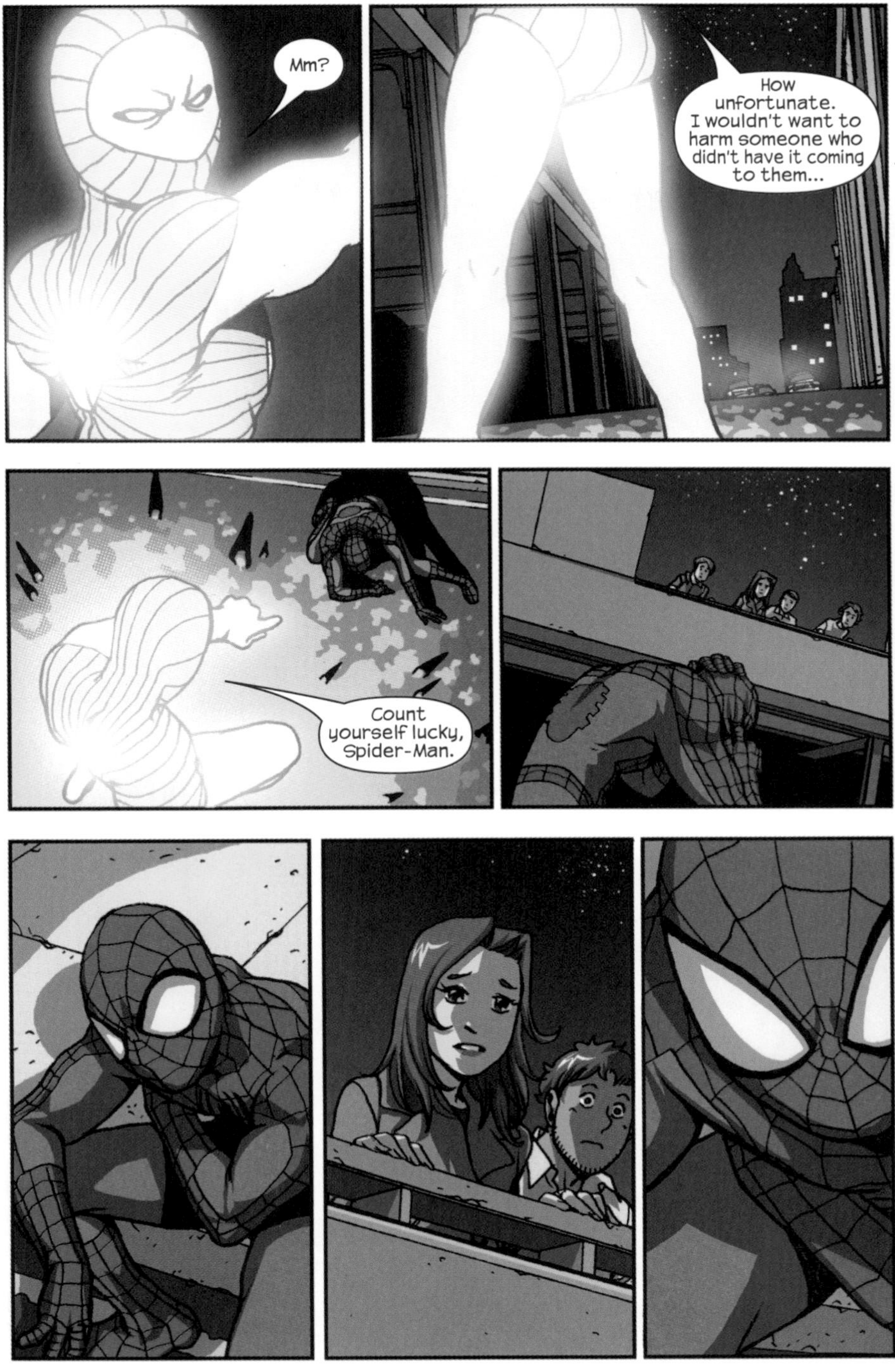
Mm?
How unfortunate. I wouldn't want to harm someone who didn't have it coming to them...
Count yourself lucky, Spider-Man.

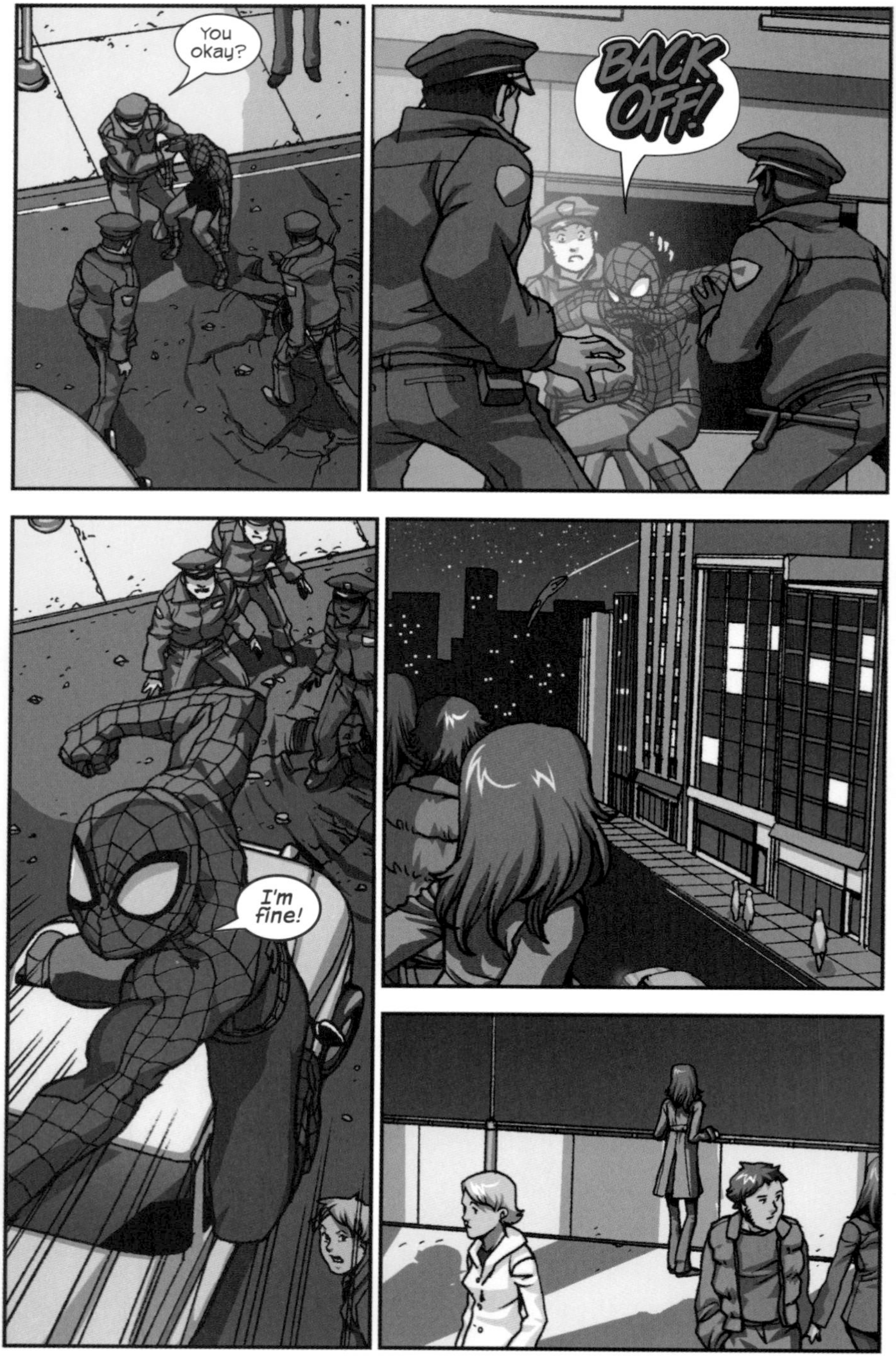
You okay?
BACK OFF!
I'm fine!

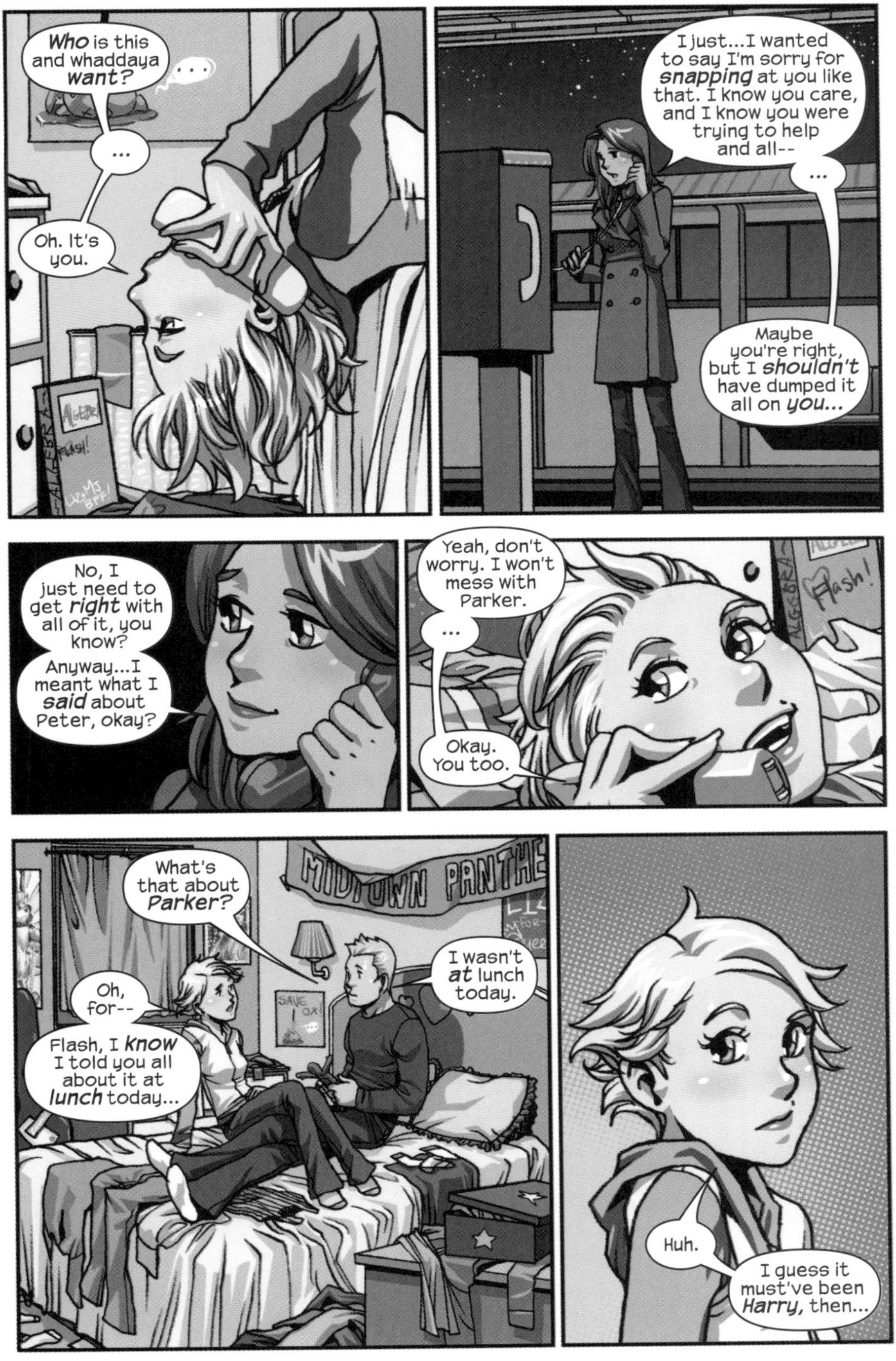
Who is this and whaddaya want?
...
...
Oh. It's you.
ALGEBRA
FLASH!
I just...I wanted to say I'm sorry for snapping at you like that. I know you care, and I know you were trying to help and all--
...
Maybe you're right, but I shouldn't have dumped it all on you...
No, I just need to get right with all of it, you know?
Anyway...I meant what I said about Peter, okay?
Yeah, don't worry. I won't mess with Parker.
...
Okay. You too.
MIDTOWN PANTHE
What's that about Parker?
I wasn't at lunch today.
Oh, for--
Flash, I know I told you all about it at lunch today...
Huh.
I guess it must've been Harry, then...

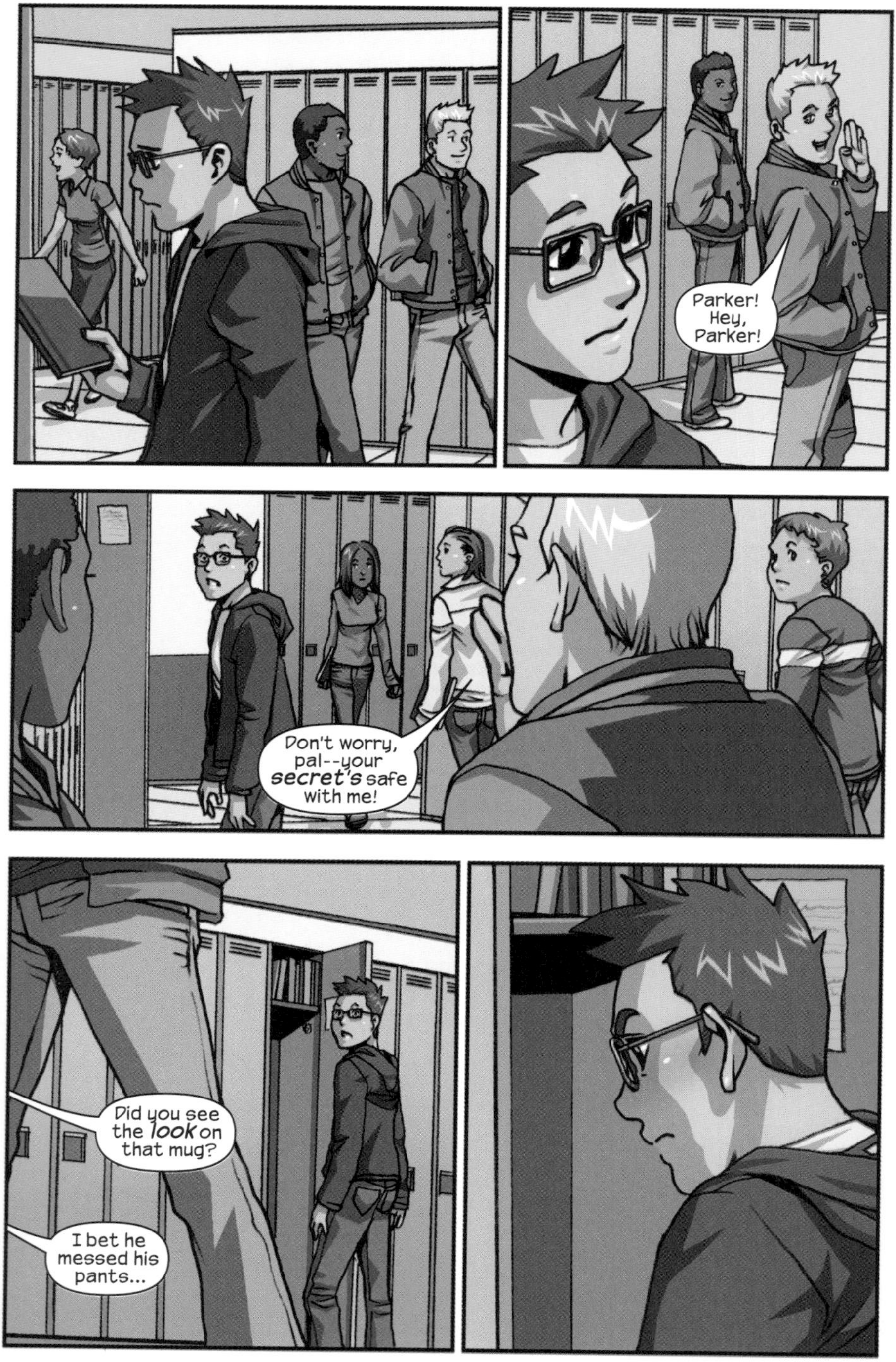
Parker! Hey, Parker!
Don't worry, pal--your *secret's* safe with me!
Did you see the *look* on that mug?
I bet he messed his pants...

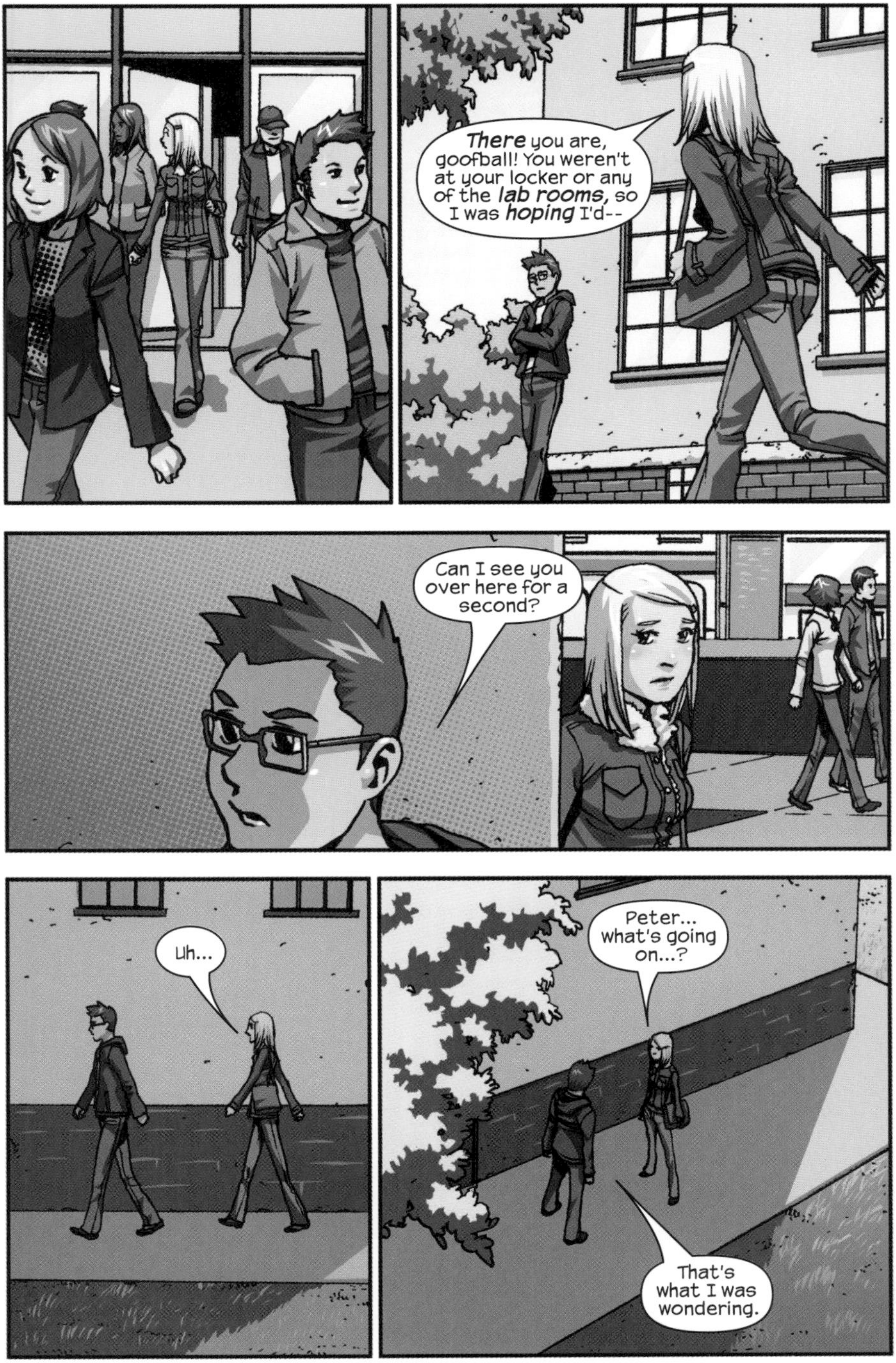
There you are, goofball! You weren't at your locker or any of the *lab rooms,* so I was *hoping* I'd--
Can I see you over here for a second?
Uh...
Peter... what's going on...?
That's what I was wondering.

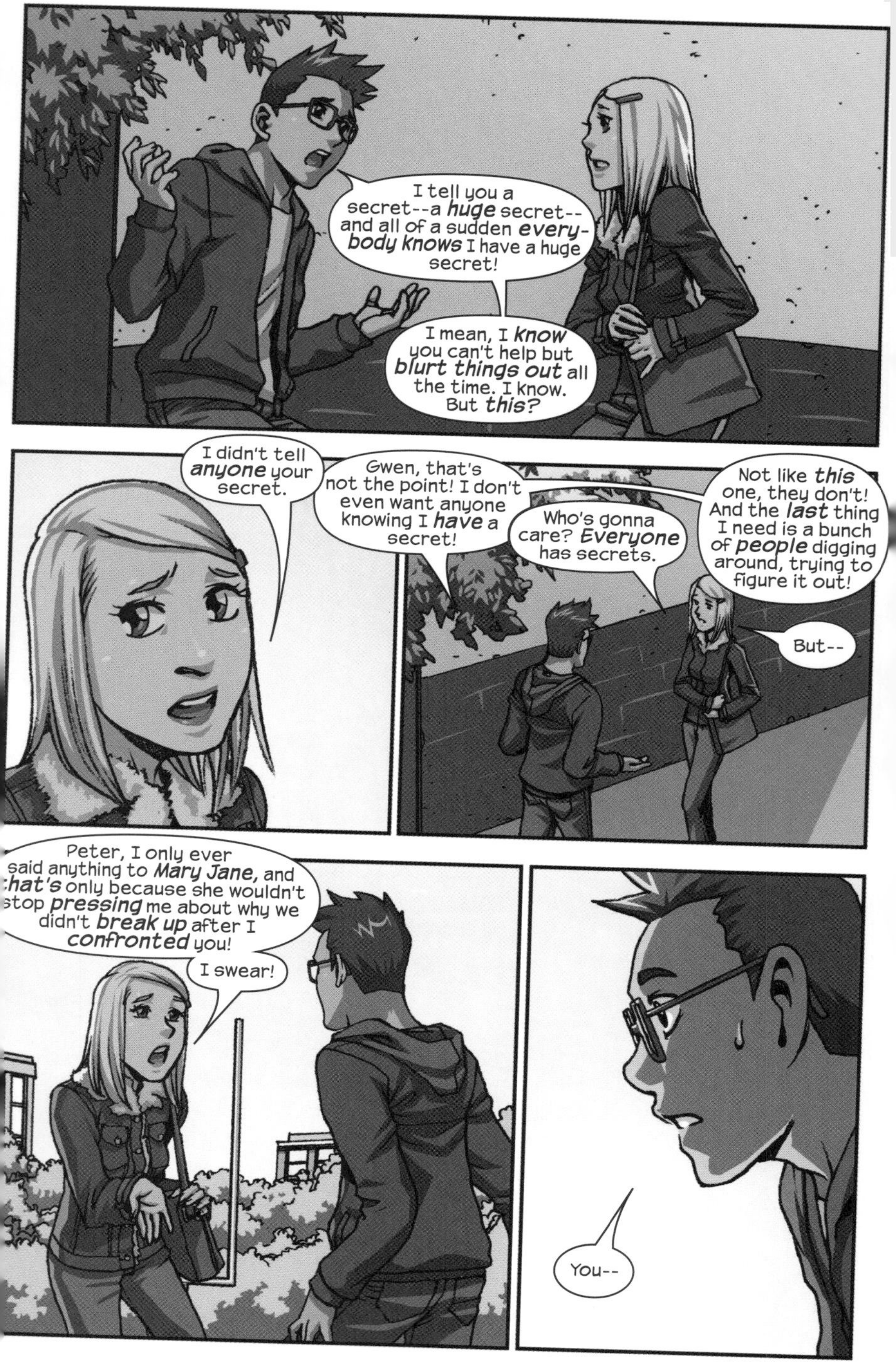
I tell you a secret--a huge secret--and all of a sudden everybody knows I have a huge secret!
I mean, I know you can't help but blurt things out all the time. I know. But this?
I didn't tell anyone your secret.
Gwen, that's not the point! I don't even want anyone knowing I have a secret!
Who's gonna care? Everyone has secrets.
Not like this one, they don't! And the last thing I need is a bunch of people digging around, trying to figure it out!
But--
Peter, I only ever said anything to Mary Jane, and that's only because she wouldn't stop pressing me about why we didn't break up after I confronted you!
I swear!
You--

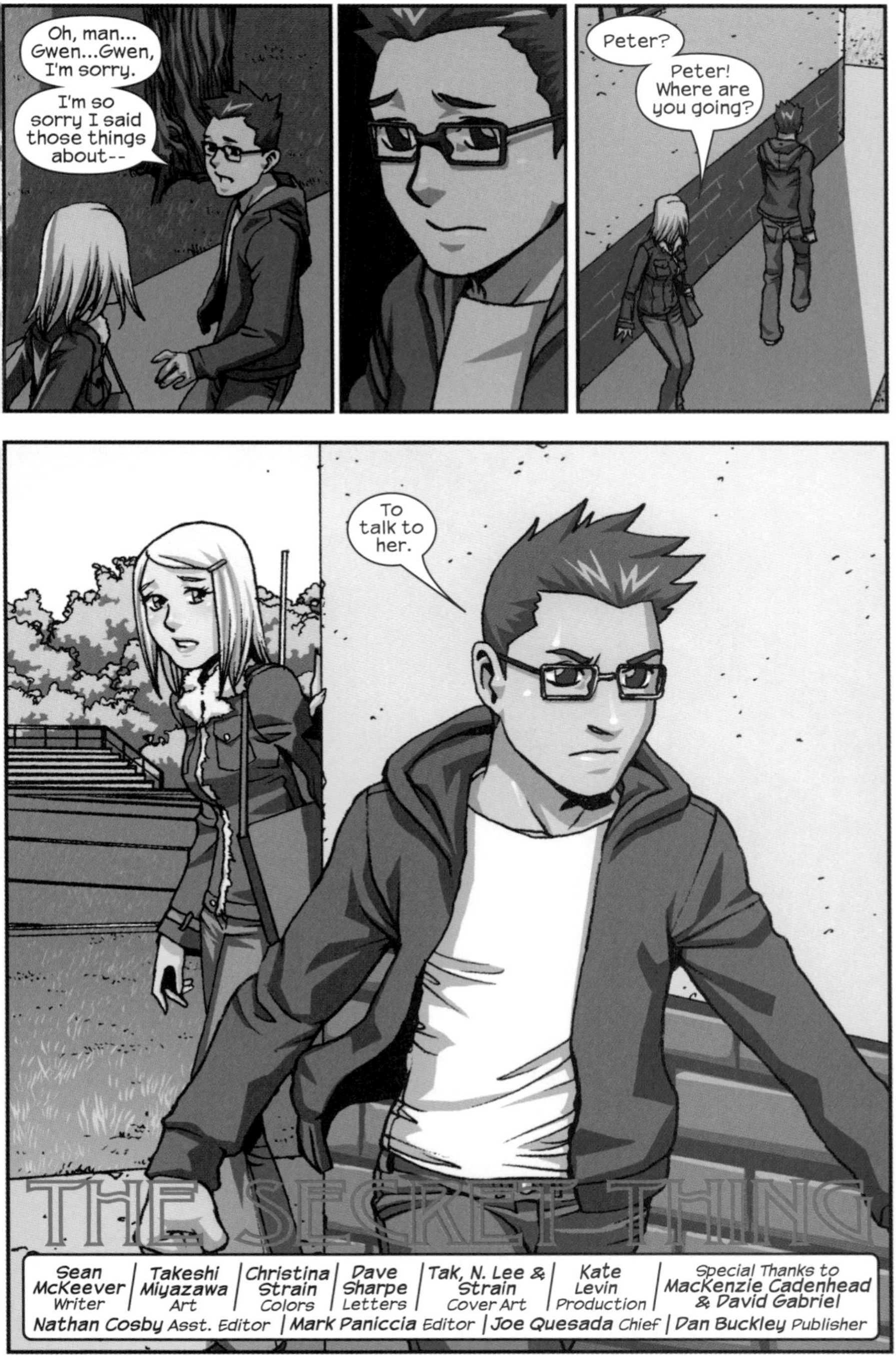

Oh, man... Gwen...Gwen, I'm sorry.
I'm so sorry I said those things about--
Peter?
Peter! Where are you going?
To talk to her.
THE SECRET THING
Sean McKeever Writer | Takeshi Miyazawa Art | Christina Strain Colors | Dave Sharpe Letters | Tak, N. Lee & Strain Cover Art | Kate Levin Production | Special Thanks to MacKenzie Cadenhead & David Gabriel
Nathan Cosby Asst. Editor | Mark Paniccia Editor | Joe Quesada Chief | Dan Buckley Publisher

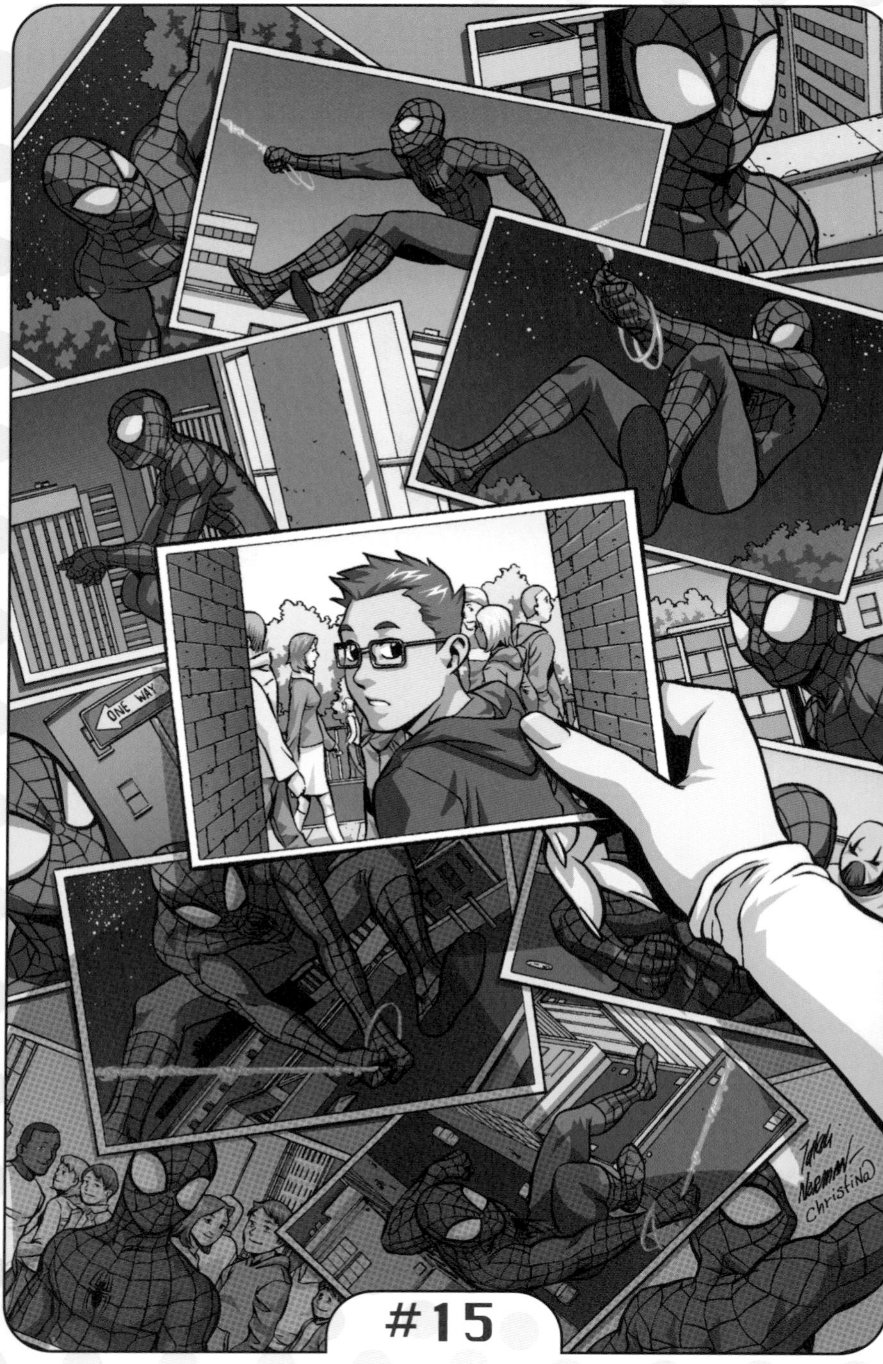
ONE WAY

#15

Queens, NY

I forgot the Bean was closed down, too--

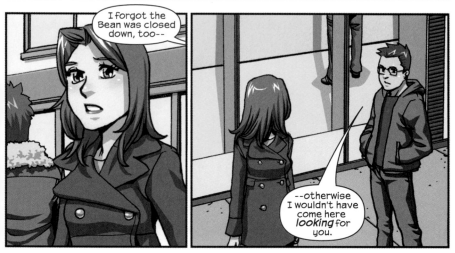

--otherwise I wouldn't have come here *looking* for you.

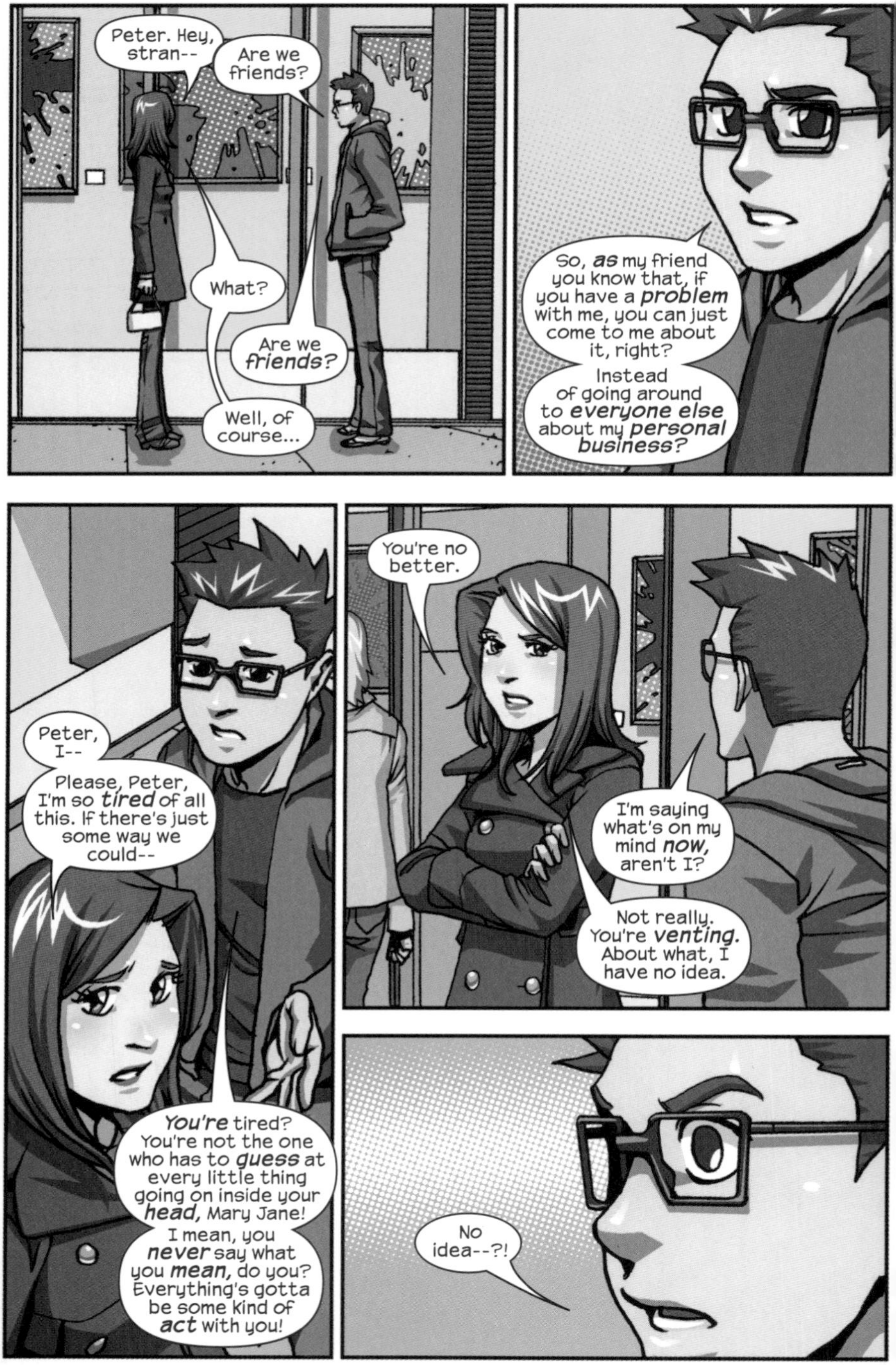
Peter. Hey, stran--
Are we friends?
What?
Are we *friends?*
Well, of course...
So, *as* my friend you know that, if you have a *problem* with me, you can just come to me about it, right?
Instead of going around to *everyone else* about my *personal business?*
Peter, I--
Please, Peter, I'm so *tired* of all this. If there's just some way we could--
You're tired? You're not the one who has to *guess* at every little thing going on inside your *head,* Mary Jane!
I mean, you *never* say what you *mean,* do you? Everything's gotta be some kind of *act* with you!
You're no better.
I'm saying what's on my mind *now,* aren't I?
Not really. You're *venting.* About what, I have no idea.
No idea--?!

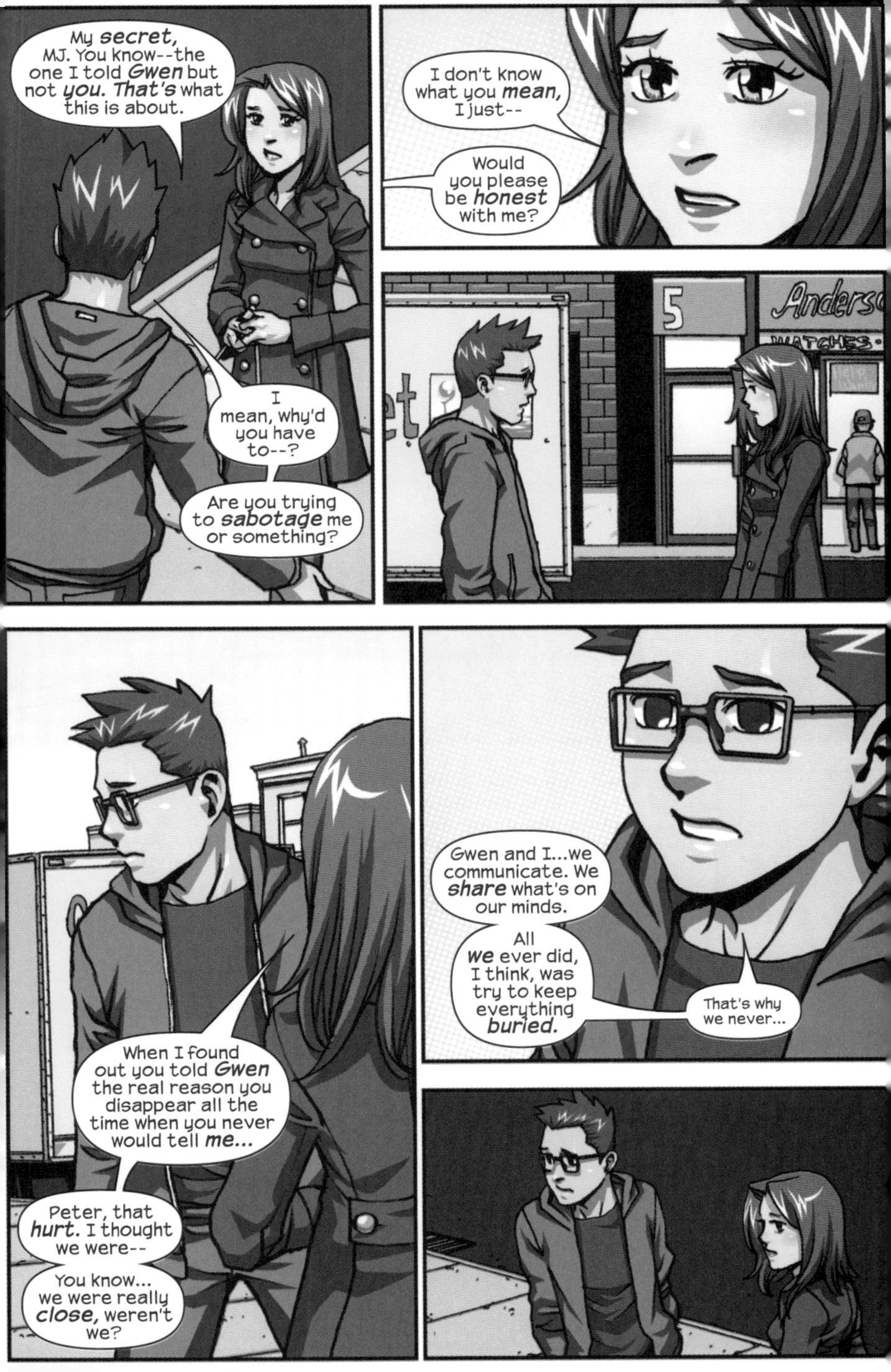
My secret, MJ. You know--the one I told Gwen but not you. That's what this is about.
I mean, why'd you have to--?
Are you trying to sabotage me or something?
I don't know what you mean, I just--
Would you please be honest with me?
5
Anderso
WATCHES
When I found out you told Gwen the real reason you disappear all the time when you never would tell me...
Peter, that hurt. I thought we were--
You know... we were really close, weren't we?
Gwen and I...we communicate. We share what's on our minds.
All we ever did, I think, was try to keep everything buried.
That's why we never...

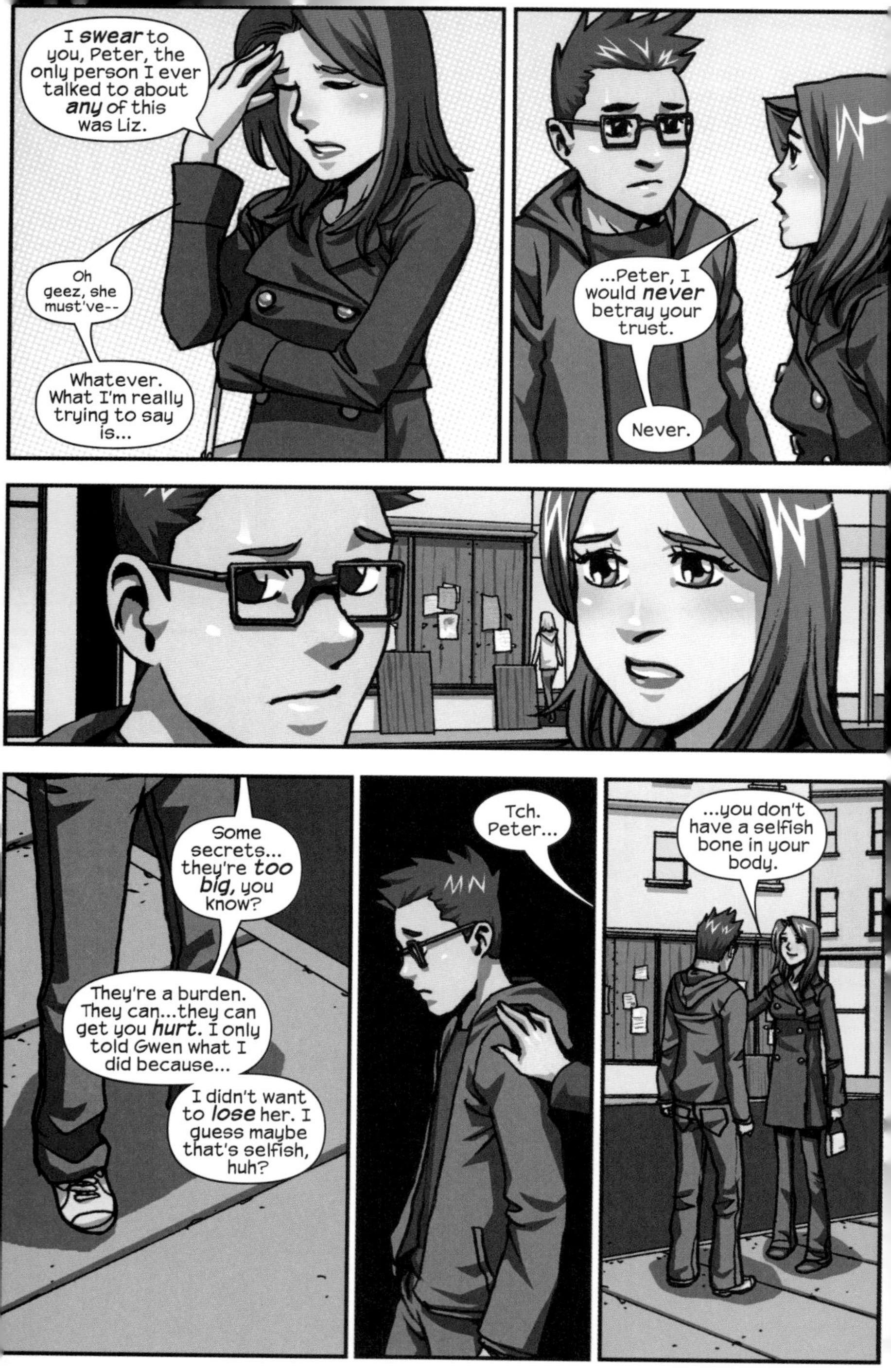
I *swear* to you, Peter, the only person I ever talked to about *any* of this was Liz.
Oh geez, she must've--
Whatever. What I'm really trying to say is...
...Peter, I would *never* betray your trust.
Never.
Some secrets... they're *too big,* you know?
They're a burden. They can...they can get you *hurt*. I only told Gwen what I did because...
I didn't want to *lose* her. I guess maybe that's selfish, huh?
Tch. Peter...
...you don't have a selfish bone in your body.

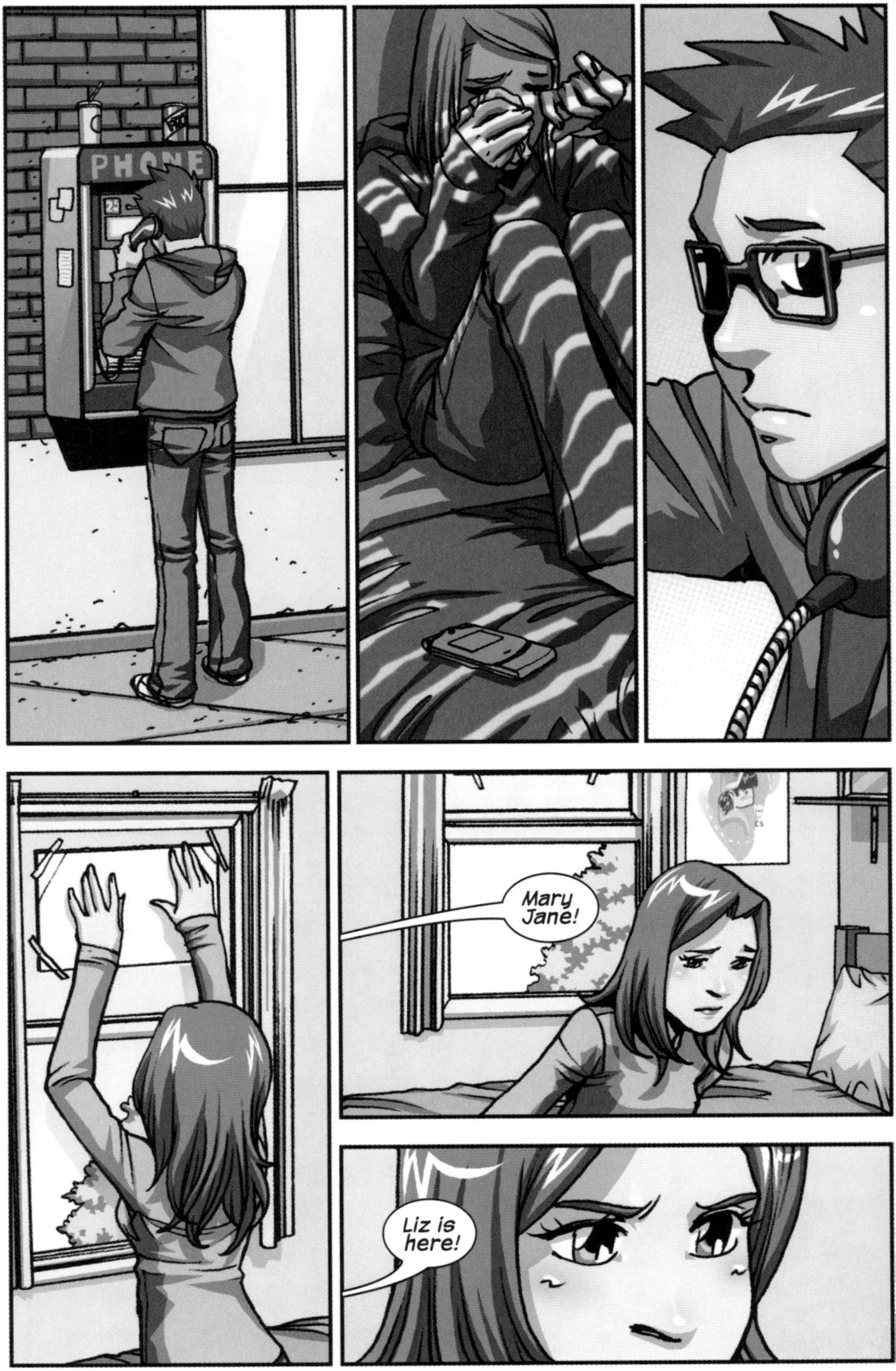
PHONE
Mary Jane!
Liz is here!

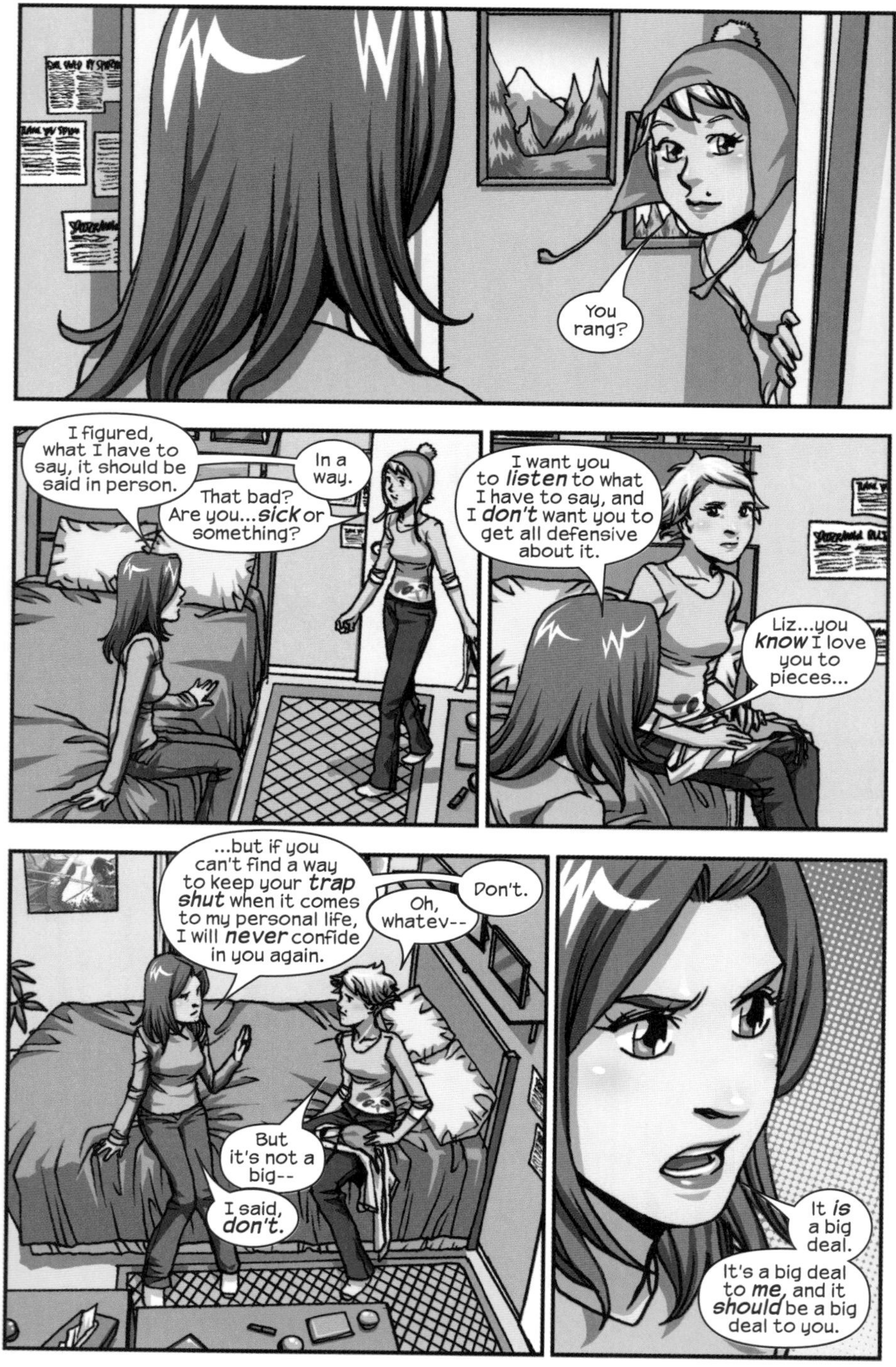
You rang?
I figured, what I have to say, it should be said in person.
That bad? Are you...*sick* or something?
In a way.
I want you to *listen* to what I have to say, and I *don't* want you to get all defensive about it.
Liz...you *know* I love you to pieces...
...but if you can't find a way to keep your *trap shut* when it comes to my personal life, I will *never* confide in you again.
Oh, whatev--
Don't.
But it's not a big--
I said, *don't.*
It *is* a big deal.
It's a big deal to *me*, and it *should* be a big deal to you.

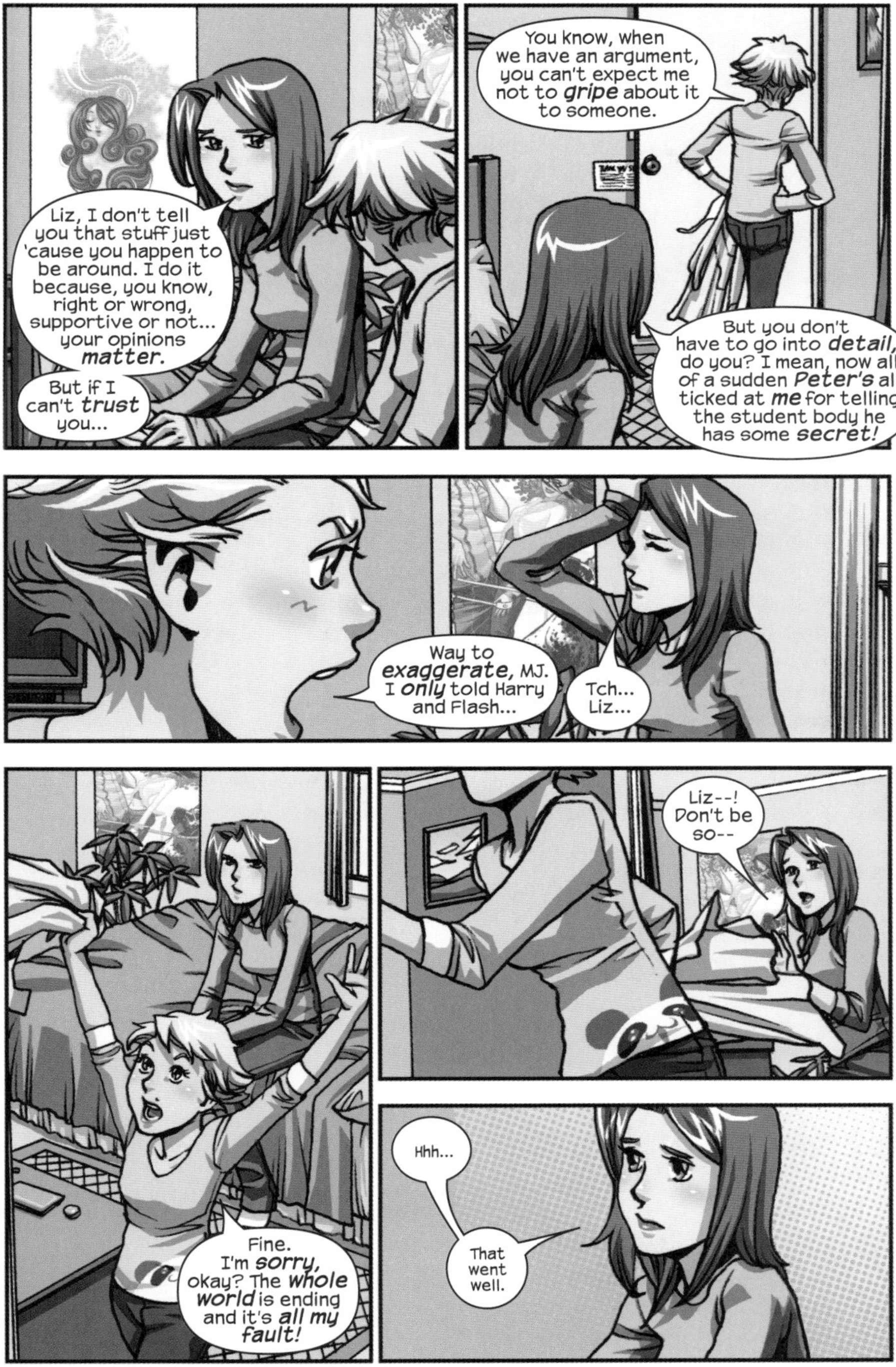
Liz, I don't tell you that stuff just 'cause you happen to be around. I do it because, you know, right or wrong, supportive or not... your opinions *matter*.
But if I can't *trust* you...
You know, when we have an argument, you can't expect me not to *gripe* about it to someone.
But you don't have to go into *detail*, do you? I mean, now all of a sudden *Peter's* all ticked at *me* for telling the student body he has some *secret!*
Way to *exaggerate*, MJ. I *only* told Harry and Flash...
Tch... Liz...
Fine. I'm *sorry*, okay? The *whole world* is ending and it's *all my fault!*
Liz--! Don't be so--
Hhh...
That went well.

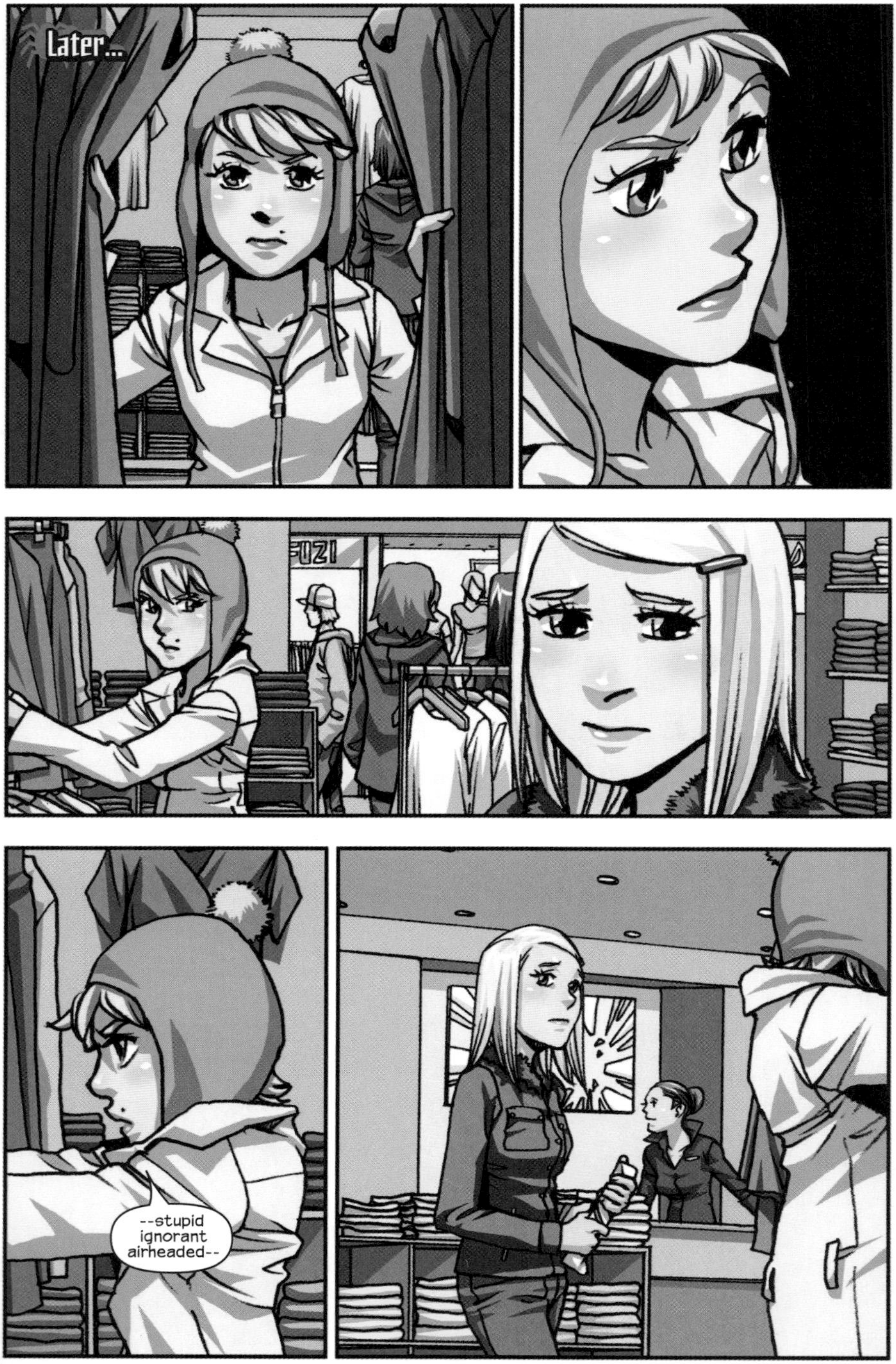
Later...
FUZI
--stupid
ignorant
airheaded--

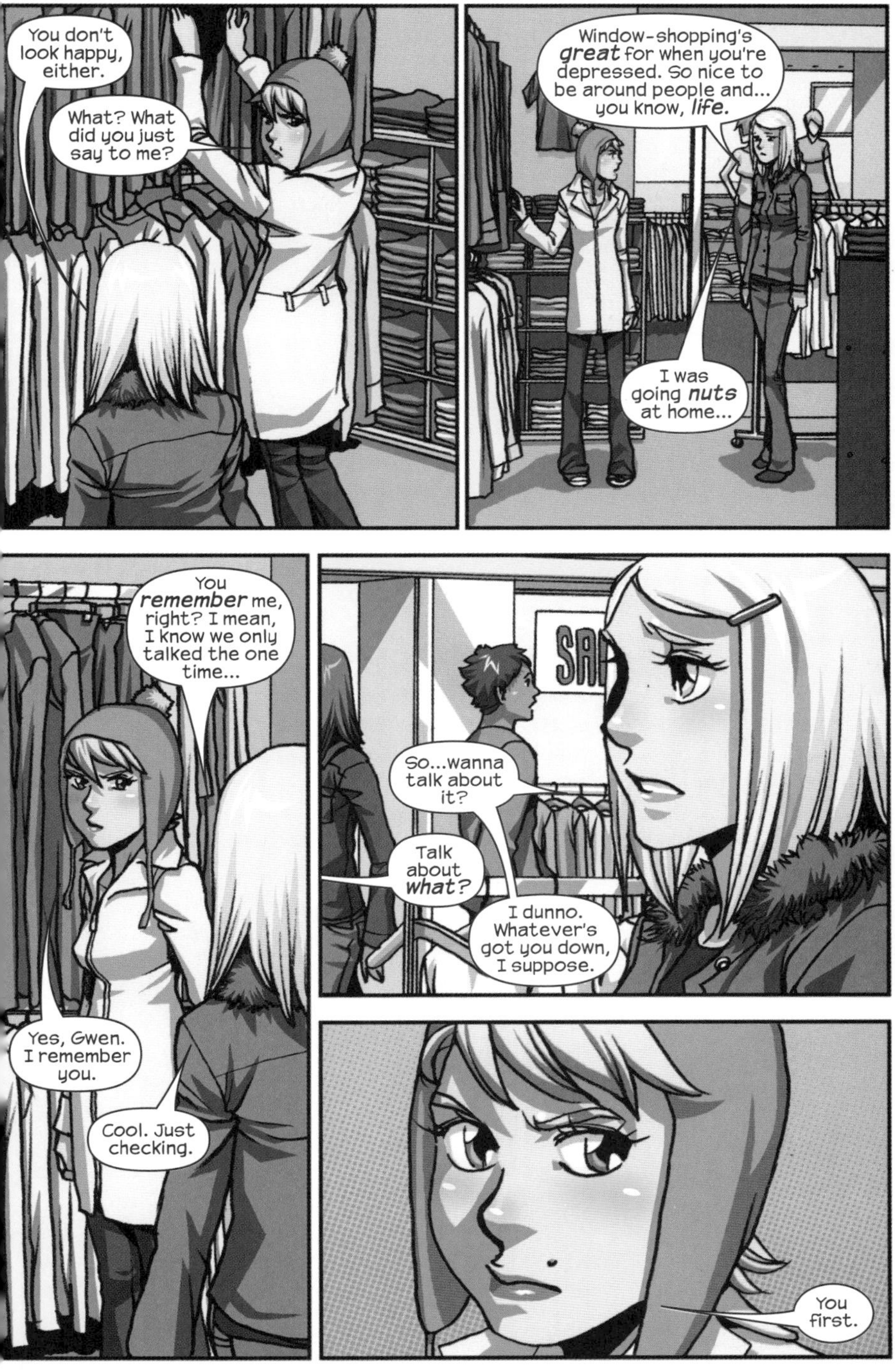
You don't look happy, either.
What? What did you just say to me?
Window-shopping's *great* for when you're depressed. So nice to be around people and... you know, *life.*
I was going *nuts* at home...
You *remember* me, right? I mean, I know we only talked the one time...
Yes, Gwen. I remember you.
Cool. Just checking.
SA
So...wanna talk about it?
Talk about *what?*
I dunno. Whatever's got you down, I suppose.
You first.

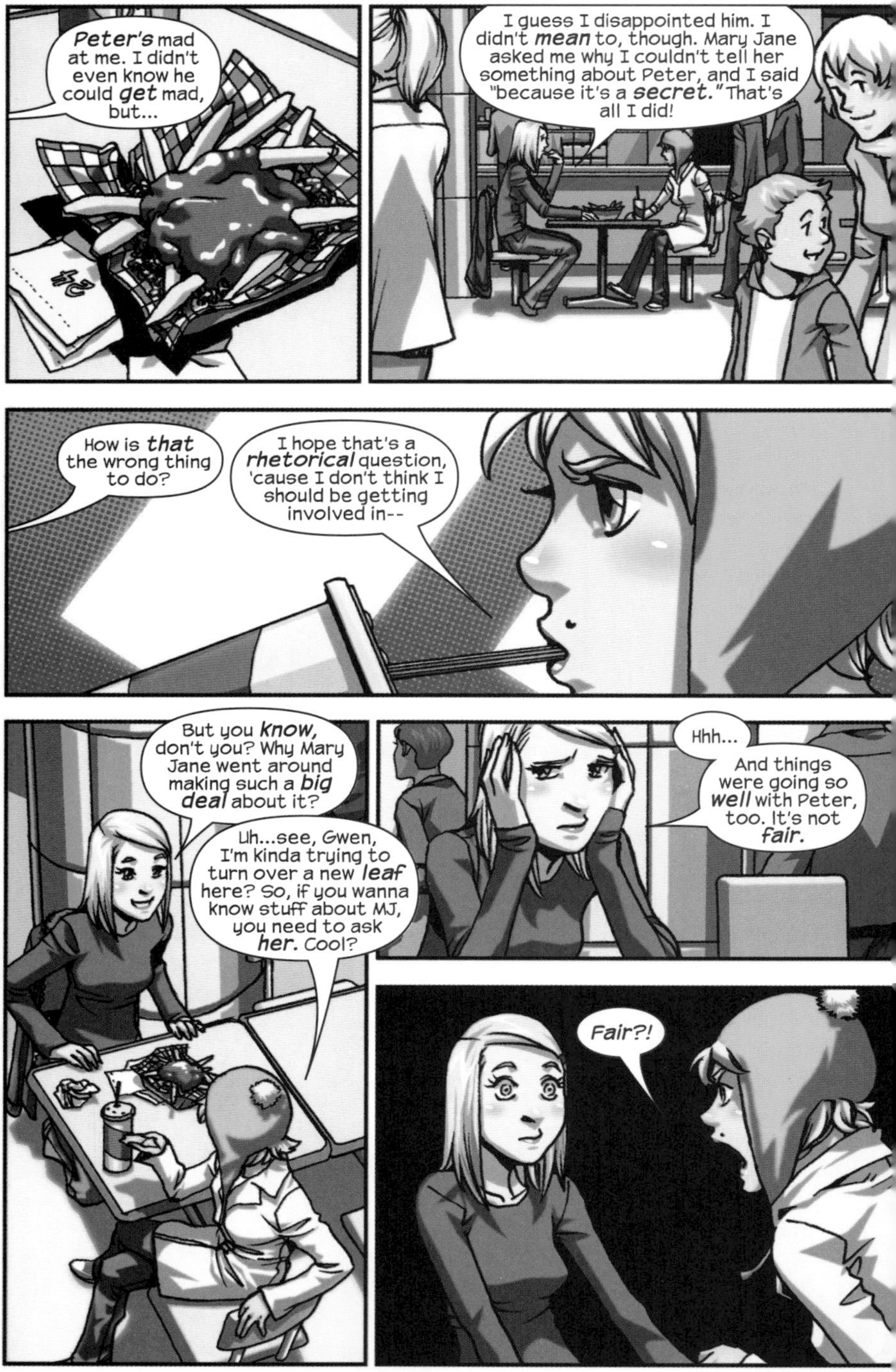
Peter's mad at me. I didn't even know he could get mad, but...
I guess I disappointed him. I didn't mean to, though. Mary Jane asked me why I couldn't tell her something about Peter, and I said "because it's a secret." That's all I did!
How is that the wrong thing to do?
I hope that's a rhetorical question, 'cause I don't think I should be getting involved in--
But you know, don't you? Why Mary Jane went around making such a big deal about it?
Uh...see, Gwen, I'm kinda trying to turn over a new leaf here? So, if you wanna know stuff about MJ, you need to ask her. Cool?
Hhh...
And things were going so well with Peter, too. It's not fair.
Fair?!

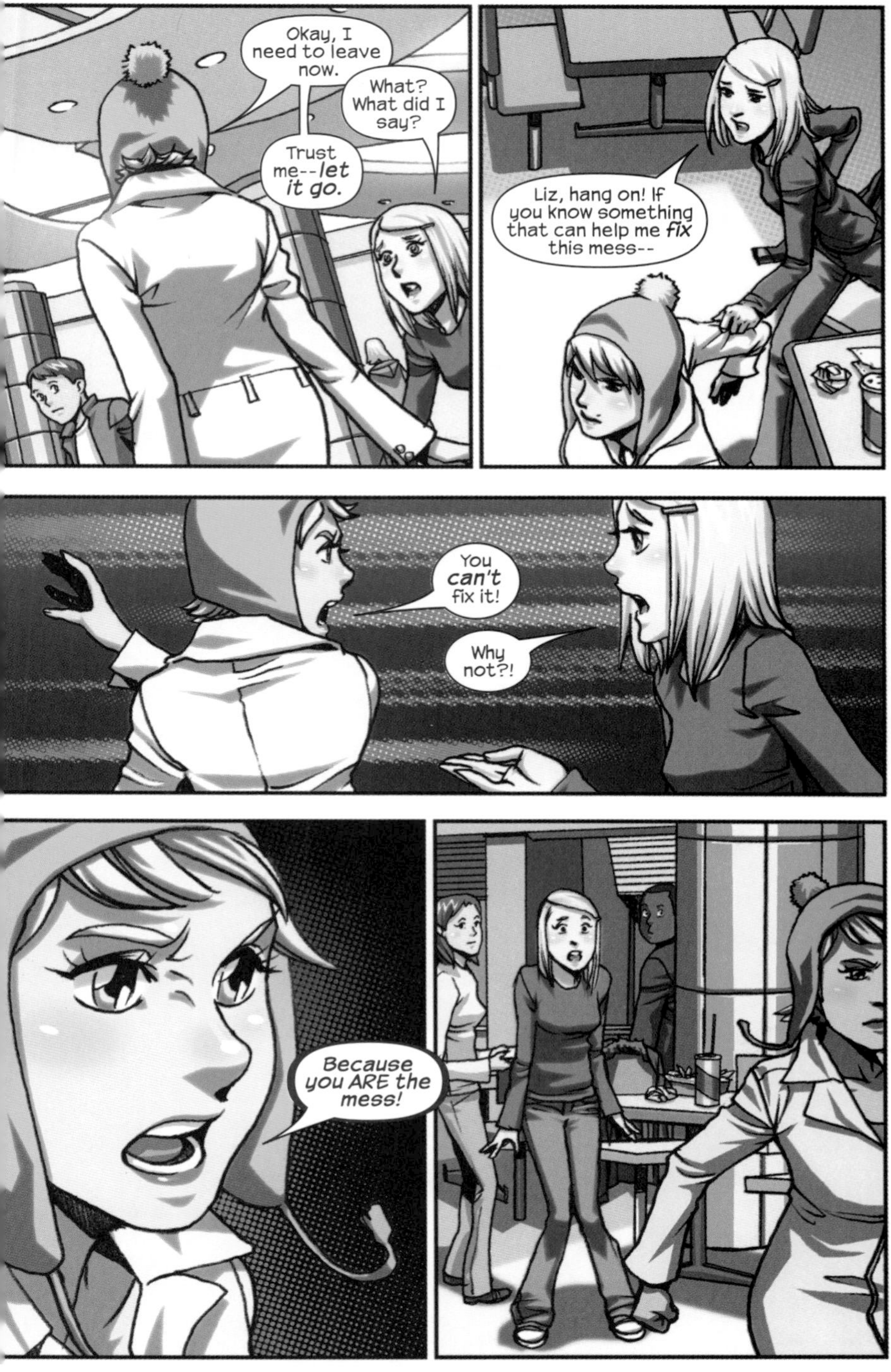
Okay, I need to leave now.
What? What did I say?
Trust me--*let it go.*
Liz, hang on! If you know something that can help me *fix* this mess--
You *can't* fix it!
Why not?!
Because you ARE the mess!

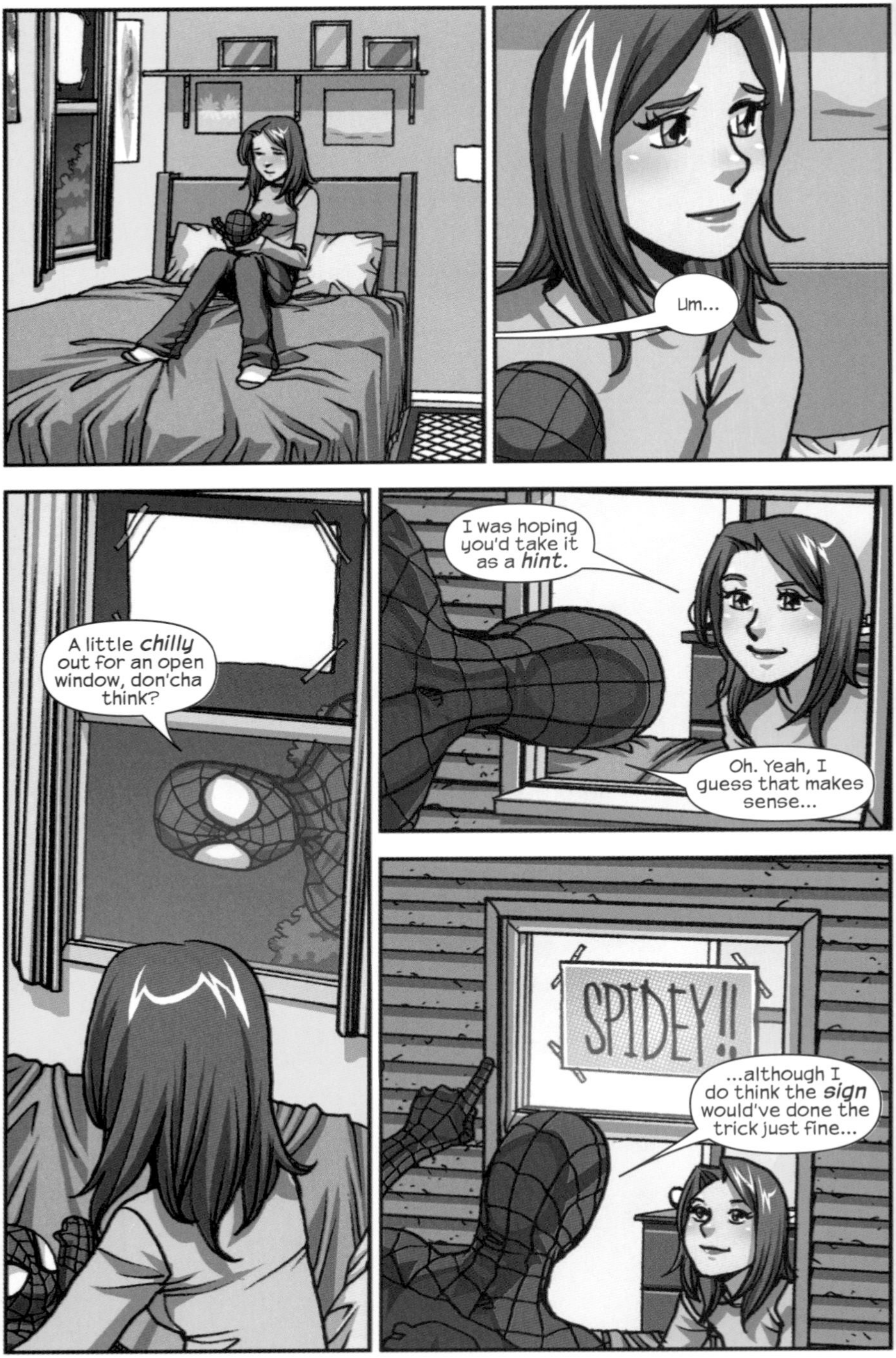
Um...
A little chilly out for an open window, don'cha think?
I was hoping you'd take it as a hint.
Oh. Yeah, I guess that makes sense...
SPIDEY!!
...although I do think the sign would've done the trick just fine...

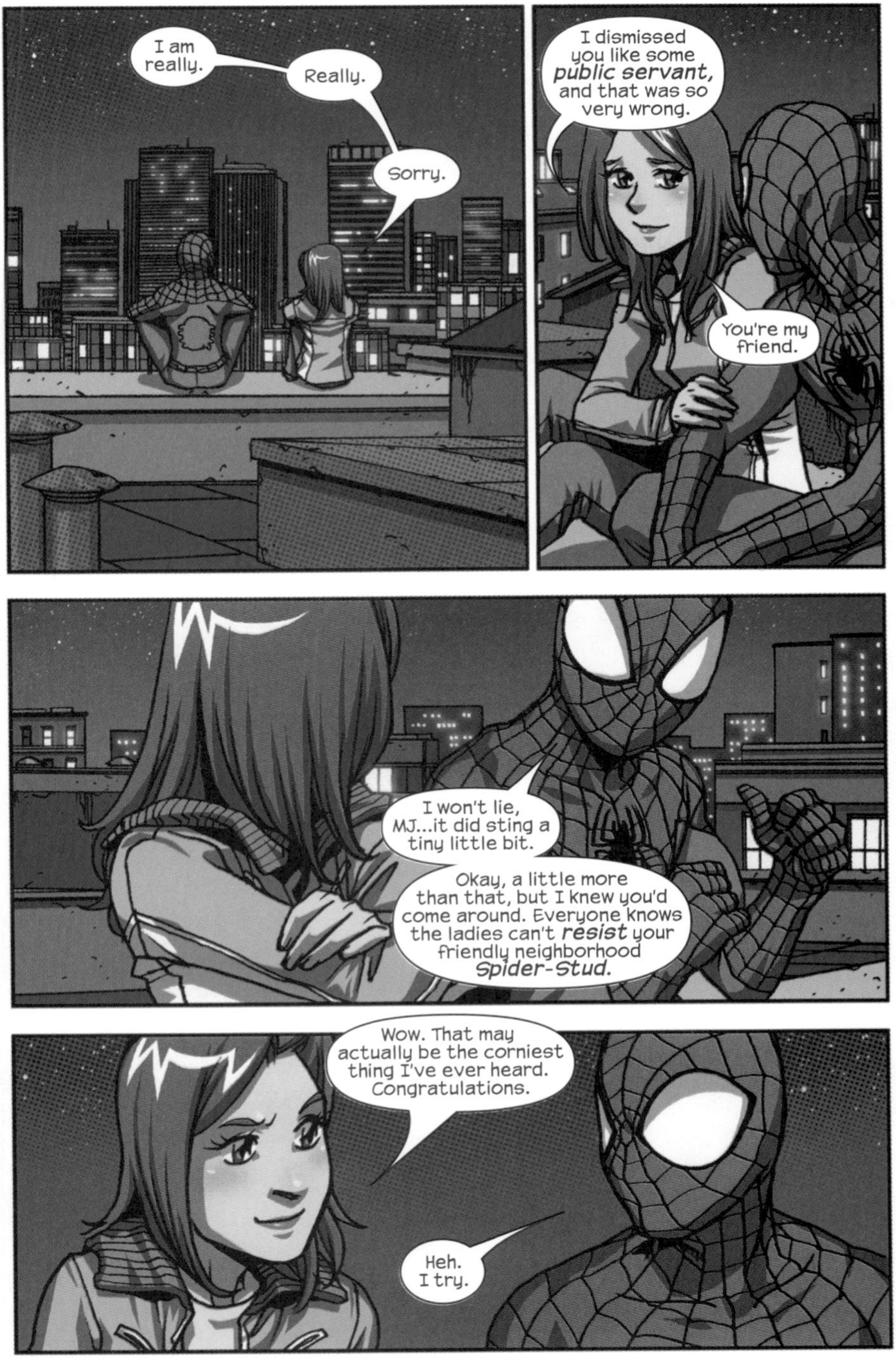
I am really.
Really.
Sorry.
I dismissed you like some *public servant,* and that was so very wrong.
You're my friend.
I won't lie, MJ...it did sting a tiny little bit.
Okay, a little more than that, but I knew you'd come around. Everyone knows the ladies can't *resist* your friendly neighborhood *Spider-Stud.*
Wow. That may actually be the corniest thing I've ever heard. Congratulations.
Heh. I try.

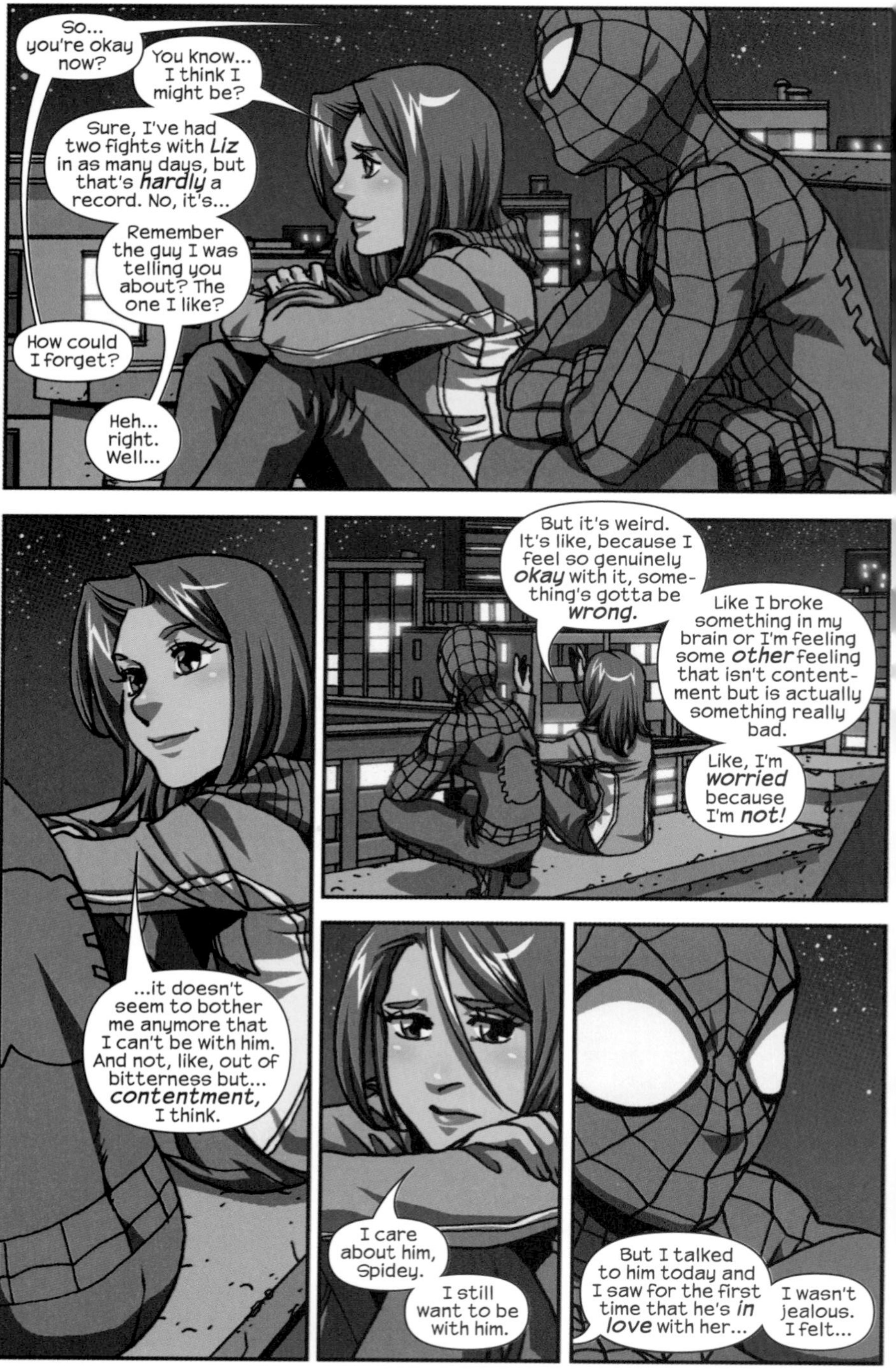
So... you're okay now?
You know... I think I might be?
Sure, I've had two fights with *Liz* in as many days, but that's ***hardly*** a record. No, it's...
Remember the guy I was telling you about? The one I like?
How could I forget?
Heh... right. Well...
...it doesn't seem to bother me anymore that I can't be with him. And not, like, out of bitterness but... *contentment,* I think.
But it's weird. It's like, because I feel so genuinely ***okay*** with it, something's gotta be ***wrong.***
Like I broke something in my brain or I'm feeling some ***other*** feeling that isn't contentment but is actually something really bad.
Like, I'm ***worried*** because I'm ***not!***
I care about him, Spidey.
I still want to be with him.
But I talked to him today and I saw for the first time that he's *in love* with her...
I wasn't jealous. I felt...

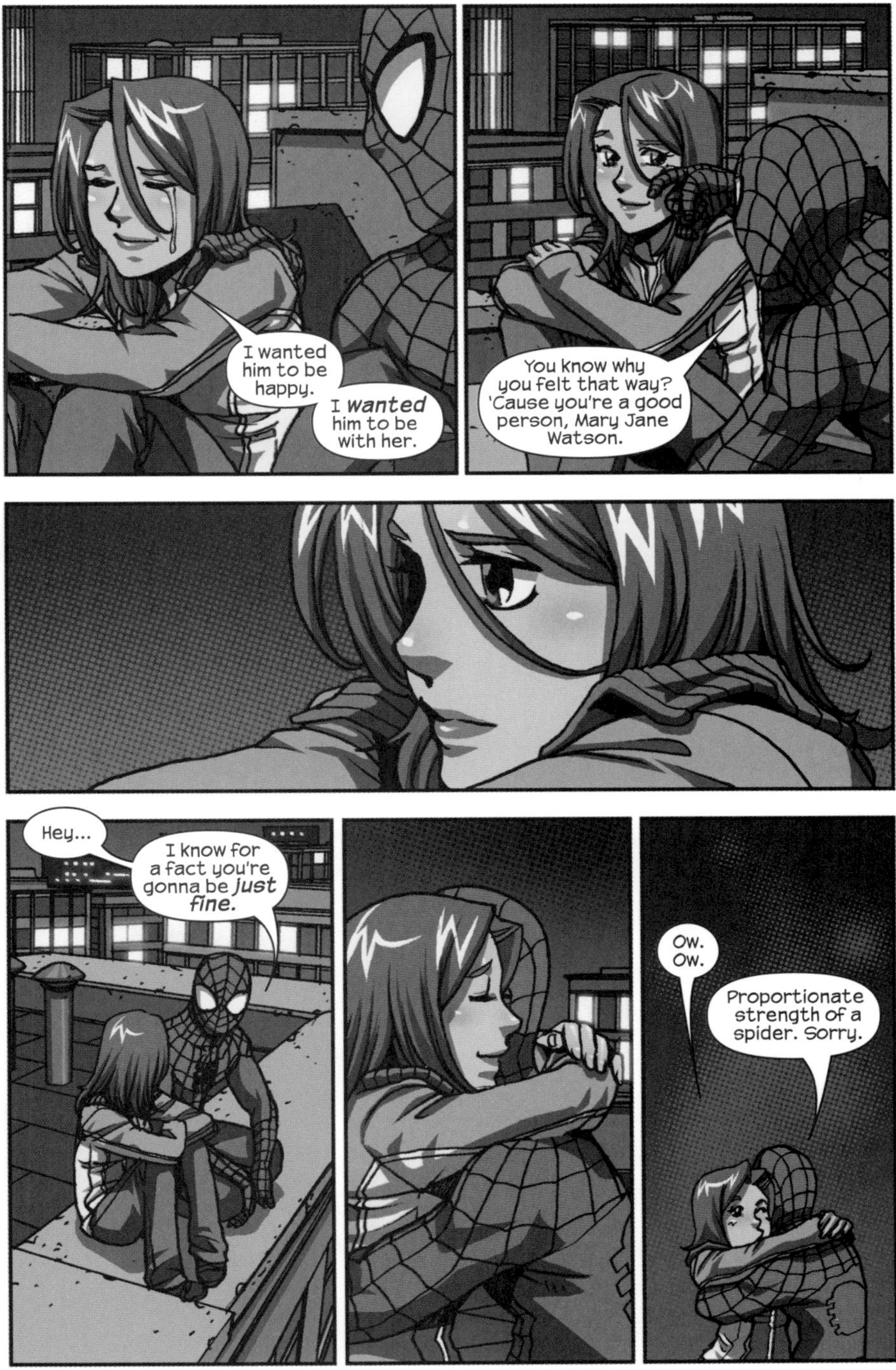
I wanted him to be happy.
I *wanted* him to be with her.
You know why you felt that way? 'Cause you're a good person, Mary Jane Watson.
Hey...
I know for a fact you're gonna be *just fine.*
Ow. Ow.
Proportionate strength of a spider. Sorry.

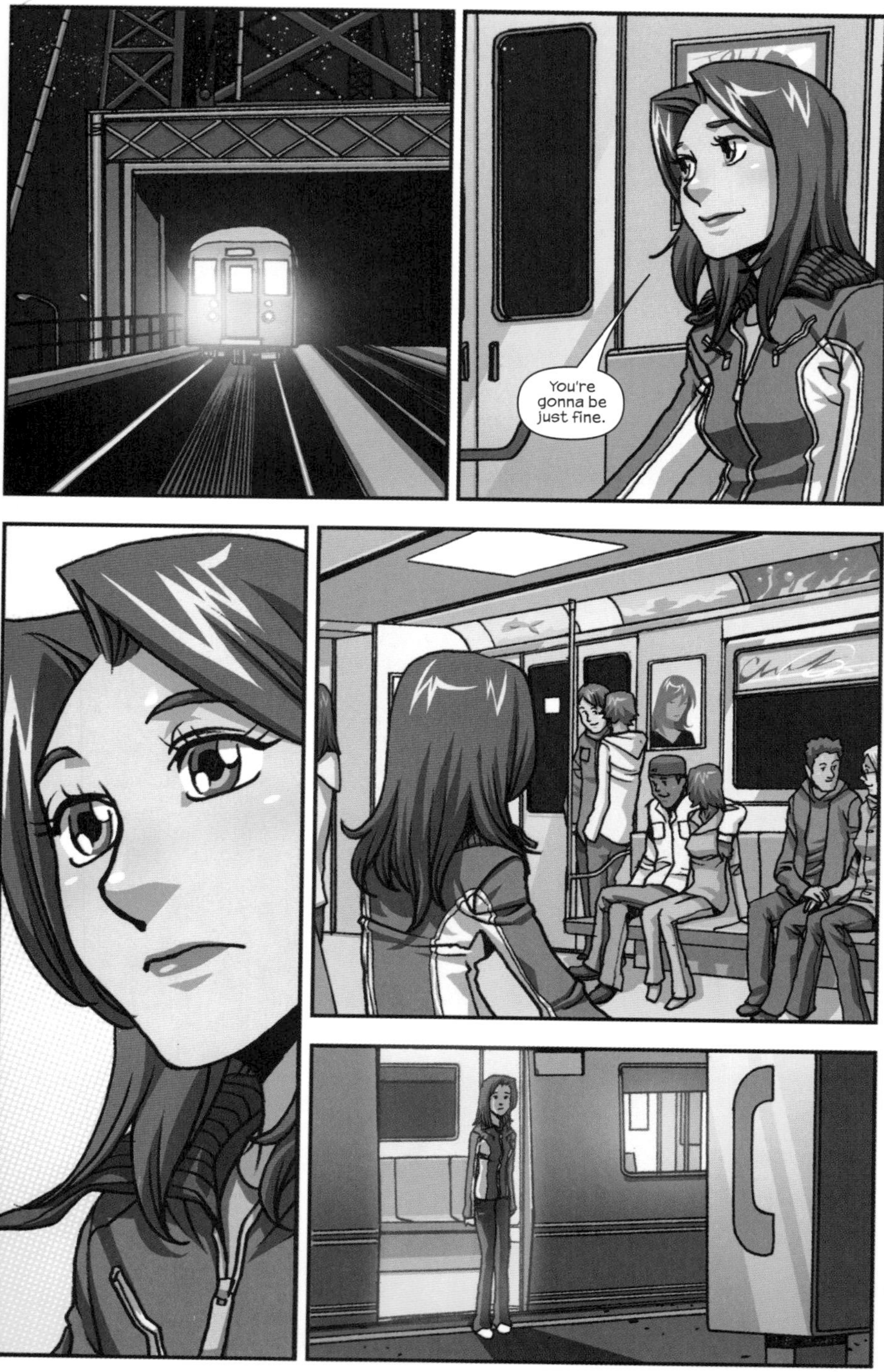
You're gonna be just fine.

Gwen!

Oh man, I'm so glad you're here! I've been trying to--

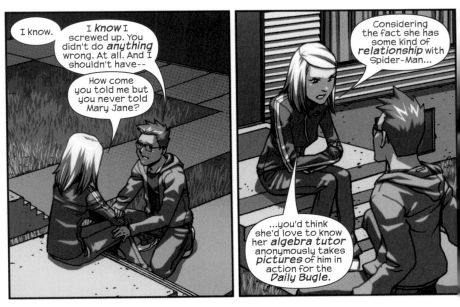

I know.

I *know* I screwed up. You didn't do *anything* wrong. At all. And I shouldn't have--

How come you told me but you never told Mary Jane?

Considering the fact she has some kind of *relationship* with Spider-Man...

...you'd think she'd love to know her *algebra tutor* anonymously takes *pictures* of him in action for the *Daily Bugle*.

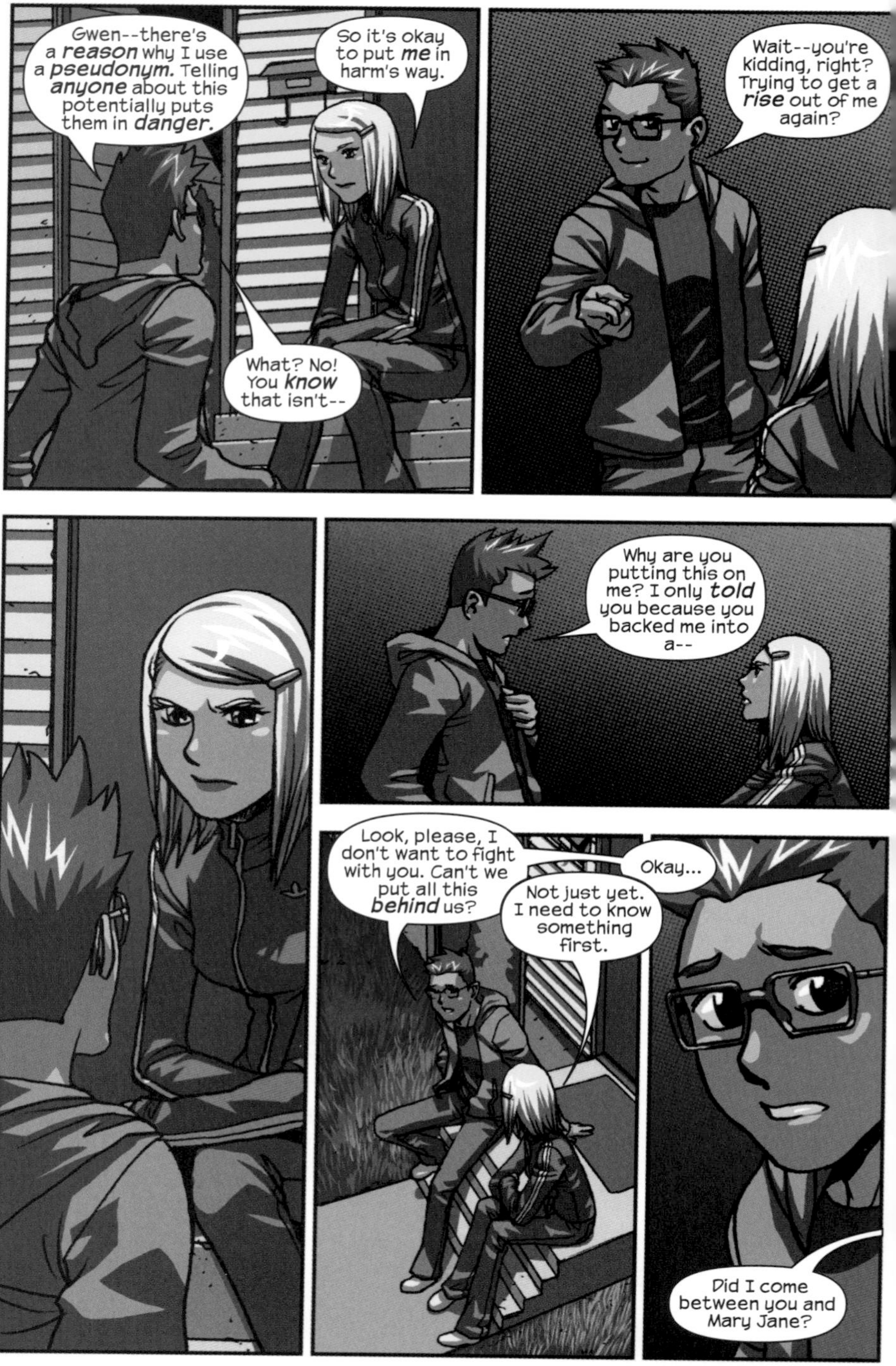
Gwen--there's a reason why I use a pseudonym. Telling anyone about this potentially puts them in danger.
So it's okay to put me in harm's way.
What? No! You know that isn't--
Wait--you're kidding, right? Trying to get a rise out of me again?
Why are you putting this on me? I only told you because you backed me into a--
Look, please, I don't want to fight with you. Can't we put all this behind us?
Not just yet. I need to know something first.
Okay...
Did I come between you and Mary Jane?

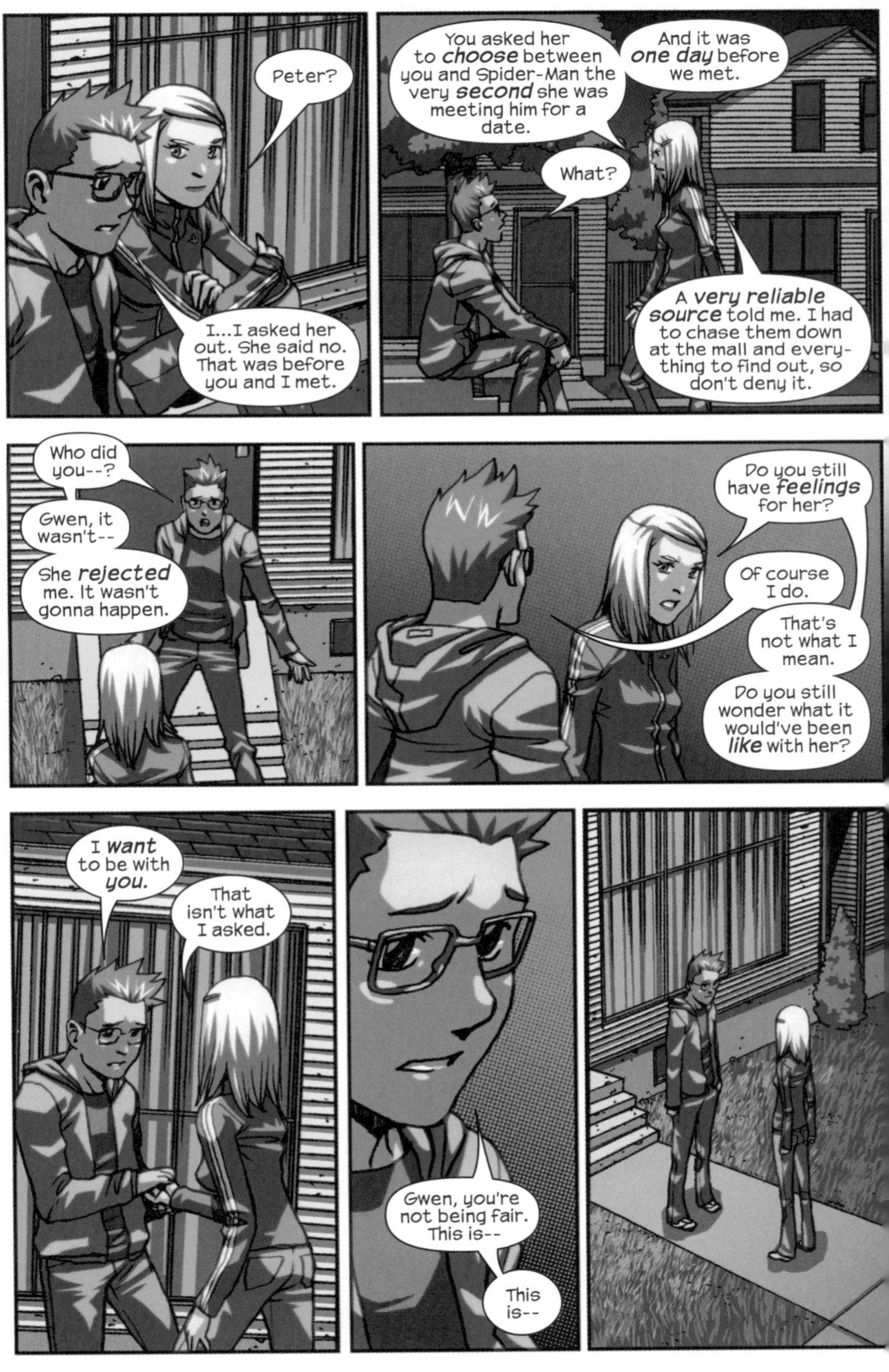
Peter?
I...I asked her out. She said no. That was before you and I met.
You asked her to choose between you and Spider-Man the very second she was meeting him for a date.
And it was one day before we met.
What?
A very reliable source told me. I had to chase them down at the mall and every-thing to find out, so don't deny it.
Who did you--?
Gwen, it wasn't--
She rejected me. It wasn't gonna happen.
Do you still have feelings for her?
Of course I do.
That's not what I mean.
Do you still wonder what it would've been like with her?
I want to be with you.
That isn't what I asked.
Gwen, you're not being fair. This is--
This is--

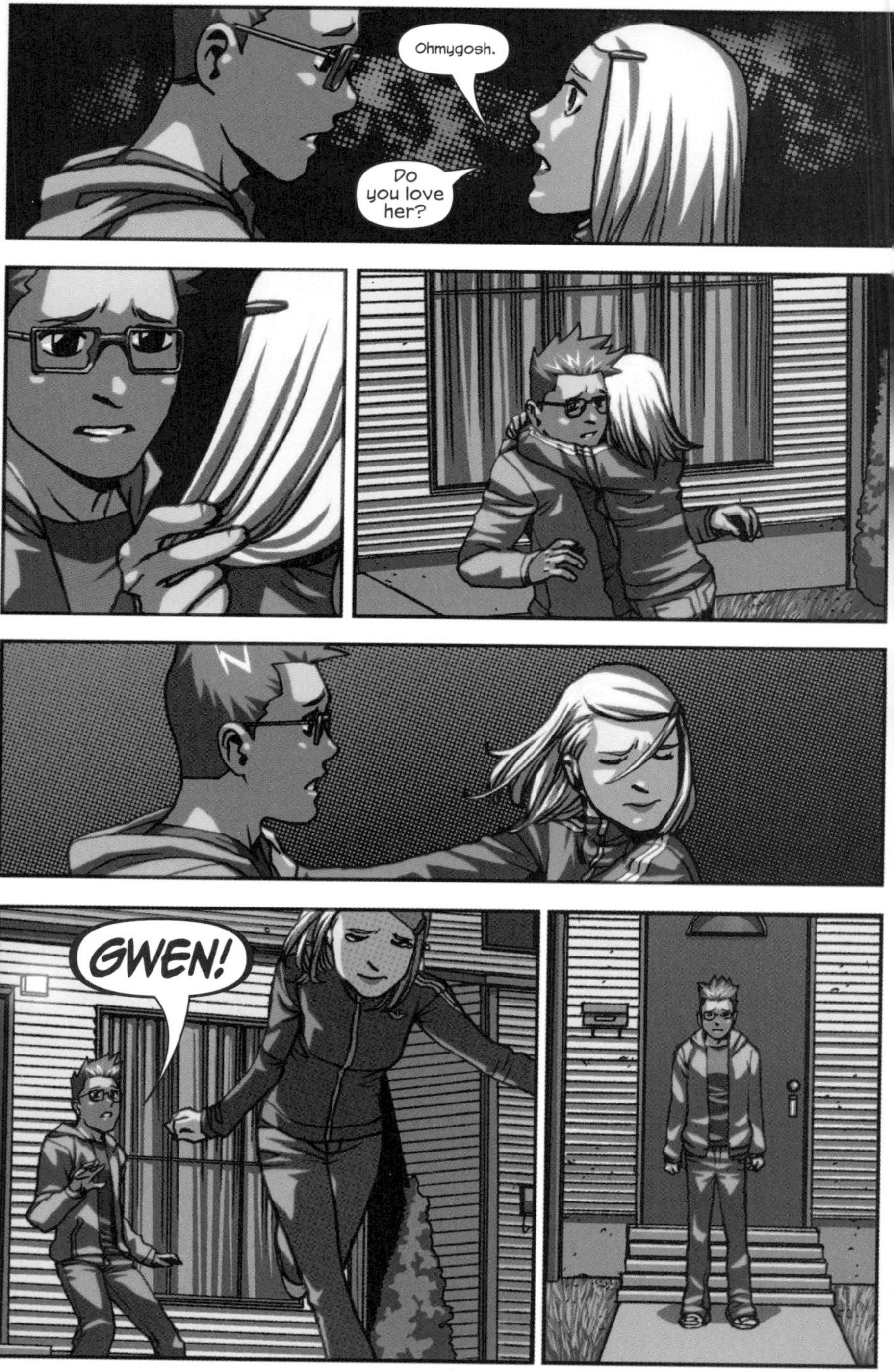
Ohmygosh.
Do you love her?
GWEN!

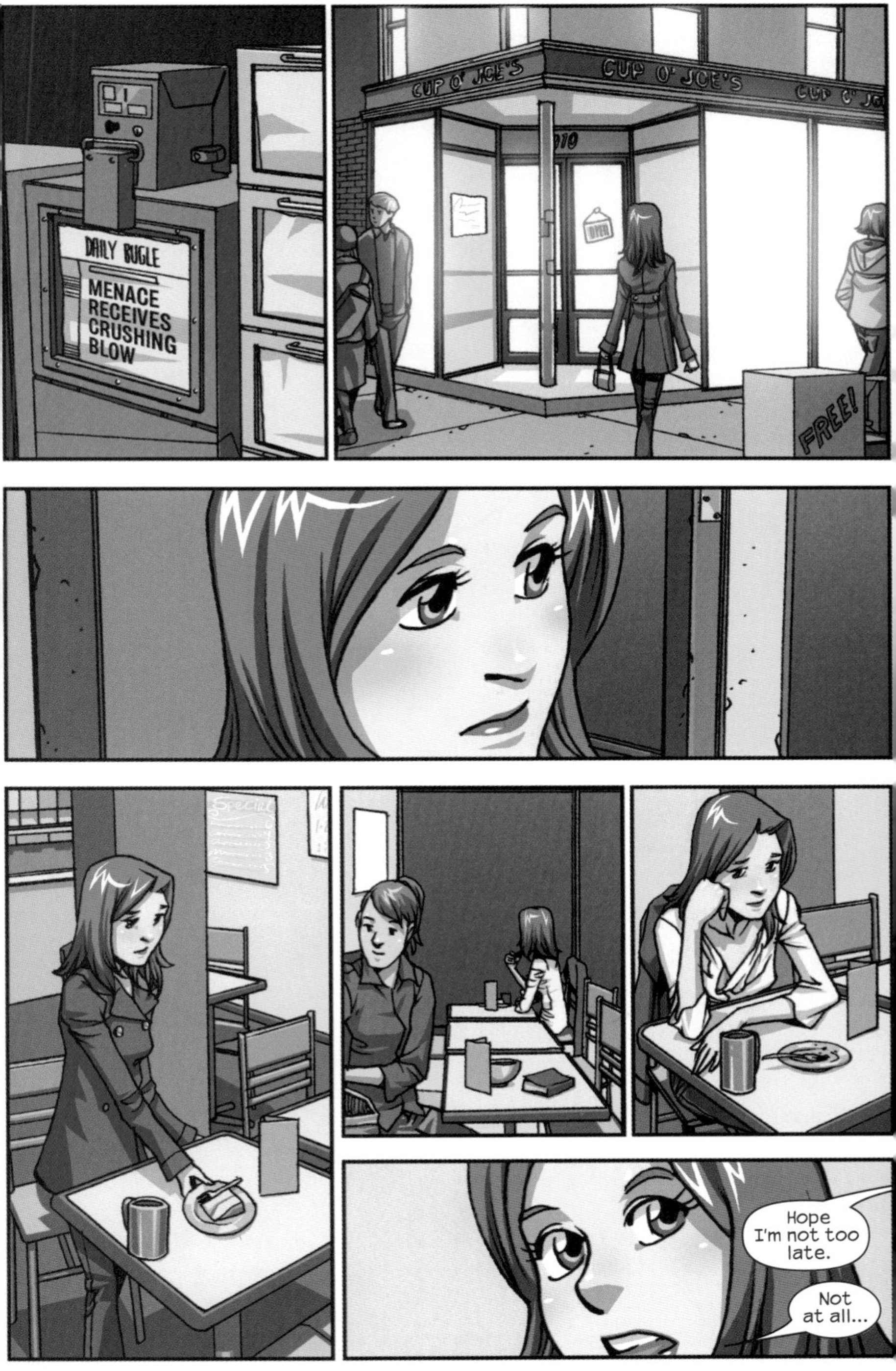
DAILY BUGLE
MENACE RECEIVES CRUSHING BLOW
CUP O' JOE'S
CUP O' JOE'S
FREE!
Hope I'm not too late.
Not at all...

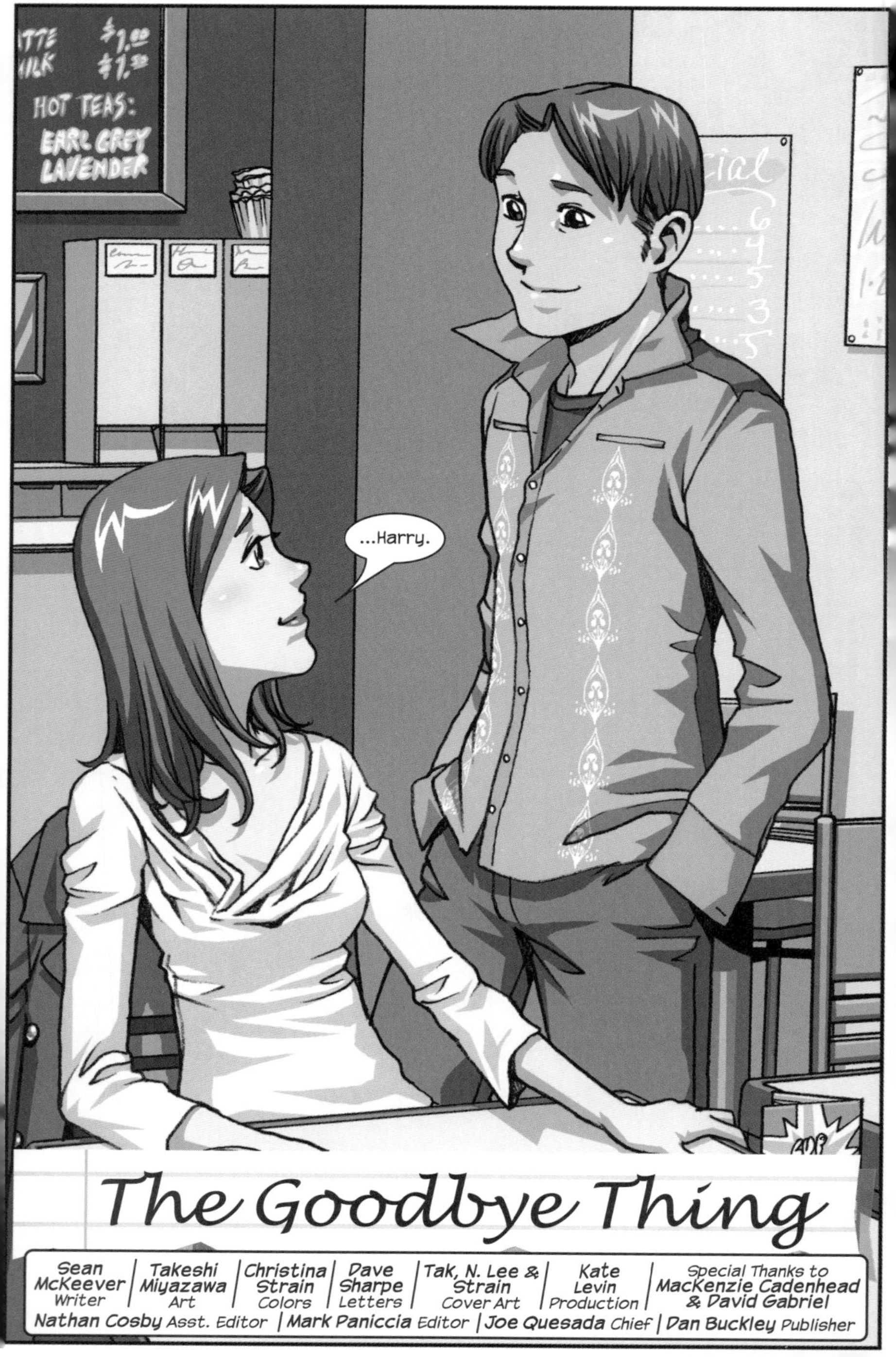
HOT TEAS:
EARL GREY
LAVENDER
...Harry.

The Goodbye Thing

Sean McKeever Writer | **Takeshi Miyazawa** Art | **Christina Strain** Colors | **Dave Sharpe** Letters | **Tak, N. Lee & Strain** Cover Art | **Kate Levin** Production | Special Thanks to **MacKenzie Cadenhead & David Gabriel**

Nathan Cosby Asst. Editor | **Mark Paniccia** Editor | **Joe Quesada** Chief | **Dan Buckley** Publisher

Issue #13 Cover Concepts
by
TAKESHI MIYAZAWA

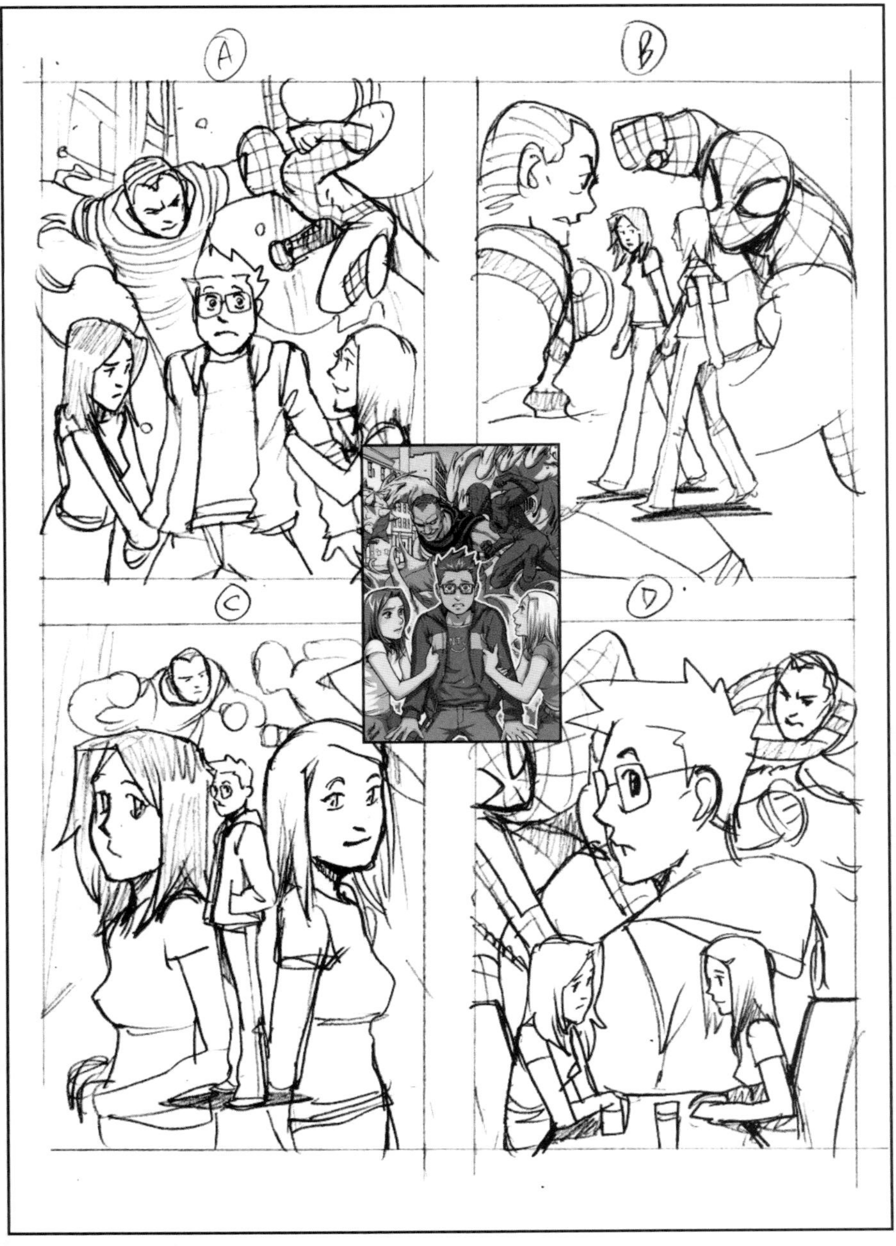
A
B
C
D

Issue #13, Pages 14-17 Layouts by

RICK MAYS

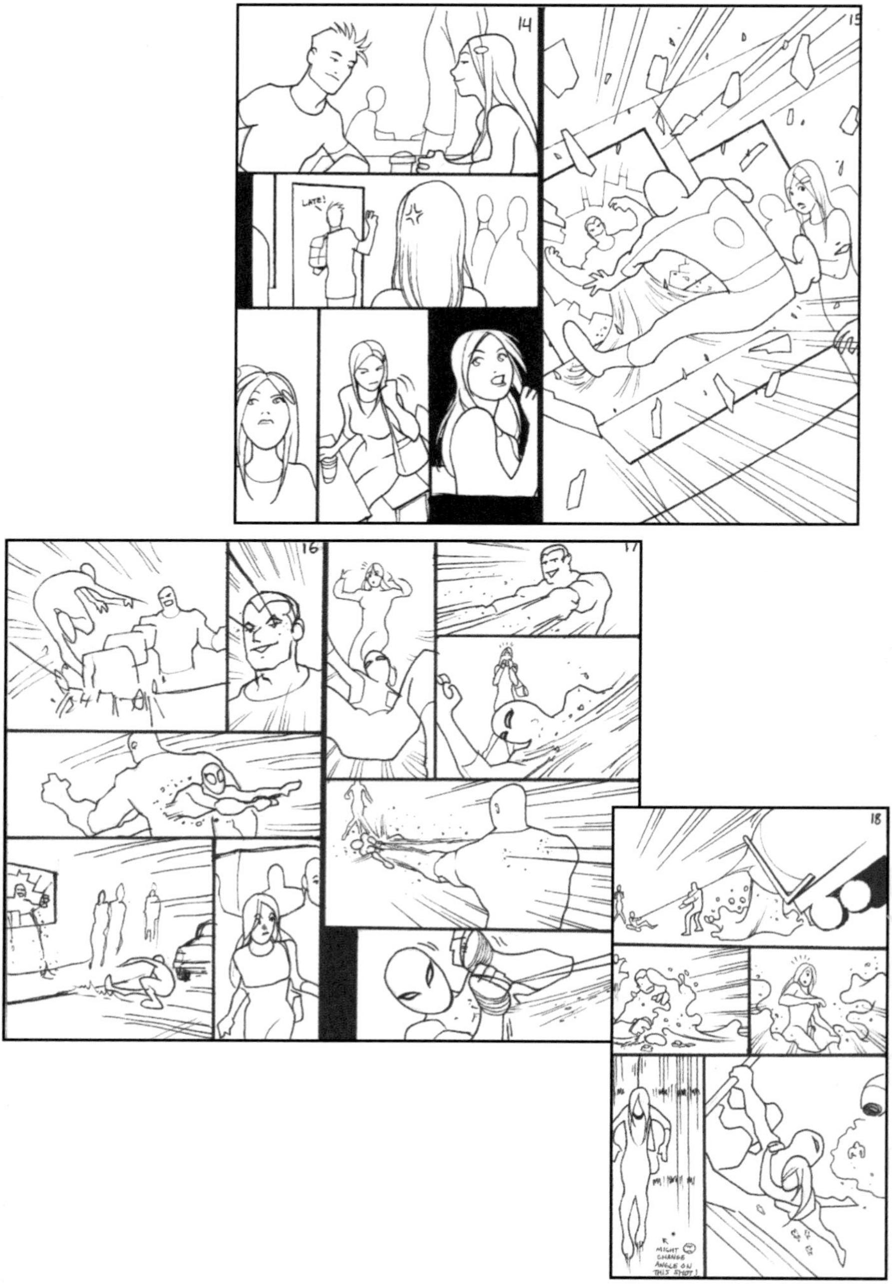

14
15
LATE!
16
17
18
MIGHT CHANGE ANGLE ON THIS SHOT!